Adopting Medicare Fee Schedules

Considerations for the California Workers' Compensation Program

Barbara O. Wynn

Prepared for the
California Commission on Health and Safety and Workers' Compensation

RAND
INSTITUTE FOR
CIVIL JUSTICE

The research presented in this report was prepared for the California Commission on Health and Safety and Workers' Compensation. This research was conducted by RAND's Institute for Civil Justice.

Library of Congress Cataloging-in-Publication Data

Wynn, Barbara O.
Adopting medicare fee schedules : considerations for the California workers' compensation program / Barbara O. Wynn.
p. cm.
"MR-1776."
Includes bibliographical references.
ISBN 0-8330-3476-6 (pbk.)
1. Medical fees—California. 2. Medicare—California. 3. Workers' compensation—California.
[DNLM: 1. Fee Schedules—economics—California. 2. Medicare—economics—California. 3. Economics, Hospital—California. 4. Patient Care—economics—California. 5. Workers' Compensation—economics—California. W 74 AC2 A239 2003] I.Title.

R728.5.W96 2003
368.4'2'009794—dc22

2003016718

Published 2003 by RAND
1700 Main Street, P.O. Box 2138, Santa Monica, CA 90407-2138
1200 South Hayes Street, Arlington, VA 22202-5050
201 North Craig Street, Suite 202, Pittsburgh, PA 15213-1516
RAND URL: http://www.rand.org/
To order RAND documents or to obtain additional information, contact Distribution Services: Telephone: (310) 451-7002; Fax: (310) 451-6915; Email: order@rand.org

RAND Institute for Civil Justice

The mission of the RAND Institute for Civil Justice (ICJ) is to improve private and public decisionmaking on civil legal issues by supplying policymakers and the public with the results of objective, empirically based, analytic research. The ICJ facilitates change in the civil justice system by analyzing trends and outcomes, identifying and evaluating policy options, and bringing together representatives of different interests to debate alternative solutions to policy problems. The Institute builds on a long tradition of RAND research characterized by an interdisciplinary, empirical approach to public policy issues and rigorous standards of quality, objectivity, and independence.

ICJ research is supported by pooled grants from corporations, trade and professional associations, and individuals; by government grants and contracts; and by private foundations. The Institute disseminates its work widely to the legal, business, and research communities, and to the general public. In accordance with RAND policy, all Institute research products are subject to peer review before publication. ICJ publications do not necessarily reflect the opinions or policies of the research sponsors or of the ICJ Board of Overseers.

For more information about the Institute for Civil Justice, contact:

Robert Reville, Director

Institute for Civil Justice

RAND

1700 Main Street

Santa Monica, CA 90407-2138

TEL: (310) 393-0411 x6786

FAX: (310) 451-6979

Email: Robert_Reville@rand.org

A profile of the ICJ, abstracts of its publications, and ordering information can be found on the World Wide Web at http://www.rand.org/centers/icj.

ICJ Board of Overseers

California Commission on Health and Safety and Workers' Compensation

Appointed by the Governor of California

Jill A. Dulich, Marriott International, *representing employers*

Leonard C. McLeod, California Correctional Peace Officers Association, *representing labor*

Darrel "Shorty" Thacker, Bay Counties District Council of Carpenters, *representing labor*

John C. Wilson, Schools Excess Liability Fund, *representing employers*

Appointed by the Speaker of the California Assembly

Allen Davenport, Service Employees International Union California State Council, *representing labor*

Robert B. Steinberg, Law Offices of Rose, Klein and Marias, *representing employers*

Appointed by the Senate Rules Committee

Tom Rankin, California Labor Federation, AFL-CIO, *representing labor*

Kristen Schwenkmeyer, Gordon and Schwenkmeyer, *representing employers*

Executive Officer

Christine Baker

Preface

In response to concerns about rapidly increasing medical costs in the California workers' compensation program, the California Commission on Health and Safety and Workers' Compensation (CHSWC) is recommending changes in the current fee schedule that determines the amounts health care providers are paid for medical services given to the state's injured workers. Specifically, the CHSWC proposes that the fee schedule be linked to Medicare fee schedules. This report describes research funded by the Commission to examine issues that would arise if such a link were to occur. The study addresses policy issues emanating from the differences between the two fee schedules, describes modifications that are likely to be necessary to tailor the Medicare fee schedules to California's injured workers, and explores the implications of automatic annual updates to those fee schedules.

The research for this study was conducted by the RAND Institute for Civil Justice. The summary of this report is intended for a broad audience of policymakers and others interested in this issue. The main body of the report should be of most interest to those concerned with technical issues regarding health care provider reimbursement under California's workers' compensation program.

Contents

Tables

Figures

Summary

Background

Medical costs are the fastest increasing component of the California workers' compensation program (CWCP). They have increased from 45 percent of benefit costs in the mid-1990s to an estimated 55 percent in 2003. During this same period, the average medical benefits paid per indemnity claim have been increasing 15 percent annually (CHSWC, 2002).

Currently, the Division of Workers' Compensation (DWC) uses an Official Medical Fee Schedule (OMFS) to set the maximum allowable amounts that may be paid to providers for medical services. The OMFS covers most medical services provided by a physician or other health care provider to whom the patient has been referred. However, maximum allowable amounts have not been established for facility fees associated with surgical procedures performed in hospital outpatient settings and ambulatory surgical centers. Moreover, the DWC has not had the resources to update the existing fee schedules on a regular basis. The portions of the OMFS that apply to inpatient hospital services and to physician and other practitioner services have not been updated since 2001 and 1999, respectively.

The California Senate Labor and Industrial Relations Committee asked the Commission on Health and Safety and Workers' Compensation (CHSWC) to develop proposals for medical cost savings. In response to this request, the CHSWC is recommending that California consider linking the OMFS to Medicare's fee schedules for all services other than pharmaceuticals.

Medicare is the federal health insurance program for the aged, the disabled, and persons with end-stage renal disease. Medicare is administered by the Centers for Medicare and Medicaid Services (CMS). With few exceptions, Medicare uses fee schedules that are regularly updated to pay for medical care provided to its beneficiaries. The fee schedules are intended to relate payments to the resources required to provide the services.

The California workers' compensation program already models its OMFS for inpatient hospital services on Medicare's payment system and has adopted elements of other Medicare fee schedules, such as the global billing periods[1] for surgery and relative values[2] for orthotics and prosthetics. Because Medicare does not cover most outpatient prescription drugs, the CHSWC is recommending that the California Medicaid (MediCal) program's fee schedule for pharmaceuticals be used. Under the commission's proposal, the only component of the OMFS

[1]The global billing period is the period during which the pre- and post-operative care provided by a surgeon is covered by the payment for the surgical procedure.

[2]As discussed later, most fee schedules include a relative value or weight that measures the resources required for a given service or group of services relative to other services.

that would require regulatory action is the multiplier, or adjustment, to the Medicare rates that would establish the overall payment levels for the California workers' compensation program. Linking the OMFS to the Medicare fee schedule would expand the services covered by the OMFS and shift the administrative burden of ongoing fee schedule refinement and regular updates to the CMS.

The CHSWC asked RAND to identify the issues that would need to be addressed if the OMFS were linked to Medicare fee schedules, including:

- issues that are likely to arise from existing differences between the two fee schedules
- issues surrounding the modifications that might be necessary to tailor the Medicare fee schedules to CWCP patients
- issues regarding the implications of automatic annual updates of fee schedules.

Prior research by other organizations has explored many of the issues that need to be considered in adopting the Medicare fee schedules. Given the limited amount of time available for this study, RAND drew heavily from this previous work and from other information to identify the policy options and potential impact if the link to Medicare fee schedules were to occur. Except for limited analyses of readily available hospital inpatient data, primary data analyses were not within the scope of this study.

This study focuses on the features of the Medicare fee schedule that are at variance with the existing OMFS fee schedule and the issues that should be considered in deciding whether to retain particular features of the OMFS. Some issues, such as whether the fee schedules for physician services should have a single conversion factor or multiple conversion factors that account for current payment differentials, primarily involve a trade-off between redistributing payments across physician specialties and improving the match between payments and the costs of providing services. Other issues, such as whether adjustments are needed to reflect the differences in the populations covered by Medicare and the California workers' compensation program, involve a trade-off between administrative burden and payment accuracy. Administrative burden is minimized if the Medicare fee schedule payment parameters are adopted without modification. However, the populations covered by Medicare and workers' compensation differ from one another, and some modifications may be needed to ensure that payments are generally appropriate.

Other workers' compensation programs have adopted the structure of the Medicare fee schedules, with different multipliers, to the Medicare payment rates. The experience of these programs and their modifications for workers' compensation–specific services could inform the decisions the DWC would need to make in adapting the Medicare fee schedules for the CWCP.

- At least 17 states, the District of Columbia, and the federal workers' compensation program have adopted resource-based relative value scale (RB-RVS) fee schedules (although a number of states have retained service-specific conversion factors) for physician services. Key features of these fee schedules are detailed in Eccleston et al. (2002); Kominski, Pourat, and Black (1999); and The Lewin Group (2002).

- At least seven states are using the Medicare fee schedule for freestanding ambulatory surgery centers to pay for ambulatory surgery. In addition, one state has implemented a fee schedule for hospital outpatient services based on Medicare's fee schedule (CHSWC, 2003).

Summary of Overall Findings

- Generally, Medicare's fee schedules cover the broad range of services covered by the CWCP (see Table S.1). Some attention, however, needs to be given to individual services that are unique to the CWCP or to providers that are not covered by Medicare, such as acupuncturists and family therapists.

- Linking the OMFS to the Medicare fee schedules shifts the administrative burden of ongoing fee schedule refinement and updates to the CMS. Medicare fee schedules are updated on a regular basis with opportunity for public comment. An independent commission is charged with reviewing and making recommendations concerning Medicare payment policies. In addition, other advisory committees provide CMS with regular input on potential refinements to its various payment systems.

- Medicare fee schedules are more than just a set of prices. Coding standards and payment policies are implicit in the prices and often differ from those currently used by the OMFS or have features that the OMFS lacks. There are a number of individual policy issues that would need to be addressed at the outset of linking the OMFS to the Medicare fee schedules. However, after the decisions are made on these issues, they can be imbedded in the OMFS and should not preclude automatic updates in the future based on Medicare fee schedule updates.

- Medicare fee schedules have evolved over time to become systems that are organized around the *provider* who is furnishing the care and the setting where that care is delivered. When services are provided in a facility setting, separate payments are made to the physician or other practitioner and to the facility. Total payment for many ambulatory procedures varies based on the setting in which those procedures are done. In contrast, the current OMFS establishes maximum payments for services and, except for surgical procedures and emergency room services for which separate facility fees are allowed, the amounts do not vary based on the ambulatory setting in which the services are provided. This situation raises a number of important issues: (1) whether to continue to employ current OMFS rules regarding separate facility fees or establish separate facility fees for all hospital outpatient services; (2) whether to establish the same maximum facility fee payments for hospital outpatient departments and ambulatory surgical centers; and (3) whether to adopt Medicare's payment differentials for services furnished in office and facility settings by physicians and other practitioners. How these issues are addressed will affect both the incentives for where care is delivered and total California workers' compensation medical care expenditures.

Table S.1
Overview of Medicare Payment System and OMFS by Type of Service

Service	Medicare Payment System	OMFS
Inpatient Hospital	Inpatient Hospital	Inpatient Hospital
Acute care hospitals	Predetermined per-case payment based on the patient's principal and secondary diagnoses, procedures, and age.	Already incorporates a modified version of the Medicare system. Exempts certain diagnosis-related groups (DRGs).
Freestanding rehabilitation hospitals and units of acute care hospitals	Predetermined per-case payment based on impairment, functional status, age, complications, and co-morbid conditions.	Currently exempts rehabilitation services. Assessment needed to determine if Medicare system is appropriate for CWCP patients.
Freestanding psychiatric hospitals and units of acute care hospitals	Cost subject to rate of increase limit on aggregate per-discharge costs. Per-diem prospective payment system under development.	Currently exempts psychiatric facilities from the OMFS. Medicare's cost-based system is not suitable for CWCP.
Long-term care hospitals	Pre-determined per-case payment based on patient's principal and secondary diagnoses, procedures, and patient's age.	Currently exempts long-term care hospitals. Assessment needed to determine if Medicare system appropriate for CWCP patients.
Physician and Other Practitioners, Outpatient Rehabilitation, and Non-Hospital Radiology	Resource-based relative value fee schedule; Medicare does not cover some services and providers that are covered by CWCP.	Charge-based relative value fee schedule.
Outpatient clinical laboratory tests	Charge-based fee schedule with national limits applicable to independent laboratories and physician offices; professional component paid under RB-RVS.	Charge-based relative value scale (RVS) applicable to all outpatient lab tests. Separate technical and professional components.
Other Hospital Outpatient Services	Facility fee paid for all services based on 570 clinically coherent groupings of procedures with similar cost.	Separate facility fees payable only for ambulatory surgery and emergency room. Fees exempt from OMFS.
Freestanding Ambulatory Surgical Center Procedures	Facility fee based on nine payment groups for procedures on approved list; if not on approved list, physician payment same as if performed in office setting.	Facility fees currently exempt from OMFS.
Durable Medical Equipment, Prosthetics, Orthotics, and Supplies	Charge-based fee schedule	Charge-based RVS. Uses Medicare relative value units (RVUs) for orthotics and prosthetics.
Outpatient Renal Dialysis	Capitated monthly rate	Currently exempts outpatient renal dialysis
Skilled Nursing Facility Inpatient Services	Per-diem rate based on 44 resource-utilization groups	Currently exempts skilled nursing facility inpatient services
Home health agency services	Case mix adjusted payment for 60-day episodes	Currently exempts home health agency services
Ambulance	National fee schedule transition	Currently exempts ambulance services

- The unit of service covered by a Medicare fee schedule payment ranges from a bundled payment for a group of services (for example, Medicare's predetermined payment for hospital inpatient services covers all facility services provided during the inpatient stay) to a separate payment for each individual item or diagnostic test. While the current OMFS for inpatient hospital services demonstrates that the Medicare bundled payments can be adapted for workers' compensation patients, Medicare bundled payments for an inpatient stay (e.g., for services delivered in rehabilitation facilities) or an episode of care (e.g., home health care services) should be assessed to determine if the payments are appropriate for workers' compensation patients.

- Medicare has policies governing which items and services are included in payment for professional and facility fees and which services may be billed separately. As noted earlier, most fee schedules include a relative value or weight that measures the resources required for a given service or group of services relative to other services. These relative weights are consistent with the service definition and may not be appropriate if the OMFS retains different policies on items and services that may be separately billed.

- For most fee schedules, Medicare applies a dollar conversion factor to the relative value for a given service to convert that value into a payment amount. A key question is what the appropriate conversion factor would be for services furnished to California workers' compensation patients. There is no "gold standard" that can be used to answer that question, and any decisionmaking in this regard should take into account a number of factors: whether there is adequate access to care, the current maximum allowable fees, the relationship between Medicare and private payer fee levels in California, and available information on the cost of providing specific services. A multiplier can be applied to the Medicare conversion factor to establish an overall payment level that is adequate to provide access to high-quality care. Setting the rate too low may create access problems, whereas setting the rate too high may encourage unnecessary utilization and result in excessive program expenditures.

- The OMFS is not adjusted for inflation on a regular basis, and most payments have been frozen for at least several years. The result is lower aggregate expenditures than the expenditures that would have resulted with regular inflation updates. While program expenditures tend to be higher with regular updates, the annual adjustments increase payment equity and predictability and should keep payments in line with the resources required to provide medical services.

- Medicare's annual update factors are set by law and include policy adjustments as well as an inflation adjustment. The policy adjustments meet Medicare's programmatic needs and may not be appropriate for updates to the OMFS. Other inflation measures may be more suitable. Input price indices account for changes in the input costs of providing services and would relate payment changes to changes in the costs of providing medical services, and medical price indices account for changes in the amounts paid for medical services by consumers and/or third-party payers. The selection of an appropriate measure depends on the underlying policy goal in making an inflation adjustment.

- The potential payment changes are quite large for some service sectors and may require a transition period to allow providers time to adjust to the new payment levels. Depending on the service sector and whether the OMFS already applies, transition policies that might be considered include
    - thresholds for the maximum change that can occur in a single year
    - blended rates that over several years provide a decreasing proportion of the payment based on the OMFS and an increasing proportion based on the Medicare fee schedule
    - hold-harmless provisions that freeze the current maximum allowable fee until it is less than the inflation-adjusted Medicare fee schedule amount
    - reducing over time the OMFS multiplier that is applied to the Medicare conversion factor.
- While any of the aforementioned transition strategies involve some administrative burden, those that require maintaining procedure-specific information on amounts currently payable under the OMFS are the most burdensome. Transition policies that phase in the payment changes through adjustments in the conversion factor are less burdensome. The annual updating burden will be minimized if the transition policies are established at the outset of linking the OMFS to the Medicare fee schedules.
- The impact on program expenditures of tying the OMFS to Medicare fee schedules would largely depend on the decisions regarding payment levels: the multiplier used to adjust the Medicare conversion factor, the update methodology, and transition policies. Administrative savings should accrue from regular and predictable updates, but the actual level of administrative savings may be affected by the extent to which modifications are made in the Medicare fee schedules to address particular CWCP concerns.
- The decisions regarding payment levels and fee schedule modifications also have major implications for workers' compensation patients' continued access to quality care. The lack of a single statewide database containing all or a representative sample of current California workers' compensation claims makes it difficult to evaluate the impact of policy options. With the potentially large payment changes that are likely to occur in some sectors, ongoing monitoring to watch for any unintended consequences of adopting the Medicare fee schedules is highly recommended. If monitoring is done during the transitional period, potential problems can be identified and addressed promptly, and any necessary mid-course corrections can be made before final payment levels are established.
- Adopting Medicare's patient classifications will allow the DWC to compare costs for comparable services across providers, compare costs with other programs' costs for services, and monitor access and utilization trends for specific services. Such analyses are predicated on obtaining administrative data on an ongoing basis.

Summary of Policy Issues Regarding Specific Fee Schedules

In this section, we summarize RAND's key findings by service sector regarding issues that are likely to arise if the OMFS is linked to the Medicare fee schedules.

Hospital Inpatient Services

The OMFS inpatient hospital fee schedule limits payment to general acute care hospitals to a pre-determined amount per stay based on the diagnosis-related group (DRG) to which the patient is assigned and on a hospital's characteristics. The hospital's characteristics are reflected in a *composite factor,* which establishes the standard payment rate for each stay. The composite rate is further adjusted by a DRG *relative weight,* which reflects the costliness of the average patient in the DRG to patients in other DRGs. The general formula for determining payment for an inpatient stay is:

$$\text{Payment} = \text{DRG relative weight}_{ind} \times \text{composite factor}_{hosp}$$

Additional payments are made for high-cost "outlier" cases to protect the hospital from large financial losses on individual patients.

The DRG classification system, most DRG relative weights, and the adjustments embodied in the composite factor (which take into account a hospital's geographic location, teaching activities, and commitment to serving low-income patients) are based on the Medicare payment system for hospital inpatient services. However, there are several important differences between the Medicare payment system and the OMFS:

- The CMS updates Medicare's payment system annually each October 1. The OMFS currently is using outdated payment parameters. Most payment parameters are from federal fiscal year (FY) 2001.
- The OMFS multiplies the standard amount that Medicare would pay for an inpatient stay by 1.2.
- Certain DRGs are exempt from the OMFS or have a different relative weight based on payments by California group health plans.
- In addition to the DRG fee schedule payment, the hardware costs for devices implanted during back and neck surgeries are reimbursed separately under OMFS policies.
- Certain hospitals that are paid under the Medicare prospective payment system (PPS) are exempt under the OMFS because the necessary variables are not readily available to the CWCP.

The OMFS for inpatient hospital services demonstrates that the Medicare fee schedules can be adapted to meet CWCP needs. Building in some time to allow for DWC to become familiar with the annual Medicare changes and their implications for the CWCP and to notify affected parties of the changes and any clarifications on how the OMFS is impacted would help prevent any unintended consequences of automatic OMFS updates being linked to the Medicare updates.

The automatic update could be based on the Medicare update factors or on an alternative measure that would be independent of Medicare policy adjustments. Inflation measures that potentially could be used are the rate of increase in the hospital "market basket" (an input price index of goods and services used by hospitals to measure price inflation in the costs of an inpatient stay) or the Producer Price Index for hospital services (which measures changes in the prices paid for hospital care). The hospital market basket has the advantage of being an integral part of Medicare's annual update and would be less burdensome than the Producer Price Index to implement. More-frequent updating of the cost-to-charge ratios used to determine additional payments for high-cost outlier cases would reduce potential abuse from excessive charge escalation.

Currently, the OMFS applies a 1.2 multiplier to the Medicare payment rate. RAND's analysis of the California Office of Statewide Health Planning and Development (OSHPD) data for 2000 indicates that Medicare payment rates without a multiplier result in an estimated payment-to-cost ratio of 1.19 for CWCP patients. This is higher than the 1.125 national payment-to-cost ratio for private payers (MedPAC, 2003) and suggests that, on average, a multiplier is not needed to cover the estimated costs of care and provide payments that are comparable to those paid by private payers. However, the range in DRG-specific payment-to-cost ratios is substantial, and adjustments may be appropriate for some DRGs. Consistent with current OMFS policy, these adjustments can be expressed as a multiplier (greater or less than 1.0 as appropriate) so that they can be self-implementing if automatic updates are made to the fee schedule.

Other OMFS modifications to the Medicare inpatient payment system should also be reexamined:

- Consideration should be given to either incorporating the additional payments for hardware and instrumentation costs into the DRG payments for back and neck procedures or to reducing the DRG relative weight for the estimated costs that are covered by the DRG payment. The current "pass-through" or additional payments for the hardware costs result in CWCP paying for the hardware twice: once in the DRG fee schedule relative and again in the additional payment for the hardware costs.

- Similarly, consideration should be given to eliminating the exemption for certain types of care provided by acute care hospitals. Including these services under the OMFS would reduce CWCP administrative burden and vulnerability to excessive payments. The payment-to-cost ratios for the exempt DRGs indicate on average that the payment in these cases will be adequate. Moreover, the additional payments for cases that have atypically high costs provide additional protection for the hospital against financial loss.

- Payment-to-cost ratios for rural hospitals are relatively low and consideration should be given to adopting Medicare's special payment protection for hospitals that are the sole source of care that is reasonably available to patients in their communities. Under Medicare, these hospitals receive the higher of the fee schedule payment or a hospital-specific rate based on historical costs. This policy could be self-implementing with little administrative burden.

Medicare exempts the following classes of hospitals from the prospective payment system for general acute care hospitals: critical access hospitals, rehabilitation hospitals and units of acute care hospitals, psychiatric hospitals and units of acute care hospitals, long-term hospitals, children's hospitals, and cancer hospitals. Prospective payment systems are in place for rehabilitation facilities and long-term hospitals. Before adopting these fee schedules, further analysis is advisable to determine whether Medicare's new payment systems for these facilities are also appropriate for the CWCP population. Medicare payments for other exempt hospitals—psychiatric facilities, children's hospitals, and cancer hospitals—are based on the reasonable costs of providing services to individual Medicare patients. This payment methodology cannot be readily adopted by the CWCP because it requires a retroactive payment determination based on cost data.

The volume of services provided by specialty hospitals to workers' compensation patients is relatively small. In 2000, these facilities had fewer than 400 CWCP cases (mostly in rehabilitation and psychiatric hospitals) and about $9.3 million in charges. Two options that might entail less administrative burden than adapting the Medicare fee schedules would be to either (1) continue to exempt these facilities and leave the payment determination to negotiations between the hospital and payer or (2) establish a payment rate based on discounted customary charges. The latter approach could utilize recent OSHPD data to determine an appropriate discount rate on a hospital-specific basis. (For example, if the hospital's cost-to-charge ratio is 0.30, a payment based on 33 percent of billed charges would produce an estimated payment-to-cost ratio of 1.125 [1.125 x 0.30 = 0.33], which is in line with the overall hospital payment-to-cost ratio for private payers.)

RB-RVS Fee Schedule for Physicians and Other Practitioners

The Medicare resource-based relative value scale fee schedule has three basic components:

- The first component consists of relative value units (RVUs) for each medical service based on the resources associated with the physician's work (the time and skill required for the procedure), practice expenses (the staff time and costs of maintaining an office), and malpractice expenses. For some procedures, the RVUs for practice expenses vary based on whether a procedure is performed in the physician's office or in a facility. The RVUs compare the resources required for a particular service to those required for other services. They have been developed for the general patient population and are not specific to the resources required to treat Medicare patients. The RB-RVS tends to provide lower relative values for surgical procedures and higher relative values for evaluation and management services than relative value scales based on historical charging practices (such as the current OMFS).

- The second component of the fee schedule is the conversion factor (CF) that converts the RVUs into a Medicare payment amount for the procedure. The CF determines overall fee schedule payment levels. The Medicare program uses a single CF for all services except anesthesia.

- The third component of the fee schedule is a geographic adjustment factor that adjusts for geographic differences in the costs of maintaining a physician practice. Separate geographic practice cost indices (GPCIs) apply to the RVUs for the three elements of the service: physician work, malpractice expense, and practice expense. For California, there are different adjustment factors for each of nine geographic areas.

Because the structure of the Medicare RB-RVS differs from the current OMFS in a number of ways, several policy choices would need to be made before linking the OMFS to the Medicare fee schedule:

- The level at which the conversion factor should be initially established and the inflation measure that should be used to update that factor in the future

- Whether a geographic adjustment factor should apply

- Whether the site-of-service differential for the practice expense component should be adopted

- Whether anesthesia professional services should be included.

Using results from The Lewin Group (2002) analysis of the impact of adopting the RB-RVS, applying a 1.15 to 1.16 multiplier (depending on the decision with respect to anesthesia) to the Medicare conversion factor would be cost neutral to the maximum allowable fees under the current OMFS. A higher multiplier may be needed to reflect overall fee levels paid by private payers. Potential inflation measures that would be independent of Medicare policy adjustments are the Medicare Economic Index and the Producer Price Index for physician offices and clinics. The Medicare Economic Index would relate payment changes to changes in the costs of maintaining a physician practice. This index is consistent with the RB-RVS concept and has the added advantage of being an integral part of the annual Medicare update to the physician fee schedule. The Producer Price Index would account for market changes in the amounts paid for physician services.

Medicare's geographic adjustment factors and site-of-service differentials are designed to improve the match between fee payments and the resources required to provide the services but would involve additional payment redistributions. Bringing anesthesia under the RB- RVS is also consistent with the goal of relating payments to resources, but, assuming a cost-neutral multiplier of 1.16, this move would reduce payments for anesthesia services by approximately 39 percent. A cost-neutral change from a charge-based to resource-based fee schedule would involve significant payment redistributions for other services as well: evaluation and management (plus 25 percent), surgery (minus 15 percent), and medicine (minus 5 percent). The change for radiology and physical medicine would be less than 1 percent. While the actual impact will depend on the multiplier that is selected, consideration should be given to phasing in the new payment rates to soften the impact of adopting the RB-RVS on anesthesia and surgery. In any event, monitoring access and utilization to specialty services that would have lower payment levels under the RB-RVS would be important.

Hospital Outpatient and Ambulatory Surgery Center Facility Services

Payments for the facility component of hospital outpatient department and ambulatory surgical center (ASC) services represent about 16 percent of total CWCP medical costs (CHSWC, 2003). Generally, a hospital outpatient department is an integral part of a hospital and is subject to the health and safety standards and licensure requirements that are applicable to hospitals. ASCs are freestanding surgical centers that are either participating in the Medicare program or have been licensed by the State of California. Facility fees paid to either entity for ambulatory surgery and to hospitals for emergency room services are not subject to a fee schedule. The negotiated or contracted rates that are used to pay for these services are often based on discounted charges. In cases in which a contract is not in place, the facility's charges are the starting point for determining payment for workers' compensation patients. Charges are considerably higher than costs; therefore, the program is vulnerable to making unnecessarily high payments. Under Medicare, different fee schedules apply to services provided in hospital outpatient departments and services provided in ASCs.

California Assembly Bill 749 (2002) authorized the establishment of a fee schedule for ambulatory surgical services but imposed a number of requirements that will postpone a fee schedule for a number of years. An alternative would be to adapt the Medicare fee schedules to pay for ambulatory surgery services. Several policy issues would need to be resolved before doing so. The most basic issue is whether the Medicare payment scheme of paying for surgery furnished in hospital outpatient departments using one payment system and paying for surgery performed in freestanding ASCs with a different fee schedule should be adopted or whether the same fee schedule, perhaps with different conversion factors, should be used for both settings.

The current ASC fee schedule has several shortcomings that suggest it might be less burdensome to simply use the hospital outpatient prospective payment system to pay for services in either setting:

- The information used to establish the costs of procedures performed in ASCs is outdated and may not reflect the current costs of performing the procedures.
- Medicare has a relatively narrow list of Medicare-approved procedures that are covered in an ASC, and that list does not include some procedures that are currently paid for in an ASC under the OMFS. The list of approved procedures includes only procedures that can be safely performed in an ASC for Medicare patients and may be more restrictive than necessary for younger and less frail members of the workers' compensation population.
- The Medicare list does not include procedures that are commonly performed in a physician's office in order to discourage a shift of these procedures from physicians' offices to an ASC.

Procedures that are not on the approved list are paid under the RB-RVS as if they were furnished in a physician's office (i.e., no separate facility fee is payable). It appears that ASCs are already paid a facility fee for minor surgical services under the OMFS; therefore, adopting the hospital outpatient fee schedule should not create a new incentive to shift services from physicians' offices to ASCs.

Other issues that would arise if Medicare fee schedules are adapted to pay for ambulatory surgery services are the level at which the conversion factor should be established and whether the same CF should be used for both settings. The Medicare payment system for hospital outpatient services was not designed to cover the full accounting costs of furnishing services to Medicare beneficiaries. The original system was intended to be budget neutral to the prior payment system, which paid approximately 82 percent of amounts reported on the Medicare cost report. This means that the original CF was set to provide an 18 percent discount below reported cost. To some extent, these costs are overstated because the DRG payment for inpatient services encouraged shifting costs to outpatient services. Nevertheless, a multiplier somewhat higher than 1.22 is needed to cover estimated costs and provide an efficient hospital with a positive margin on outpatient services (e.g., a multiplier of 1.27 would provide a 5-percent margin, which is the average hospital margin on patient care services). To be comparable with the rates paid by private payers, i.e., an estimated payment-to-cost ratio of 1.125, the multiplier would need to be as high as 1.37 (1.125 x 1.22).

In the absence of current cost data, the empirical data needed to inform a decision regarding the appropriate conversion factor for ASC services are limited. Available information suggests ASCs do not need a conversion factor as high as the CF hospitals need for ambulatory surgery. Hospital outpatient departments have higher cost structures than ASCs because they must meet more demanding regulatory requirements, such as the Emergency Medical Treatment and Active Labor Act, and stricter Medicare certification and state licensure requirements (MedPAC, 2003), and they are more likely to incur uncompensated care costs. ASCs are also more likely than hospital outpatient departments to have higher productivity because they specialize in certain procedures, whereas most hospitals perform the full array of surgical procedures.

An examination of Medicare beneficiary characteristics found that hospitals were more likely to perform the same procedures on patients at higher risk (MedPAC, 2003). Setting the conversion factor at an unnecessarily high level would provide incentives for unnecessary utilization. However, available information also indicates ASCs will experience significant payment reductions under a fee schedule. One option is to phase in the payment reductions by setting the initial conversion factor at a relatively high level and reducing it over time. In the interim, monitoring for changes in the settings where care is delivered, analyzing the cost and quality implications of care furnished in alternative ambulatory settings, and analyzing the amounts paid by private payers can be done to better inform decisionmaking on this issue.

In summary, consideration should be given to

- using the structure of Medicare's prospective payment system for hospital outpatient services to pay for procedures performed in both hospital outpatient departments and ASCs

- establishing a higher conversion factor for hospital outpatient services than for ASC services
- phasing in the fee schedule by setting the initial conversion factor at a relatively high level and reducing it over time
- monitoring for changes in access to and quality of care in ambulatory settings.

Another important issue is whether Medicare's fee schedule for hospital outpatient services should also be used to pay for other medical and diagnostic services furnished by hospital outpatient departments. Except for emergency room services, the current OMFS does not expressly authorize separate payment for the facility fee for these services. In contrast, Medicare pays a facility fee for clinic and emergency room care. The OMFS fee schedule pays the same amount for the technical component of diagnostic tests across ambulatory settings, whereas the Medicare payments for these procedures in a hospital outpatient department differ from the amounts payable under the RB-RVS to freestanding diagnostic treatment centers and physician offices. For example, Medicare's payment for a two-view chest X-ray is $25.34 when it is furnished in a physician's office or freestanding diagnostic treatment center and $44.95 when it is furnished as a hospital outpatient service. The maximum allowable amount under the OMFS is $28.50 across all ambulatory settings.

There are two basic policymaking choices concerning medical and diagnostic services furnished in hospital outpatient departments:

- Use Medicare's policies for determining when facility fees are payable. This option would allow facility fees to be charged for both medical and surgical services and would create site-of-service differentials for radiology and other diagnostic tests.
- Retain current OMFS policies regarding when facility fees are payable (surgical procedures and emergency room only). When a facility fee is not payable, the total payment (hospital and physician) would be limited to the same total payment that would be made for an office-based service.

Overall, the benefits of linking the OMFS to existing Medicare fee schedules would be diluted if the program's basic payment policies were not adopted at the same time. The limited amount of readily available data on hospital outpatient services precludes an analysis of the financial impact of the alternative policies. Regardless of the decision, it will be important to monitor where ambulatory care is being delivered in the future and to evaluate the impact of the payment policies on cost, access, and quality of care.

Diagnostic Clinical Laboratory Tests

Currently, the OMFS uses a relative value fee schedule to pay for laboratory tests with separate technical and professional components. Medicare uses the RB-RVS to pay for the professional component and a separate fee schedule to pay for the technical component of laboratory tests. The fee schedule pays the lowest amount of the actual charge billed for the test, a locally determined fee schedule amount, or a national limitation amount. For most tests, the national limit is 74 percent of the median of the local fees and is typically the controlling payment amount. As with other fee schedules, CMS has an established process for updating the fee schedule on an annual basis. However, the fee schedule has been frozen several times since it was first established, most recently between 1998 and 2002. If the OMFS is linked to the Medicare fee schedule, one decision to be made will be whether to adopt the Medicare inflation factor or to establish an independent adjustment for inflation.

There are also secondary issues regarding how Medicare-unique codes or new codes without an established Medicare fee schedule amount should be handled. Overall, using the Medicare fee schedules would provide a mechanism for updating the codes and fee schedule amounts on an annual basis. A comparison between the aggregate maximum allowable amounts that would be allowed under the current OMFS and the Medicare fee schedule has not been made. This information is needed to estimate a cost-neutral multiplier and analyze the impact of moving from the OMFS to the Medicare fee schedule.

Durable Medical Equipment, Prosthetics, Orthotics, and Supplies

For the Medicare beneficiary, durable medical equipment (DME) is defined as equipment that can withstand repeated use, that generally serves a medical purpose, and that is intended for use in the home. DME is paid on a fee schedule reflecting local and regional prices for six categories of items that are updated annually based on the rate of change in the Consumer Price Index: All Urban Consumers (CPI-U).

- Payment for inexpensive or routinely purchased items is made on a rental or lump-sum basis using the lower of the actual charge or the fee schedule amount.
- Equipment requiring frequent servicing is reimbursed as a rental.
- Oxygen and oxygen equipment is paid a monthly fee schedule amount with an added payment for portable oxygen equipment.
- Carrier discretion is allowed for customized DME.
- Prosthetics and orthotics are generally reimbursed on a lump-sum payment basis.
- Certain rental items (hospital beds and wheelchairs) are paid at national rates based on the lesser of actual charges or 10 percent of the allowable purchase price for the first three months and then 7.5 percent of the allowable purchase price each month for up to 15 months of continuous use. Thereafter, suppliers must furnish the item at no charge other than maintenance and servicing.

One issue stemming from linking to the durable medical equipment, prosthetics, orthotics, and supplies (DMEPOS) fee schedule is whether the range of equipment covered by CWCP is broader than Medicare's coverage such that there are items and equipment that do not have Medicare prices. Analysis of DMEPOS claims would be needed to assess whether these items and equipment are used in high volumes. If they are high-volume items, a maximum allowable fee would still be appropriate to reduce program vulnerability and the administrative costs of case-by-case pricing, but the fee would need to be established independently of the Medicare fee schedule. For low-volume items, a continuation of current OMFS policies might be sufficient. These policies provide for reimbursing the lower of (1) the provider's customary charge or (2) cost (purchase price plus sales tax, shipping, and handling) plus (a) 20 percent of the cost up to $15 for supplies and materials other than DME or (b) 50 percent of the cost up to $25 for DME. A second issue is whether Medicare rules concerning rental versus purchase of equipment and other special policies should be adopted at the same time. Paid claims data would need to be analyzed to determine the impact of adopting the special policies as well as the Medicare fee schedule.

The DMEPOS fee schedules are updated on a quarterly basis in order to implement fee schedule amounts for new codes and to revise any fee schedule amounts for existing codes that were calculated in error. While the necessary information to make the changes is readily available, the frequency of the updates may pose an administrative challenge. An annual update with new services excluded from the fee schedule for up to nine months may be sufficient for purposes of the OMFS.

Skilled Nursing Services

Medicare pays for short-term skilled nursing facility (SNF) care following a three-day qualifying hospital stay using a per diem prospective payment rate. A person receiving SNF level of care is defined as needing skilled care or skilled rehabilitative care on a daily basis (five times per week for therapy) that as a practical matter can be provided only on an inpatient basis. Custodial care is not covered under the Medicare program. For Medicare payment purposes, patients are assigned to one of 44 resource utilization groups (RUGs) based on the patient's service needs and expected resource requirements. One issue that should be reviewed before linking the OMFS fee schedule to Medicare fee schedules is whether Medicare's payment for skilled nursing care is appropriate for the levels of care covered by the CWCP.

Medicare's rates are all-inclusive rates that cover all medically necessary services provided by the SNF. The SNF is required to bill directly for all services (whether those services are provided by the SNF or by an outside supplier under arrangements with the SNF) that are not expressly excluded from the provision. A comparable rule would be needed to assure that the CWCP does not pay for services twice—once through the per diem rate and again through an outside supplier (e.g., a physical therapist or pharmacy).

Home Health Services

Medicare makes a prospective payment covering all services other than DME provided during a 60-day episode of care provided by a home health agency. The payment is adjusted for clinical severity, functional severity, and service utilization. However, it also reflects the nature of the Medicare home health benefit. To be eligible for home health care, a Medicare beneficiary must be homebound and need intermittent skilled nursing care or therapy services. The per episode payment reflects the typical mix of Medicare-covered services provided during the 60-day episode.

Further analysis of the home care services provided to CWCP patients is advisable to determine if the per episode payment reflects the types and duration of home care needed by CWCP patients. If the episodic payment is not appropriate, Medicare's per visit payment for low-volume episodes might be. If fewer than five visits are provided during a 60-day episode, Medicare pays the home health agency (HHA) a per-visit amount that varies by type of visit rather than the per-episode amount. These wage-adjusted rates might be a suitable basis for a per-visit fee schedule. A per-visit payment methodology can provide incentives for excess utilization but, in the absence of a good case mix adjustment, is still preferable to excluding home care from the OMFS. The appropriateness of the per-visit rates for home health aide/homemaker services covered by the CWCP would need to be evaluated because there can be considerable variation in the duration of these visits.

Ambulance Services

CMS implemented a fee schedule for ambulance services in April 2002. Payment is based on the relative value for the service, a geographic adjustment factor, and a uniform conversion factor. Fourteen codes are used to describe the level of service, supplies and equipment used, and mileage. CMS has established a five-year transition period using a blend of old and new payment amounts, but only the new payment system is feasible for the OMFS to consider. The fee schedule rates are to be updated annually based on the rate of increase in the CPI-U. Through FY 2006, Medicare payments under the fee schedule are to be budget-neutral to estimated payments that would have been made under the prior payment system. As a result, the update factor that is applied to the conversion factor may not be appropriate for the CWCP, and consideration should be given to applying only the CPI-U.

Research Agenda

RAND's analysis of the policy considerations involved in linking the OMFS to the Medicare fee schedules highlighted the need for ongoing data collection on the services provided to CWCP patients. In the short run, the lack of readily available data limits the ability to model the impact of moving from the current OMFS to the Medicare fee schedules and to understand how overall OMFS payment levels compare with Medicare payment levels and those of private payers. This information would be helpful in establishing the OMFS conversion factor and in determining transition policies for ambulatory facility fees, laboratory tests, and DMEPOS. The Lewin Group (2002) study provides the needed information on the impact of the RB-RVS, but additional information on private payer fee levels would be beneficial. Other areas in which further analysis would benefit the policymaking process include

- evaluating the impact of adopting the geographic adjustment factor and other policy choices in adopting the RB-RVS for physician and other practitioner services
- modeling the financial implications of alternative fee schedules for ambulatory surgery center facility services and hospital outpatient services
- evaluating whether the bundled payments for inpatient services furnished in rehabilitation facilities, long-term care hospitals, and skilled nursing facilities and for home health episodes of care are appropriate for worker's compensation patients.

In the longer term, additional research is also needed to inform decisions regarding potential refinements to the payment system. Further analyses that would benefit future decisionmaking include

- assessing whether patient characteristics affect where ambulatory surgery is performed and whether there are differences in outcomes across the different settings
- determining the hardware and instrumentation costs that are included in the back and neck DRG payments for inpatient hospital services
- reviewing the medical literature on back and spinal procedures to see if the evidence would support practice guidelines for the procedures and use of new technology hardware and instrumentation.

Linking the OMFS to Medicare fee schedules would expand the services covered by the OMFS and reduce the administrative burden of keeping the rates current by capitalizing on the regular updates that the CMS performs for Medicare. The impact on patient access to quality medical care and program expenditures largely would be determined by the overall level at which payments are set. Ongoing data collection and analysis would be needed to monitor access, cost, and quality of care and to address issues of potential concern. This activity would be needed to assure that linking the OMFS to Medicare fee schedules does not have unintended consequences affecting CWCP patient access to medically appropriate services or program expenditures.

Acknowledgments

This report owes its existence to the dedicated efforts of Christine Baker, Executive Director of CHSWC, to explore the implications of linking the OMFS to the Medicare fee schedules. She had the strategic vision that provided the initial impetus for this study and its funding by CHSWC, and she facilitated efforts to gather the data and other information needed for the analyses. I thank the Commissioners of CHSWC for funding this study and for their leadership. I also appreciate the valuable support throughout this project from a number of other individuals, including Joel Gomberg and Irina Nemirovsky at the CHSWC; Frank Neuhauser of the University of California at Berkeley Survey Research Center; Rea Crane and Alex Swedlow at the California Workers' Compensation Institute; and Robert Reville and Carole Gresenz of the RAND Institute for Civil Justice. I benefited from thoughtful and constructive comments provided by Ross Anthony, Gerald Kominski, members of the ICJ Board of Overseers, members of ICJ's Insurance Advisory Committee, and other individuals who reviewed an earlier version of this report.

I would like to thank Jennifer Popovic for her programming support, Lisa Spear and Joanna Nelsen for providing general administrative support, Nancy DelFavero and Laura Zakaras for their editorial work on the final document, and Christopher Dirks for providing assistance in preparing the final document.

Acronyms

AA	Anesthesia assistant
AD	Administrative Director
AHQR	Agency for Health Care Quality Research
AMA	American Medical Association
AMI	Acute myocardial infarction
APC	Ambulatory payment classification (group)
ASA	American Society of Anesthesiologists
ASC	Ambulatory surgical center
BLS	Bureau of Labor Statistics
BR	By report
CC	Complication and/or comorbidity
CF	Conversion factor
CFR	Code of Federal Regulations
CHSWC	Commission on Health and Safety and Workers' Compensation
CMG	Case mix group
CMI	Case mix index
CMS	Centers for Medicare and Medicaid Services
CPI	Consumer Price Index
CPI-U	CPI: All Urban Consumers
CPT-4	*Physicians' Current Procedure Terminology,* Fourth Edition
CRNA	Certified registered nurse anesthetist
CWCI	California Workers' Compensation Institute
CWCP	California Workers' Compensation Program
CY	Calendar year
DHHS	Department of Health and Human Services
DME	Durable medical equipment
DMEPOS	Durable medical equipment, prosthetics, orthotics, and supplies
DoD	Department of Defense
DRG	Diagnosis-related group
DSH	Disproportionate share (adjustment for low-income patients)
DWC	Division of Workers' Compensation
E&M	Evaluation and management
FDA	Food and Drug Administration
FR	Federal Register
FY	Fiscal year
GAF	Geographic adjustment factor
GPCI	Geographic practice cost index
GROUPER	Program to assign inpatient stays into DRGs
HCFA	Health Care Financing Administration

HCPCS	HCFA Common Procedure Coding System
HCRIS	Healthcare Cost Report Information System
HHA	Home health agency
HMO	Health maintenance organization
HOPD	Hospital outpatient department
HPSA	Health Professional Shortage Areas
HUD	U.S. Department of Housing and Urban Development
ICD-9-CM	International Classification of Diseases, Ninth Revision, Clinical Modifications
ICJ	Institute for Civil Justice
IMC	Industrial Medical Council
IME	Indirect medical education (adjustment)
IPPS	Inpatient PPS
IRF	Inpatient rehabilitation facility
IV	Intravenous
LTC-DRG	Long-term care DRG
LTCH	Long-term care hospital
MB	(Hospital) market basket (of goods and services)
MDC	Major diagnostic category
MediCal	Medicaid (California)
MedPAC	Medicare Payment Advisory Commission
MEI	Medicare Economic Index
MIRCal	Medical Information Reporting for California
MRI	Magnetic resonance imaging
MSA	Metropolitan Statistical Area
N	Number
NLA	National limitation amount
OACT	Office of the Actuary, CMS
OMFS	Official Medical Fee Schedule
OPPS	Outpatient PPS
OSHPD	Office of Statewide Health Planning and Development
PEAC	Practice Expense Advisory Committee
PET	Positron emission tomography
PPI	Producer Price Index
PPS	Prospective payment system
PTCA	Percutaneous transluminal coronary angioplasty
RB-RVS	Resource-based relative value scale
RUC	Relative (Value) Update Committee (AMA)
RUG	Resource utilization group
RVS	Relative value scale
RVU	Relative value unit
SASD	State Ambulatory Surgery Databases
SGR	Sustainable growth rate
SNF	Skilled nursing facility

SWW	(Average) statewide weekly wages
TENS	Transcutaneous electrical nerve stimulator
WCIRB	Workers' Compensation Insurance Rating Bureau
WCRI	Workers' Compensation Research Institute
WI	Wage Index

1. Introduction

Background

California's workers' compensation law covers more than 14 million employees. About 800,000 job injuries occur annually, of which two-thirds are "medical-only" claims requiring only medical treatment. In the remaining one-third, the worker is unable to work for one or more days. Injured workers are entitled to receive all medical care reasonably required to cure or relieve the effects of their injury. The average age of a workers' compensation claimant is 37.7 years, and males file two-thirds of the claims (California Workers' Compensation Institute [CWCI], 2003). The most-common injuries suffered by workers' compensation claimants are sprains and strains (38.5 percent of all injuries), cuts and lacerations (7.1 percent), and bruises and contusions (5.8 percent) (CWCI, 2001a) (see Figure 1.1).

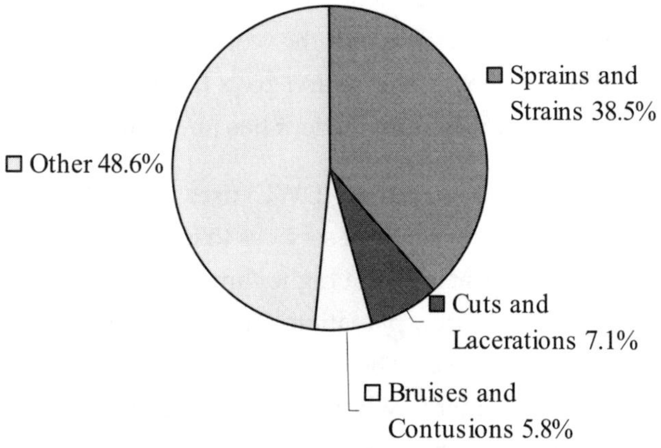

Figure 1.1—Most Common Injuries of Workers' Compensation Claimants

In 2001, system-wide medical payments for California workers' compensation patients totaled about $4.4 billion (California Commission on Health and Safety and Workers' Compensation [CHSWC], 2002). Figure 1.2 shows the distribution of those payments.

About 36 percent of payments to physicians cannot by classified by physician specialty. As a percentage of the remaining payments to physicians, the top specialties were: chiropractic, 17.0 percent; physical therapy, 15.8 percent; orthopedic, 10.9 percent; and general and family practice, 10.7 percent. Clinics received 12.8 percent of the classified payments (Workers' Compensation Insurance Rating Bureau [WCIRB], 2002).

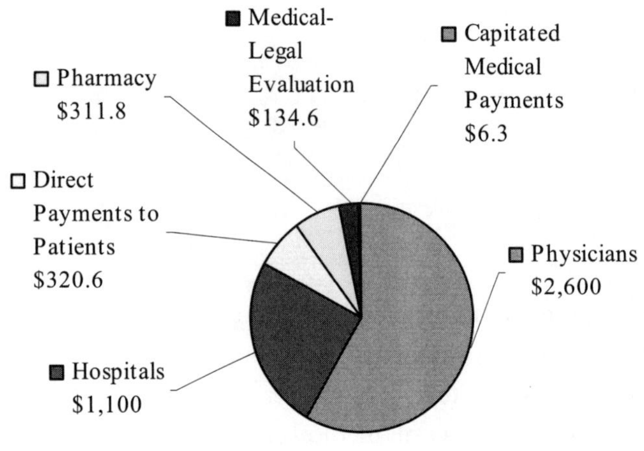

Figure 1.2—System-Wide Distribution of Medical Payments (in millions $)

Approximately two-thirds of the total payroll in California is covered for workers' compensation through insurance policies issued by about 100 private for-profit insurers and one public nonprofit insurer. The remaining third of the state payroll is covered through self-insurance (CHSWC, 2002). When an injured worker files a workers' compensation claim and seeks medical care, the provider files a claim with the workers' compensation insurer for payment. If the medical claim is accepted, the insurer pays for the service in accordance with the Official Medical Fee Schedule (OMFS) and the patient has no liability for the service.

The Division of Workers' Compensation (DWC) uses the OMFS to set the maximum allowable amounts that may be paid for medical services to providers. The OMFS does not apply if the insurer and provider have contracted for a higher amount or if a higher charge is reasonable, itemized, and justified by an explanation of extraordinary circumstances related to the unusual nature of the medical services. The OMFS covers most medical services provided by a physician or other health care provider to whom the patient has been referred; however, maximum allowable amounts have not been established for facility fees associated with surgical procedures performed in hospital outpatient settings and ambulatory surgical centers. These procedures represent about 16 percent of expenditures for medical services (CHSWC, 2003). The negotiated or contracted rates that are used to pay for these services are often based on discounted charges. Where a contract is not in place, the facility's charges are the starting point for determining payment for workers' compensation patients. In this case, the program is vulnerable to making excessive payments for these services because charges are considerably higher than facility costs.

DWC has not had the resources to update the existing fee schedules on a regular basis. The portions of the OMFS applying to inpatient hospital services and to physician and other practitioner services have not been updated since 2001 and 1999, respectively. For physician and diagnostic services, California has low fee schedule payments relative to the workers' compensation programs of other states. According to a Workers' Compensation Research Institute study (Eccleston et al., 2002), California ranked the sixth lowest of 40 states in 2001 with an overall payment level for physician and diagnostic services that was 12 percent higher than Medicare fee levels.[3]

Medical costs are the fastest increasing component of the California workers' compensation program (CWCP), increasing from 45 percent of benefit costs in the mid-1990s to an estimated 55 percent in 2003. During this period, the average medical benefits paid per indemnity claim have been increasing 15 percent annually (CHSWC, 2002). Most of the higher costs are attributable to utilization increases. However, there are inefficiencies in the payment system as well. For example, the lack of regular updates imposes an administrative burden on both insurers and providers. They are forced to maintain outdated procedure codes in their billing and claims processing systems and negotiate on a claim-by-claim basis any payments for new procedures that do not have maximum allowable fees. Most important, the lack of maximum allowable fees for ambulatory surgery results in not only higher treatment costs but also additional administrative costs because payments must be negotiated.

In January 2003, the California Senate Labor and Industrial Relations Committee requested that the CHSWC develop medical cost savings proposals. CHSWC is recommending that CWCP adopt Medicare's[4] fee schedules for all services other than pharmaceuticals. With few exceptions, the program uses fee schedules that are regularly updated to pay for medical care provided to its beneficiaries. These fee schedules cover most of the medical services covered by the CWCP (see Table 1.1).

CWCP already models its OMFS for inpatient hospital services on Medicare's payment system and has adopted elements of other fee schedules, such as the global billing periods for surgery[5] and Medicare relative values[6] for orthotics and prosthetics. Because Medicare does not cover most outpatient prescription drugs that can be self-administered, CHSWC is recommending that the California Medicaid (MediCal) program's fee schedule be used for pharmaceuticals. Under CHSWC's proposal, the only component of the OMFS that would require regulatory action is the multiplier, or adjustment, to the Medicare rates that would establish the overall payment levels for the California workers' compensation program.

---

[3]The relationship between California workers' compensation program (CWCP) fee levels and Medicare fee levels was determined by comparing the amounts that would be payable for a standard market basket of procedures under the two fee schedules; it was not determined through claims analysis of the actual distribution of CWCP claims. We estimate that California's 12-percent premium has increased to about 15 percent since 2001 because Medicare's conversion factor has decreased 3.8 percent while California's fee levels have remained unchanged.

[4]Medicare is the federal health insurance program for the aged, the disabled, and persons with end-stage renal disease.

[5]For surgical services, the "global billing period" is the period during which the pre- and post-operative care provided by the surgeon is covered by the payment for the surgical procedure.

[6]Most fee schedules include a relative value or weight that measures the resources required for a given service or group of services relative to other services.

Table 1.1
Overview of Medicare Payment System and OMFS by Type of Service

Service	Medicare Payment System	OMFS
Inpatient Hospital	Inpatient Hospital	Inpatient Hospital
Acute care hospitals	Predetermined per-case payment based on the patient's principal and secondary diagnoses, procedures, and age.	Already incorporates a modified version of the Medicare system. Exempts certain diagnosis-related groups (DRGs).
Freestanding rehabilitation hospitals and units of acute care hospitals	Predetermined per-case payment based on impairment, functional status, age, complications, and co-morbid conditions.	Currently exempts rehabilitation services. Assessment needed to determine if Medicare system is appropriate for CWCP patients.
Freestanding psychiatric hospitals and units of acute care hospitals	Cost subject to rate of increase limit on aggregate per-discharge costs. Per-diem prospective payment system under development.	Currently exempts psychiatric facilities from the OMFS. Medicare's cost-based system is not suitable for CWCP.
Long-term care hospitals	Pre-determined per-case payment based on patient's principal and secondary diagnoses, procedures, and patient's age.	Currently exempts long-term care hospitals. Assessment needed to determine if Medicare system appropriate for CWCP patients.
Physician and Other Practitioners, Outpatient Rehabilitation, and Non-Hospital Radiology	Resource-based relative value fee schedule; Medicare does not cover some services and providers that are covered by CWCP.	Charge-based relative value fee schedule.
Outpatient clinical laboratory tests	Charge-based fee schedule with national limits applicable to independent laboratories and physician offices; professional component paid under RB-RVS.	Charge-based relative value scale (RVS) applicable to all outpatient lab tests. Separate technical and professional components.
Other Hospital Outpatient Services	Facility fee paid for all services based on 570 clinically coherent groupings of procedures with similar cost.	Separate facility fees payable only for ambulatory surgery and emergency room. Fees exempt from OMFS.
Freestanding Ambulatory Surgical Center Procedures	Facility fee based on nine payment groups for procedures on approved list; if not on approved list, physician payment same as if performed in office setting.	Facility fees currently exempt from OMFS.
Durable Medical Equipment, Prosthetics, Orthotics, and Supplies	Charge-based fee schedule	Charge-based RVS. Uses Medicare relative value units (RVUs) for orthotics and prosthetics.
Outpatient Renal Dialysis	Capitated monthly rate	Currently exempts outpatient renal dialysis
Skilled Nursing Facility Inpatient Services	Per-diem rate based on 44 resource-utilization groups	Currently exempts skilled nursing facility inpatient services
Home health agency services	Case mix adjusted payment for 60-day episodes	Currently exempts home health agency services
Ambulance	National fee schedule transition	Currently exempts ambulance services

There are several potential advantages to linking the OMFS to the Medicare fee schedule:

- It would shift the administrative burden of ongoing fee schedule refinement and regular updates to the Centers for Medicare and Medicaid Services (CMS) and allow the DWC to concentrate its limited resources on issues specific to workers' compensation.
- It would expand the services covered by the OMFS. In addition, most Medicare fee schedules relate payments to the resources required to provide the services, which creates incentives for the efficient delivery of appropriate services. If payments are substantially less than the costs, there may be problems with access to care. If payments are substantially higher than costs, excessive expenditures occur, and incentives are created for providing unnecessary services.
- Regular updating of the fee schedules will eliminate the need for providers and payers to maintain outdated procedure codes in their billing and claims-processing systems.
- Most providers have relatively few workers' compensation patients but a substantial number of Medicare patients. The administrative burden of treating workers' compensation patients will be reduced if those providers no longer need to remain current on a separate set of OMFS payment rules.

Concerns with linking the OMFS to the Medicare fee schedules focus on (1) establishing an appropriate overall payment level that is sufficient to provide injured workers with access to high-quality medically necessary care and (2) payment redistributions that would occur across physician specialties. Overall, Medicare payment rates are generally lower than private payer rates. For physician services, Medicare's payment rates are a lower percentage of private payer payment rates for surgery and anesthesia than for evaluation and management services.

Workers' compensation programs in other states have adopted the structure of the Medicare fee schedules, but with different multipliers. The experience of those programs and their modifications for workers'-compensation–specific services could inform the decisions that DWC would need to make in adapting the Medicare fee schedules for the CWCP.

- At least 17 states, the District of Columbia, and the federal workers' compensation program have adopted Medicare's resource-based relative value scale (RB-RVS) to pay physicians and other practitioners (although a number of states have retained service-specific conversion factors).[7]
- At least seven states are using the Medicare fee schedule for freestanding ambulatory surgery centers to pay for ambulatory surgery. In addition, one state has implemented a fee schedule for hospital outpatient services based on Medicare's fee schedule (CHSWC, 2003).

---

[7]Key features of these fee schedules are detailed in Eccleston et al. (2002); Kominski, Pourat, and Black (1999); and The Lewin Group (2002).

Study Purpose and Approach

CHSWC asked RAND to identify the issues that would need to be addressed if the OMFS were to be linked to Medicare fee schedules. Those issues include

- issues that are likely to arise from existing differences between the two fee schedules
- issues surrounding the modifications that might be necessary to tailor the Medicare fee schedules to CWCP patients
- issues regarding the implications of automatic annual updates.

Our focus was on features of the Medicare fee schedule that are at variance with the existing OMFS fee schedule and the issues that need to be considered in deciding whether to retain particular features of the OMFS or adopt the Medicare policies. Generally, these decisions involve a trade-off between policy objectives, administrative burden, and/or payment redistributions. Some issues, such as whether the fee schedule for physician services should have a single conversion factor or multiple conversion factors that account for current payment differentials, primarily involve a trade-off between improving the match between payments and the costs of providing services and redistributing current payments across geographic areas or physician specialties. Other issues, such as whether adjustments are needed to reflect the differences in the populations covered by Medicare and the California workers' compensation program, involve a trade-off between administrative burden and payment accuracy. Administrative burden is minimized if the Medicare fee schedule payment parameters are adopted without modification. However, the populations and services covered by Medicare and workers' compensation are different, and some modifications may be needed to ensure that payments are generally appropriate. This concern is primarily applicable to payments that are based on a "bundle" of individual services furnished to Medicare patients. For example, the facility payments for hospital inpatient care cover all the services provided during the stay.

Prior research by other organizations has explored many of the issues that need to be considered in adopting the Medicare fee schedules. Given the limited amount of time available for this study, RAND drew heavily from this previous work as well as from detailed information on the OMFS and Medicare fee schedules to identify the policy options and potential impact if the link to Medicare fee schedules were to occur. In particular, we drew extensively on several studies that have examined issues related to adopting Medicare fee schedules:

- The Industrial Medical Council asked Kominski, Pourat, and Black (1999) to investigate the use of relative value scales for provider reimbursement in state workers' compensation programs. Their report identifies a number of issues that need to be considered in establishing a fee schedule for physician and other practitioner services. This study was followed by a study by The Lewin Group (2002) that specifically examined the Medicare RB-RVS. RAND used the impact analyses by The Lewin Group to model alternative policies for transitioning from the current charge-based relative value scale to the RB-RVS.

- CHSWC asked Kominski and Gardner (2001) to compare current CWCP payments for inpatient hospital services and ambulatory surgery with the Medicare fee schedules for those services. RAND used the impact analyses from the Kominski and Gardner report to determine the range of surgical procedures for which facility fees are being paid and to assess the overall impact of establishing maximum allowable fees for these services at the Medicare payment rate.

- The Workers' Compensation Research Institute has done a number of comparative studies of payment levels across state workers' compensation programs that benchmark to the Medicare RB-RVS fee schedule. The comparisons are based on a market basket of high-volume procedures performed on worker's compensation patients. We used this market basket to make our comparisons of OMFS and Medicare payments for specific procedures.

Organization of This Report

The remaining chapters of this report present detailed findings regarding the policy issues involved in linking the OMFS to the Medicare fee schedules. In-depth reviews were done of three types of services that constitute most medical care costs: inpatient hospital services, physician and other practitioner services, and hospital outpatient and ambulatory surgery center services. These are the areas for which earlier studies provide information that can be used to estimate the impact of adopting the Medicare fee schedules.

Chapter 2 analyzes the OMFS for inpatient hospital services. The OMFS for services furnished by acute care hospitals is based on the Medicare fee schedule for these services with certain modifications. The RAND research team focused its study on those aspects of the OMFS that differ from the Medicare fee schedule and that inform the discussion of issues related to automatic linking of the OMFS to the Medicare fee schedule. Chapter 2 presents a comparison of the costs of inpatient stays for workers' compensation patients with the Medicare payment rates for those stays. Particular attention is given to

- the 1.2 multiplier that the OMFS applies to the Medicare rate
- the acute care hospital services that are excluded from the OMFS
- the OMFS "pass-through" (additional payments based on cost) for hardware used in neck and back procedures
- additional protections that hospitals receive under Medicare policies if they are the sole source of hospital care reasonably available in their community.

Chapter 3 compares the current charge-based relative value scale (RVS) that the OMFS uses for physician and other practitioner services to the Medicare RB-RVS for these services. The Medicare RB-RVS and the OMFS have a number of structural differences that require several policy choices to be made before linking to the Medicare fee schedule:

- The overall payment level (as determined by a multiplier to the Medicare rate)

- Whether a geographic adjustment factor should be implemented
- Whether the site-of-service differential for the practice expense component should be adopted
- Whether anesthesia should be included in the RB-RVS
- Policies that could be used to transition from the current charge-based RVS to the RB-RVS.

Chapter 4 discusses the issues involved in linking the OMFS to Medicare fee schedules for hospital outpatient services and surgical procedures performed in freestanding ambulatory surgery centers. The three most important policy choices in that area are the following:

- Whether the Medicare payment scheme of paying for surgery furnished in hospital outpatient departments using one payment system and paying for surgery performed in freestanding ambulatory surgical centers (ASCs) with a different fee schedule should be adopted, or whether the same fee schedule—perhaps with different conversion factors—should be used for both settings
- Whether Medicare's fee schedule for hospital outpatient services should also be used to pay for services that are not currently eligible for a facility fee (currently, facility fees are payable only for surgical procedures and emergency room services)
- The overall payment levels (as determined by a multiplier to the Medicare rate).

Chapter 5 covers the major issues that are likely to arise from linking the OMFS to the remaining Medicare fee schedules for other medical services, items, and supplies including non-hospital clinical laboratory diagnostic tests; durable medical equipment, prosthetics, orthotics, and supplies; ambulance services; and post-acute care services provided by skilled nursing facilities and home health agencies. Except for post-acute services, the main issues are the overall payment levels, whether ancillary payment-related policies should be adopted at the same time that the OMFS is linked to the Medicare fee schedules, and whether there are some services covered by CWCP for which Medicare has not established payment rates. For post-acute care services, a major issue is whether the bundle of Medicare services included in the payment rate is appropriate for the workers' compensation population.

Finally, Chapter 6 highlights the general conclusions drawn from the comparison of each Medicare fee schedule, summarizes specific study findings, and identifies the areas in which additional research and analysis would benefit the policy decisions that need to be made in linking the OMFS to Medicare fee schedules.

2. Hospital Inpatient Fee Schedule

Overview of the Current OMFS Fee Schedule

The OMFS inpatient hospital fee schedule for acute care hospitals is based on the Medicare prospective payment system (PPS). Payment is limited to a predetermined amount per stay based on the diagnosis-related group (DRG) to which the patient is assigned and the hospital's characteristics. In general, cases are classified into DRGs based on principal diagnosis (the condition which caused the admission); up to eight additional diagnoses; up to six procedures performed during the stay; age; sex; and discharge status.

Most patients are assigned to DRGs that are defined by major diagnostic categories (MDCs) based on a single etiology or organ system. A few DRGs involve multiple body systems (e.g., major multiple trauma). In addition, classification to certain high-cost DRGs is based on procedures rather than on principal diagnosis (e.g., for transplants and tracheostomies). Because patients can have multiple procedures within a single inpatient stay, surgical DRGs in each MDC are assigned in hierarchical order so that patients with multiple procedures are assigned to the surgical DRG with the highest relative weight. Patients are assigned to DRGs using the Medicare GROUPER program that contains the DRG logic (i.e., the set of classification rules) for the payment year.

A hospital's characteristics are reflected in a composite factor, which establishes the standard payment rate for each stay. The composite rate is further adjusted by a DRG relative weight, which reflects the costliness of the average patient in the DRG as compared with patients in other DRGs. Most DRG relative weights and the adjustments embodied in the composite factor (which take into account a hospital's geographic location, teaching activities, and commitment to serving low-income patients) are based on the Medicare PPS. The information for the composite rate is taken from the Medicare PPS impact file that is made available as a public-use file each year when the Medicare rates are updated.

Although the OMFS is based on the Medicare PPS policies and rates, there are several important differences between the two payment systems:

- CMS updates Medicare's prospective payment system annually each October 1, i.e., the payment system was last updated (as of this writing) for federal fiscal year (FY) 2003. The OMFS is using outdated payment parameters—DRG relative weights, standard payment amounts, payment adjustments, and other parameters—from FY 2001 (October 2000–September 2001) and the cost outlier threshold for FY 2000.

- The OMFS multiplies the standard amount that Medicare would pay for an inpatient stay by 1.2; i.e., payments for workers' compensation patients are 20 percent higher than Medicare's payments for patients assigned to the same DRG.
- Certain DRGs are exempt from the OMFS or have a different relative weight based on payments by California group health plans.
- In addition to the DRG fee schedule payment, the costs of "hardware" (implanted devices and instrumentation used during back and neck surgeries) are reimbursed separately under OMFS policies as a pass-through.
- A few hospitals that are paid under the Medicare PPS are exempt under the OMFS because the necessary variables are not readily available to the CWCP. An example is a new hospital whose payment parameters are not reported on the Medicare PPS impact file.

Currently, DWC uses the California administrative rulemaking process to make changes in the inpatient fee schedule. In the following sections, we explore technical and financial issues related to an automatic update in the OMFS for inpatient hospital services that would be based on the annual Medicare update to its PPS. First, the types of changes that are made annually in the Medicare PPS and the process for making the changes are summarized. Next, potential adjustment factors for inflation and the likely impact an automatic update would have on CWCP hospital payments and administrative costs are discussed.

The automatic updates could retain the unique features of the OMFS fee schedule, such as the multiplier, excluded services, and pass-through for hardware used in back and neck procedures. However, following the section on the update process, we identify aspects of the inpatient hospital fee schedule for which modifications might produce savings without adversely impacting patient access. Where feasible, we used readily available administrative data to explore some of these issues by estimating what the payment-to-cost ratio would be for CWCP inpatient stays assuming Medicare payment rates. The data and our general methodology used for these analyses are discussed next. The results are presented in the pertinent sections of the following chapters that draw on the analyses.

Analysis of CWCP Inpatient Records

Data Sources

OSHPD Claims Data. We[8] used inpatient administrative data obtained from the California Office of Statewide Health Planning and Development (OSHPD) for discharges occurring in 2000. In total, there were 3,816,887 discharges, 29,768 of which indicated that the expected primary payer is workers' compensation. In addition to the expected payer, the OSHPD data elements for each discharge include the primary diagnosis and up to 24 secondary

[8]The RAND study team involved in this project.

diagnoses, the principal procedure and up 20 additional procedure codes, FY 2000 DRG assignment, total charges, length of stay, and discharge disposition. We eliminated 503 discharges for workers' compensation patients for which no charges were reported. Most of those discharges were following stays in facilities owned by Kaiser Permanente that are not required to report charges. With no charge data, one cannot estimate the cost of the stay or determine any outlier payments that might be payable. We retained all discharges, regardless of expected primary payer, for any hospital that had at least one workers' compensation patient. In total, there were 3,416,838 inpatient records in our final database. Most of our analyses used 28,684 records for CWCP stays in acute care hospitals other than children's hospitals and cancer hospitals, which are excluded from the Medicare prospective payment system.

Medicare Cost Report Data. We used Medicare cost report data from the Healthcare Cost Report Information System (HCRIS) December 31, 2002, update for hospital cost reporting periods during calendar year 2000. A Medicare cost report is submitted by each Medicare participating hospital based on its own fiscal year.[9] The HCRIS files contain data on costs and charges for routine, ancillary, and outpatient services. The cost report uses a step-down cost accounting methodology to allocate overhead costs to patient care cost centers. The stepped-down costs and charges can be used to develop cost-to-charge ratios by department and an overall cost-to-charge ratio for inpatient services.

Medicare PPS Impact Files. CMS produces the PPS impact files each year as part of the annual PPS update. The files contain the current payment parameters (e.g., the applicable wage index) that can be used to estimate each hospital's payments for the upcoming fiscal year. The CWCP used the FY 2001 file to develop the current composite factors for the OMFS. We used the impact files from FY 2000 and FY 2001 to estimate Medicare payments in 2000. To understand the implications of DRG and payment parameter changes that occurred after 2000, we also used the FY 2003 impact file.

Methodology

Earlier studies have evaluated the adequacy of the Medicare PPS rates for CWCP patients by comparing on a DRG-specific basis the average charges for a CWCP patient with the average charges for Medicare patients. Implicit in this comparison is an assumption that the payment rate is adequate for the Medicare patients assigned to the particular DRG. A more direct indication of whether payments are adequate can be obtained by comparing the Medicare payments that would be made for CWCP patients assigned to the DRG with the estimated costs for their care.

A payment-to-cost ratio of 1.0 indicates that on average Medicare payments are sufficient to cover the estimated costs of workers' compensation patients. According to the Medicare Payment Advisory Commission (MedPAC), the payment-to-cost ratio for Medicare patients for both inpatient and outpatient services in 2000 was 1.002, i.e., payments were only slightly higher

---

[9]Medicare allows hospitals with low Medicare utilization, such as children's hospitals, to file low-volume reports that do not contain all the cost information required for the full cost report.

than the costs (MedPAC, 2003). However, a higher payment-to-cost ratio is needed for a hospital to accumulate capital and remain financially viable. Overall, including non-patient care revenues, hospital financial gains were 4.8 percent of total hospital costs (i.e., a payment-to-cost ratio of 1.048). The private payer payment-to-cost ratio is generally higher than the overall payment-to-cost ratio in order to cross-subsidize patients receiving uncompensated care and Medicaid patients. The overall payment-to-cost ratio for private payers was 1.125 in 2000 (MedPAC, 2003). In summary, a payment-to-cost ratio of 1.0 is sufficient to cover the estimated costs of care and a payment-to-cost ratio of 1.125 is comparable to that of private payers. A payment-to-cost ratio substantially in excess of 1.125 indicates the payment rate may be higher than necessary to provide access to appropriate care.

Developing a payment-to-cost ratio involves two basic steps at the individual claim level: (1) simulating what Medicare would pay for the stay and (2) estimating the costs for the stay. The results can then be aggregated into meaningful analysis categories, e.g., by DRG or other patient characteristics, specific procedures, or hospital characteristics. To support the analyses described in the sections that follow, we developed payment-to-cost ratios for 2000 and 2003. We used the following methodology:

2000 Payment Simulation. To simulate what the maximum allowable amounts would have been in 2000 if the OMFS had used Medicare payment rules without modification, we applied the payment parameters in the PPS impact file to the OSHPD administrative data. We used all records that (1) involved an acute care hospital stay that had at least one CWCP discharge and (2) reported total charges. We applied the FY 2000 Medicare payment parameters to discharges occurring on or before September 30, 2000. We applied the FY 2001 parameters to the remaining discharges that occurred during the last quarter of the fiscal year. OSHPD made all DRG assignments for calendar year 2000 based on the FY 2000 DRG GROUPER. There were only minor DRG changes between FY 2000 and FY 2001 that would have negligible effect on our results. The general formula that we used to estimate payment was

$$\text{Basic Payment}_{ind} = [(\text{Labor-related rate}_{hosp} \times \text{Wage Index}_{hosp} + \text{Non-labor related rate}_{hosp}) \times \text{DRG relative weight}_{ind} \times (1 + \text{OperDSH}_{hosp} + \text{OperIME}_{hosp})] + \text{Capital rate}_{hosp} \times \text{GAF}_{hosp} \times (1 + \text{CapDSH}_{hosp} + \text{CapIME}_{hosp})$$

where

- labor-related and non-labor–related operating rates and the capital rate depend on whether the hospital is located in a large urban area or other type of area
- Wage Index (WI) and Geographic Adjustment Factor (GAF) values are based on the hospital's location. The WI value is determined for each Metropolitan Statistical Area (MSA) and the remaining non-MSAs of the state.
- DRG relative weight is determined by the DRG to which the patient is assigned
- the disproportionate share (DSH) adjustment and indirect medical education (IME) adjustment are the hospital's percentage add-ons for serving a disproportionate share of low-

income patients and for its teaching activities. The add-ons are different for operating and capital payments.

Our payment simulation included Medicare's policy for short-stay transfer cases to another acute care hospital[10] and additional payments for high-cost outlier cases (see discussion below). For various reasons, some acute care hospitals with OSHPD administrative data are not on the Medicare PPS impact file. We assigned a wage index to those hospitals based on their geographic location and estimated other payment parameters from Medicare cost report data.

2000 Cost Estimation. We estimated the costs for each inpatient stay in our analysis file by applying a hospital-specific cost-to-charge ratio for inpatient services to the total charges reported on the OSHPD record.[11] We used the Medicare cost report data to develop the cost-to-charge ratios. For each cost center, the total charges, inpatient and outpatient charges, and total costs are reported. We estimated the departmental costs for inpatient services by developing a ratio of total costs to total charges and applying it to the reported inpatient charges for the department.[12] We determined the overall inpatient cost-to-charge ratio by summing the departmental inpatient costs and dividing them by the sum of the departmental inpatient charges. The overall cost-to-charge ratio is a dollar-weighted average markup for services that are received by hospital inpatients.[13]

In cases in which the hospital's fiscal year does not coincide with the calendar year, we calculated the cost-to-charge ratios as a weighted average of values in the two cost-reporting periods that had portions occurring in 2000. We used the proportion of the calendar year occurring in each of the two cost-reporting periods as our weight. We were missing Medicare cost reporting data for 77 hospitals with CWCP discharges in our analysis file. We assigned the statewide average inpatient cost-to-charge ratio to these hospitals in order to retain the maximum number of hospitals in our analysis. We also assigned the statewide average inpatient cost-to-charge ratio to three other hospitals that we identified as being statistical outliers (having a cost-to-charge ratio that was more than plus or minus three standard deviations from the mean log of

---

[10]The transfer policy applies to stays with an average length that is less than the geometric mean length of stay for the DRG. The general formula provides a per diem amount up to the full DRG amount; the payment for joint replacements provides 0.5 the DRG payment on the first day and a 0.5 per diem thereafter. The transfer policy also applies to short-stay cases in ten DRGs that are discharged to post-acute care (a skilled nursing facility [SNF] or home health agency [HHA]). We did not model the post-acute transfer policy.

[11]We used the Medicare cost report data to develop the cost-to-charge ratios instead of the OSHPD financial data because the Medicare data enable us to calculate a cost-to-charge ratio that is specific to inpatient hospital services. We can determine only an overall cost-to-charge ratio for all (inpatient and outpatient) services from OSHPD data.

[12]We did not include labor and delivery room costs and charges in our calculations because the markup is often considerably different for those services, and they are not likely to be CWCP-covered services. We also excluded the data for distinct part rehabilitation, psychiatric, and SNF units of acute care hospitals because they are not acute care cost centers.

[13]We note that this not the same as the cost-to-charge ratio used to determine outlier payments. That ratio is specific to Medicare patients and is from the hospital's latest settled cost report rather than the cost report for the payment year.

the cost-to-charge ratios). Medicare uses the statewide cost-to-charge ratio in a comparable manner in estimating the costs of inpatient stays for high-cost outlier determinations.

The methodology assumes that costs are consistently related to charges at the departmental level, and that the markup for the mix of services received by CWCP patients is similar to the markup for all inpatient hospital services. We were unable to use the departmental cost-to-charge ratios directly in our cost estimation because the OSHPD data report only total charges for the stay. Having departmental charge data for each record would improve the cost estimate because markups vary across departments and because the mix of services provided to CWCP patients differs from that provided to all patients. CWCP patients represent less than 1 percent of all inpatient stays but account for a significant proportion of stays for orthopedic procedures. We believe our estimates are sufficient to provide a general understanding of the relationship between the Medicare payment rates and the estimated cost of workers' compensation inpatient stays. However, further analyses using departmental charges would be advisable if estimated costs are used to establish any DRG-specific adjustments.

Accounting for Subsequent Changes in DRGs and Other Payment Parameters. We also estimated what the payment-to-cost ratios would have been if the 2003 DRG classification changes and other payment parameters had been in effect. The purpose of this step was to estimate the impact of intervening changes in the DRG classification system and other payment adjustments, such as the hospital wage index and any additional payments for indirect teaching costs and for serving a disproportionate share of low-income patients. This required updating several variables in our estimation:

- We accounted for changes in the DRG classification system between FY 2000 and FY 2003. Where feasible, we mapped hospital discharges from their old DRG assignment to their new DRG assignment based on the ICD-9-CM diagnosis and procedure codes reported in the administrative data (i.e., claims data). Where that mapping was not feasible, we computed a weighted average of the FY 2003 relative weights for the revised DRGs and used it to determine payment for inpatient stays assigned to the old DRG(s). This weighted average approximates what the relative weight would have been for the cases if the DRG classification changes had not occurred. A detailed description of our methodology is in Appendix A.

- We used the Medicare payment adjustments in the FY 2003 impact file to estimate what the 2000 payments would have been using the updated payment adjustments. The updated payment adjustments reflected in the FY 2003 impact file were as follows:

    - The wage index adjustment was updated based on more-current wage data. Along with the DRG changes, the wage index adjustment is budget neutral (that is, the changes do not affect aggregate Medicare payments).

    - The formula for the IME adjustment for operating costs was reduced so that additional payments to teaching hospitals decreased on average about 15 percent (MedPAC, 2003).

- A temporary reduction in the additional payments to hospitals that serve a disproportionate share of low-income patients ended so that additional payments to these hospitals increased by 3 percent. In addition, increases in the formula that primarily benefit rural and small urban hospitals went into effect.

We held the 2000 standard payment rate and outlier thresholds constant and did not adjust hospital charges or estimated costs for inflation. This approach has the effect of updating the payment adjustments without our having to make assumptions about inflation and behavioral changes, such as a reduction in the average length of stay or increased use of new technology.

Results

We report our results that are relevant to specific issues in the following sections that appear later in this chapter: "Applying an OMFS Multiplier to the Medicare PPS Rate," "Pass-Through for Hardware Used in Back and Spinal Procedures," "Payments for Exempted Services," and "Payments to Medicare-Exempt Hospitals."

Process for Updating the PPS for Hospital Inpatient Services

Medicare's statutory and regulatory framework governs its process for making annual changes in the PPS for inpatient hospital services.[14] By law, changes in the payment parameters are effective each October 1. They are preceded by a proposed rule setting out the changes in the forthcoming federal fiscal year. The changes involve virtually all aspects of the payment system, including

- modifications in the DRG classification system to account for coding changes in the *International Classification of Diseases, Ninth Revision, Clinical Modifications* (ICD-9-CM) and to reduce the amount of resource variation among cases assigned a given DRG
- recalibration of the DRG relative weights based on more recent Medicare claims data that reflect changes in patterns of care and use of new technology
- revisions in the hospital wage index used to adjust the standard payment rate based on more recent Medicare cost reporting data
- adjustment to the standard payment rate for inflation and other policy considerations
- adjustments in the outlier threshold used to determine additional payments for extremely high-cost cases
- other policy changes implementing statutory changes or addressing issues that have arisen.

---

[14]The Medicare law governing inpatient hospital services is in Section 1866 of the Social Security Act (available at http://www.ssa.gov/OP_Home/ssact/title18/1866.htm). The regulations governing inpatient hospital services are found in 42 CFR Part 412, "Prospective Payment Systems for Inpatient Hospital Services" (available at http://www.access.gpo.gov/nara/cfr/waisidx_02/42cfr412_02.html).

The proposed rule is scheduled for publication each year by April 1 with a 60-day public comment period; however, it is typically published 30 to 60 days late. The final rule is published on a timely basis by August 1 each year. It is often followed within a relatively short time by a correction notice fixing any errors that were identified in the published rule. Occasionally, legislative action may also produce mid-year changes.

In linking OMFS updates to the Medicare PPS updates, three considerations arise: (1) what the normal effective date of the OMFS update should be, (2) whether mid-year changes should be automatically incorporated, and (3) whether changes that affect OMFS-specific policies should also be automatically adopted. From the provider perspective, an October 1 effective date is attractive because it means ICD-9-CM coding changes can be implemented simultaneously with Medicare's adoption of the code revisions. This would allow 60 days for payers to make the necessary systems changes and for DWC to evaluate the implications of any policy changes and decide whether clarifications are needed for the OMFS. If automatic updates are anticipated, the 60-day period should provide a sufficient window for DWC to notify affected parties of the fee schedule update and to issue any additional instructions it determines are needed. A somewhat shorter timeframe might be involved if the Medicare effective date is used for mid-year changes, and consideration should be given to making mid-year changes effective 60 days after publication.

The annual update includes regulatory changes in the policies that determine how payments are made. An across-the-board rule regarding whether these changes are also automatically incorporated into the OMFS payment rules may not be desirable because the changes might be at odds with existing OMFS policies or may not be appropriate for the OMFS. For example, a Medicare DRG classification change may obviate the need for an existing DWC modification to the Medicare DRG relative weight. DWC needs some flexibility to decide whether certain Medicare rules should be adopted and/or current OMFS policies should be modified without going through administrative rulemaking. A general policy that automatically incorporates Medicare payment policy changes unless DWC overrides a change within 60 days would serve this purpose.

Establishing the Annual Update Factor

Medicare's annual adjustment to its standard prospective payment rate reflects the projected rate of inflation in hospital costs per discharge over the coming year and other factors that may not be appropriate for DWC to take into account in updating OMFS payment rates. These other factors include budget neutrality requirements for revisions in certain payment parameters and policy adjustments that include federal budget constraints.[15] Because the inpatient payment covers all services provided during an inpatient stay, an ideal measure would

[15]The Medicare law requires that the annual DRG changes, the hospital wage index updates, and the pass-through for new technology be budget neutral. Further, hospitals are allowed to request geographic reclassification to a higher wage area, and the effect of these reclassifications must be budget neutral. Budget neutrality is established by making an adjustment to the standard payment amount.

take into account not only price inflation but also new technology and changes in practice patterns that affect the nature of the inpatient stay and cost per discharge. The new technology and practice pattern factors are difficult to measure and the adjustment, if any, for these factors is ultimately a policy judgment. Using an inflation measure that does not take into account new technology and changes in practice patterns may not be that important an issue because, to some extent, new technology costs are offset by productivity gains through more efficient service delivery. An alternative would be for DWC to periodically reevaluate the adequacy of the OMFS rates.

CMS uses an *input price index* composed of a market basket (MB) of goods and services used by hospitals to measure price inflation in the costs of an inpatient stay. Separate MBs apply to operating and capital costs. (Further information on the hospital MB is in Appendix B.) An advantage to using the hospital MB as the inflation measure is that it is an integral part of the PPS annual update process. The projected rates of increase for the coming fiscal year are published in the proposed rule. In addition, the CMS Office of the Actuary's forecast of changes in the hospital operating market basket over the coming decade are included in the trustees' report released each March on the Medicare trust funds. Thus, the projected rates of increase are available in advance for budgeting purposes.

The Producer Price Index (PPI) for hospital services is another economic indicator that would be an appropriate inflation measure to use. The PPI measures changes in the transaction prices paid by purchasers of hospital services. It differs from the Consumer Price Index (CPI),[16] which measures the changes in consumer out-of-pocket costs, and those costs are frequently based on "list" prices for services. One PPI series is specific to general medical and surgical hospitals. Both public and private payers are included in this series, and there are sub-series for prices paid by Medicare, Medicaid, and all other payers. Also, while there are separate sub-series for inpatient major diagnostic categories, there is no sub-series specifically for all inpatient services. Another disadvantage besides the lack of a sub-series for all inpatient services is that the federal government does not forecast changes in the PPI the same way it does for the hospital market basket.

Figure 2.1 compares the historic rates of increase in the Medicare hospital MB, the PPI series for general medical and surgical hospitals, and the CPI for inpatient hospital services. The higher rates of inflation in the CPI reflect the escalation in charge increases that began in 2000. Managed care growth and aggressive price discounting reduced the rate of increase in the PPI through early 2000. The higher rates of increase reflect in part the shift in employer insurance from managed care plans to preferred provider organizations. Between 1997 and the first quarter of 2003, the PPI for hospital services increased 15.5 percent relative to a 21 percent increase in the hospital market basket.

---

[16]The U.S. Bureau of Labor Statistics produces the Consumer Price Index (CPI) yearly. The CPI measures average price changes in relation to prices in an arbitrarily selected base year.

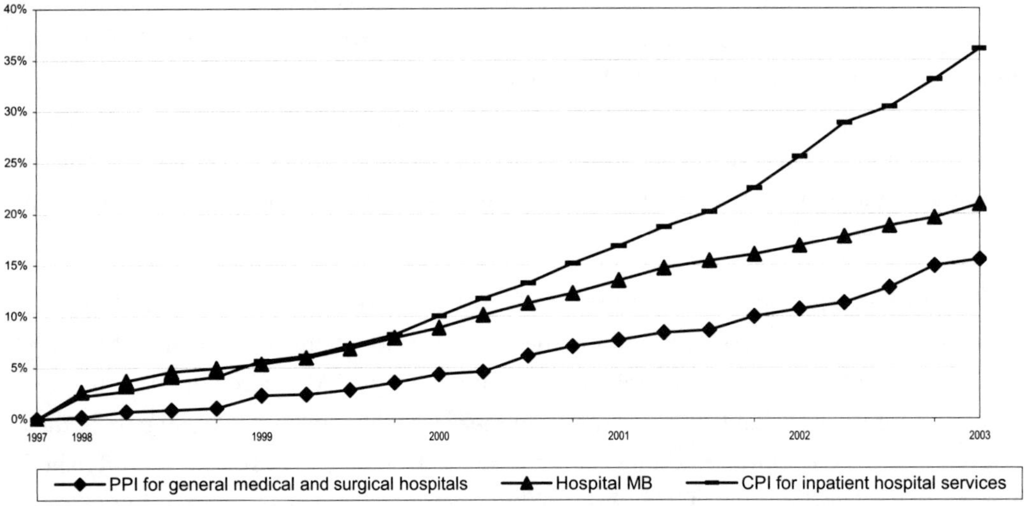

Figure 2.1 – Cumulative Percentage Change in Inflation Measures for Hospital Inpatient Services: 1997–2003

The policy objectives for the update factor should determine whether Medicare's hospital MB or the PPI is the more appropriate inflation measure. If the primary goal is to assure the rates are adequate by adjusting for estimated increases in costs per discharge, the hospital market basket is the more appropriate measure. The MB also has the added administrative advantage of being readily available as part of the Medicare PPS annual update process with forecasted values that could be used for budgeting and premium-setting purposes. However, if the primary goal is to keep pace with market prices for hospital services, the PPI is the more appropriate measure.

Applying an OMFS Multiplier to the Medicare PPS Rate

In theory, by applying a 1.2 multiplier to the Medicare payment rate, the OMFS payment is 20 percent higher than the amount Medicare pays for a patient assigned to the same DRG in the same hospital. In actuality, the current OMFS does not provide for an across-the-board multiplier. This is because it adjusts the relative weights for 48 DRGs by a payment-to-cost ratio before the multiplier is applied. This ratio varies by DRG and is based on a comparison of workers' compensation charges and the charges and payment rates for patients covered by group health plans. In some cases, the adjustment increases the amount payable under the OMFS and in other cases it reduces the amount. For example, the ratio for DRG 4 Spinal Procedures is 0.6283, so that the maximum allowable amount for a non-outlier case is 62.83 percent of Medicare's payment times 1.20, or 75 percent of the Medicare payment amount.

Medicare patients are primarily over age 65, or have been disabled for at least two years, or have end-stage renal disease. In contrast, CWCP patients are considerably younger (their average age was 37.7 years in 2000) and most are in the workforce (CWCI, 2003). Earlier studies have concluded that CWCP patients are not more resource-intensive or more severely ill than Medicare patients (CWCI, 2001a; Kominski and Gardner, 2001). To better understand the need for and implications of a multiplier, we calculated DRG-specific payment-to-cost ratios for the CWCP inpatients in the OSHPD data. We did not model the impact of the exemption for Level 1 or 2 trauma centers treating life-threatening injuries. The payment-to-cost ratios reported in all analyses include discharges that may have qualified for this exemption. If these cases are more costly on average than others assigned to the same DRG, the payment-to-cost ratios are understated relative to what they would be if the excluded cases were removed.

In total, there were 28,684 records for acute care hospital stays (other than in cancer hospitals and children's hospitals) that reported CWCP as the expected payer. The estimated average cost per case was $8,443 and, with an average payment per case of $10,082, the estimated average payment-to cost ratio using Medicare rates with no ratio adjustment and multiplier is 1.19. In Table 2.1, we summarize the information for high-volume DRGs. The top 20 DRGs by volume account for 60 percent of CWCP stays and 62 percent of the payments that would be made using Medicare rates. Overall, CWCP patients account for less than 1 percent of all inpatient stays; however, they are more than 15 percent of the patients in several DRGs, including those for spinal fusion and hand and wrist procedures. Assuring adequacy is particularly important for these DRGs. The payment-to-cost ratios are above 1.0 for all DRGs; in other words, the average payment is greater than the estimated average costs for CWCP patients across all DRGs. The ratios range from a low of 1.03 and 1.05, respectively, for DRG 498, Spinal Fusion Without CC (Complication and/or Comorbidity), and DRG 441, Hand Procedures for Injuries, to a high of 2.13 for DRG 415, Operating Room Procedure for Infectious and Parasitic Diseases. We examine spinal procedures in greater detail later in this chapter because there have been recent DRG changes that affect the payment for these cases. Another measure of the adequacy of payment is the proportion of stays that qualify as high-cost outliers and the percentage of total payments that are outlier payments. DRG 229 (Hand or Wrist Procedures, Except Major Joint Procedures Without CC) warrants further examination. The average payment-to-cost ratios look reasonable, but there are seven very high-cost cases with outlier payments of nearly 16 percent of total payments. A similar pattern exists for DRG 217 (Wound Debridement and Skin Graft Except Hand) except that a fairly significant number of cases—14 percent—would qualify for outlier payments using Medicare rates.

Table 2.1
Top 20 DRGs by Volume: Payment-to-Cost Ratios and Outlier Payments Using Medicare Rates and Payment Parameters for 2000

				CWCP Patients Only							
DRG	Description	CWCP Stays (N)	% of California DRG Stays	Average Cost per Case ($)	Average Payment per Case ($)	Average Payment-to-Cost Ratio	Payment-to-Cost Ratio: 25th Percentile	Payment-to-Cost Ratio: 75th Percentile	Outlier Cases (N)	Average Outlier Pay ($)	Outlier Pay as % of Total Pay
	ALL CWCP INPATIENT STAYS	28,684	0.82	8,443	10,082	1.19	0.92	1.92	1524	21,987	11.5
498	SPINAL FUSION W/O CC	3,490	26.07	10,803	11,126	1.03	0.82	1.54	289	7,619	5.7
500	BACK & NECK PROCEDURES EXCEPT SPINAL FUSION W/O CC	3,229	17.49	5,224	5,638	1.08	0.90	1.53	27	4,215	0.6
209	MAJOR JOINT & LIMB REATTACHMENT PROCEDURES OF LOWER EXTREMITY	1,280	2.53	11,206	12,314	1.10	0.95	1.36	45	7,876	2.2
243	MEDICAL BACK PROBLEMS	1,126	6.19	3,298	4,303	1.30	1.03	2.83	10	8,214	1.7
497	SPINAL FUSION W CC	1,071	18.09	16,067	17,968	1.12	0.87	1.65	130	11,421	7.7
219	LOWER EXTREMITY & HUMERUS PROCEDURES EXCEPT HIP, FOOT, FEMUR AGE >17 W/O CC	1,065	8.64	6,110	6,270	1.03	0.84	1.57	28	8,274	3.5
231	LOCAL EXCISION & REMOVAL OF INTERNAL FIXATION DEVICES EXCEPT HIP & FEMUR	767	15.47	5,268	8,245	1.57	1.34	2.32	13	23,964	4.9
224	SHOULDER, ELBOW OR FOREARM PROCEDURES, EXCEPT MAJOR JOINT PROCEDURES, W/O CC	700	10.74	4,368	4,675	1.07	0.89	1.60	6	7,881	1.4
503	KNEE PROCEDURES W/O PRINCIPAL DIAGNOSIS OF INFECTION	657	13.36	5,884	7,065	1.20	0.96	1.83	7	14,228	2.1
223	MAJOR SHOULDER/ELBOW PROCEDURES, OR OTHER UPPER EXTREMITY PROCEDURES W CC	556	14.90	4,083	5,395	1.32	1.05	2.04	3	2,587	0.3
496	COMBINED ANTERIOR/POSTERIOR SPINAL FUSION	543	35.31	20,077	33,682	1.68	1.45	2.29	47	12,233	3.1
499	BACK & NECK PROCEDURES EXCEPT SPINAL FUSION W CC	443	8.16	7,240	8,658	1.20	1.02	1.84	17	7,048	3.1
229	HAND OR WRIST PROCEDURES, EXCEPT MAJOR JOINT PROCEDURES, W/O CC	385	18.79	4,622	5,407	1.17	0.99	1.84	7	47,307	15.9
217	WOUND DEBRIDEMENT & SKIN GRAFT EXCEPT HAND, FOR MUSCULOSKELETAL & CONNECTIVE TISSUE DISORDERS	370	7.39	14,319	21,683	1.51	1.14	3.93	53	26,929	17.8
227	SOFT TISSUE PROCEDURES W/O CC	344	10.92	4,497	5,035	1.12	0.95	1.67	4	26,656	6.2
278	CELLULITIS AGE >17 W/O CC.	310	3.01	2,649	3,386	1.28	0.95	2.29	2	755	0.1
441	HAND PROCEDURES FOR INJURIES	302	34.53	6,529	6,888	1.05	0.76	2.31	22	10,783	11.4
4	SPINAL PROCEDURES	280	10.56	9,264	17,009	1.84	1.51	5.15	19	28,390	11.3

				CWCP Patients Only							
DRG	Description	CWCP Stays (N)	% of California DRG Stays	Average Cost per Case ($)	Average Payment per Case ($)	Average Payment-to-Cost Ratio	Payment-to-Cost Ratio: 25th Percentile	Payment-to-Cost Ratio: 75th Percentile	Outlier Cases (N)	Average Outlier Pay ($)	Outlier Pay as % of Total Pay
116	OTHER PERMANENT CARDIAC PACEMAKER IMPLANT OR PERCUTANEOUS TRANSLUMINAL CORONARY ANGIOPLASTY W CORONARY ARTERY STENT	277	0.53	10,672	13,672	1.28	1.09	1.72	12	4,100	1.3
415	OPERATING ROOM PROCEDURE FOR INFECTIOUS & PARASITIC DISEASES	258	3.54	10,526	22,460	2.13	1.85	4.77	14	26,841	6.5

NOTES: DRG titles were in effect during FY 2000 (DHHS, 1999). In all tables, N = number.

The degree to which hospitals specialize in providing certain inpatient procedures is also an important consideration in evaluating payment adequacy. If hospitals provided a disproportionate share of procedures with relatively low payment-to-cost ratios, we would expect them to have lower payment-to-cost ratios. Table 2.2 shows the distribution of cases by hospital characteristic. Nearly two-thirds of the stays are in hospitals located in a large urban area, defined as a Metropolitan Statistical Area with a population of more than one million. CWCP patients constitute a slightly higher proportion of stays in other urban and rural hospitals, but across all three geographic classifications, CWCP patients on average constitute less than 1 percent of hospital stays. The average case mix index (CMI) is the average DRG relative weight and is a measure of the hospital's case complexity. On average, the CMI is 1.5 and, as expected, it is lower than average in rural hospitals, smaller hospitals, and non-teaching hospitals. Generally, these hospitals have a lower percentage of surgical cases than other hospitals; somewhat surprisingly, however, major teaching hospitals also have a lower than average CMI and percentage of surgical cases than do minor teaching hospitals.[17]

Across the hospital classes, the estimated average payment-to-cost ratios range from a low of 0.95 for rural hospitals to a high of 1.27 for major teaching hospitals. The latter figure reflects the additional payments these hospitals receive for teaching and serving a disproportionate share of low-income patients. Although rural hospitals do not have a large number of CWCP patients, the low payment-to-cost ratios could potentially create access problems. Medicare has special payment provisions for critical access hospitals and sole community hospitals, which are covered later in this chapter.

The payment-to-cost ratios presented thus far have been for 2000. We also estimated what the payment-to-cost ratio would be using a hybrid model of 2000 payment rates and costs but with 2003 DRG relative weights and payment adjustments (see Table 2.3). By estimating what the payments would have been if the 2003 DRG classification system and payment adjustments had been in effect in 2000, we avoid having to make assumptions about hospital cost and charge increases between 2000 (the most recent year for which claims data are available) and 2003 (the current payment year). As discussed later, significant changes in the DRG classification logic for spinal procedures occurred in 2003, which have the effect of increasing the overall case mix index from 1.50 to 1.57 and reducing the percentage of outlier payments from 0.115 percent to 0.086 percent of total payments. The average payment-to-cost ratio increases from 1.19 to 1.23.

---

[17]Major teaching hospitals are defined as teaching hospitals with an average resident-to-bed ratio of 0.25 or greater.

Table 2.2
Distribution of CWCP Discharged by Hospital Characteristics: Estimated Payment-to-Cost Ratios and Outlier Payments Using Medicare Rates and Payment Parameters in 2000

	Hospitals (N)	CWCP Discharges (N)	Total California Discharges (%)	Average CMI	Medical DRGs (%)	Average Cost Per Case ($)	Total Payment Per Case ($)	Average Payment-to-Cost Ratio	Standardized Cost Per Case ($)	Outlier Cases (N)	Average Outlier Payment ($)	Outlier Payments as % of Total Payments
All	342	28,841	0.82	1.50	29.3	8,443	10,082	1.19	3,871	1524	21,988	0.12
Location by Beds												
Large Urban	199	19,119	0.76	1.51	29.2	8,417	10,354	1.23	3,630	1032	17,403	0.09
<100 beds	37	853	0.85	1.37	33.1	6,628	7,932	1.20	3,749	102	7,727	0.07
100–199 beds	79	4,786	0.72	1.51	29.8	8,594	10,081	1.17	3837	274	14,850	0.09
200–299 beds	53	7,383	0.72	1.53	27.6	7,591	9,359	1.23	3,490	232	14,169	0.05
300–399 beds	15	1997	0.77	1.53	30.0	10,053	12,320	1.23	3,687	192	29,531	0.15
400+ beds	15	4,100	0.86	1.51	29.7	9,121	11,957	1.31	3,542	232	17,868	0.10
Other Urban	108	9,100	0.99	1.51	28.5	8,722	9,863	1.13	4,341	468	32,986	0.17
<100 beds	40	1,077	1.07	1.36	23.4	6,246	6,552	1.05	4,070	33	11,418	0.05
100–199 beds	38	2,069	0.73	1.39	33.2	8,496	9,771	1.15	4,559	152	33,604	0.22
200–299 beds	17	2,661	1.17	1.55	27.2	7,678	9,028	1.18	3,565	83	21,802	0.09
300–399 beds	9	2,527	1.15	1.60	26.6	11,231	11,549	1.03	5,792	132	45,954	0.28
400+ beds	4	766	1.18	1.67	29.1	9,386	11,724	1.25	3,481	68	30,551	0.12
Rural	34	621	0.78	1.12	45.0	5,199	4,929	0.95	4,395	24	4,671	0.04
<100 beds	33	557	0.77	1.14	44.1	5,297	4,998	0.94	4,469	22	4,941	0.04
100–199	1	64	0.91	1.03	51.3	4,497	4,436	0.99	3,863	2	1,707	0.01
Control												
Government	62	3,453	0.64	1.41	41.5	11,619	13,420	1.15	4,863	353	37,209	0.27
Not-for-profit	175	19,266	0.84	1.52	28.0	8,012	9,642	1.20	3,670	766	19,432	0.08
Investor-owned	87	5,129	0.90	1.51	26.3	7,865	9,430	1.20	3,919	405	13,554	0.10
Missing	18	993										
Teaching Status												
Non-teaching	245	15,953	0.85	1.45	28.9	7,370	8,513	1.16	3,831	679	17,967	0.08
Minor teaching	65	9,180	0.79	1.60	27.2	9,159	11,169	1.23	4,046	332	27,850	0.13
Major teaching	21	3,165	0.79	1.57	33.6	11,222	14,286	1.27	3,715	503	23,840	0.17
Missing	11	543										

Table 2.3
Comparison of Payments Using 2000 Medicare Rates and Rules to Payments Using Hybrid Model with 2000 Rates and 2003 Rules

		Average Per Case		Payment-to-Cost Ratio				Outlier Cases	
	Average CMI	Payment	Cost	Average	25th Percentile	75th Percentile	Cases (N)	Average Outlier Pay	Outlier Pay as % of Total Pay
2000 Medicare rates and rules	1.502	$10,082	$ 8,443	1.194	0.921	1.93	1,524	$ 21,988	0.115
Hybrid 2000 rates/2003 rules	1.574	$10,406	$ 8,443	1.232	0.940	2.01	1,032	$ 25,130	0.086

In summary, our analysis indicates that the Medicare DRG payment-to-cost ratio without a multiplier was nearly 1.20 in 2000 and would have been 1.23 if the DRG changes and other payment policy changes had been in effect. The payment-to-cost ratio on average was already higher than the national ratio for private payers in 2000 (1.125), and we believe the additional 1.20 across-the-board multiplier was not needed to ensure access for workers' compensation patients. A DRG-specific adjustment would be appropriate for certain high-volume procedures:

- Those DRGs with a relatively low payment-to-cost ratio, particularly if CWCP patients constitute a substantial proportion of the cases in the DRG, such as with DRGs 219, 224, 441, and 500. The payment-to-cost ratios for these high-volume DRGs were less than 1.10 in 2000.
- The estimated average payment-to-cost ratios for some DRGs are quite high, and even without a 1.20 multiplier they could provide incentives to provide care on an inpatient basis that could be appropriately performed in an outpatient setting. The payment-to-cost ratios are greater than 1.5 for DRGs 217, 231, and 415. (The findings for spinal fusion surgery are discussed later).

The current OMFS uses an adjustment ratio to modify the DRG relative weight for the CWCP patient population. This mechanism essentially develops DRG-specific multipliers when determined to be appropriate. The flexibility to continue these adjustments would be an important feature of an update process that is linked to annual Medicare updates. By continuing to specify the adjustment as a ratio, it can be automatically applied to updated DRG relative weights. Generally, the relative weight changes are fairly minor from year to year unless DRG changes are involved. If the DRG classification rules change for an affected DRG, DWC would need to assess whether the adjustment ratio for that DRG should be modified.

Pass-Through for Hardware Used in Back and Spinal Procedures

Under the OMFS, implantable hardware and/or instrumentation for back and spinal procedures (DRGs 496–500) are reimbursed separately at the hospital's documented costs plus 10 percent (up to $250) and any shipping and handling charges. Only limited information is available on the amounts that are being paid for hardware and instrumentation. A conservative estimate projects the costs at between $7.1 million and $28.6 million (Kominski and Gardner, 2001). Another estimate placed the costs at between $25 million and $72 million and concluded that the additional payments would increase hospital payment levels 11–33 percent (CWCI, 2001b). After CWCP established the pass-through in 2001 for hardware used in back and spinal procedures, Medicare made several changes that may affect whether the pass-through is still needed. First, the DRGs for spinal fusion were refined to better account for cost variation among patients having these procedures. Second, Medicare established a temporary pass-through exception for quality-enhancing new technology. Later, we discuss these changes and explore options for further consideration and analysis.

In FY 2002, changes in the DRG logic resulted in cervical fusions and re-fusions with and without complications being assigned to new DRGs. We modeled the impact of the new DRGs by mapping hospital discharges with the applicable procedure codes into the new DRGs. Table 2.4 summarizes two payment simulations for the CWCP stays. Simulation A reports the distribution of cases, estimated costs, payment-to-charge ratios, and the estimated percentage of outlier payments for 2000. This is the same simulation as was reported in Table 2.1. The simulation uses Medicare rules and does not include a multiplier or pass-through for hardware and instrumentation. The cost-to-charge ratio for DRG 498, Spinal Fusion Without CC, at 1.03 is lower than the average payment-to-cost ratio for all CWCP patients (1.19). Simulation B shows how the distribution of cases and payment-to-cost ratios are affected by the DRG changes. In this simulation, we held costs per case, the standardized payment amounts, and the outlier thresholds constant. We used the revised DRG relative weights and updated WI, DSH, and IME adjustment factors. The simulation shows significant improvements in the estimated payment-to-cost ratios for spinal procedures. Thus, even without the pass-through for hardware and instrumentation and before consideration of the multiplier, payments for spinal fusions are on average more than sufficient to cover the estimated costs of the average stay.

Table 2.4
Simulation of Impact of DRG Refinements to Spinal Fusion DRGs

DRG	Name	CWCP Patients (N)	DRG Relative Weight	Estimated Cost Per Case ($)	Payment-to-Cost Ratio	Outlier Payments
A. Payment Simulation Using 2000 Medicare Payment Rates and Rules						
496	COMBINED ANTERIOR/ POSTERIOR SPINAL FUSION	543	5.6871	20,077	1.68	3.1%
497	SPINAL FUSION W CC	1,071	2.8441	16,067	1.12	7.7%
498	SPINAL FUSION W/O CC	3,490	1.7952	10,803	1.03	5.7%
B. Payment Simulation Using FY 2003 DRG Relative Weights and Payment Rules and 2000 Rates						
496	COMBINED ANTERIOR/ POSTERIOR SPINAL FUSION	725	5.7988	18,905	1.86	1.1%
497	SPINAL FUSION EXCEPT CERVICAL W CC	837	3.3938	17,089	1.22	4.2%
498	SPINAL FUSION EXCEPT CERVICAL W/O CC	2,042	2.4738	12,651	1.18	2.1%
519	CERVICAL SPINAL FUSION W CC	168	2.3551	10,435	1.40	4.1%
520	CERVICAL SPINAL FUSION W/O CC	1,325	1.5389	7,671	1.17	0.8%

Several ICD-9-CM coding revisions may affect the DRG logic for spinal fusions in the future. In FY 2002, new ICD-9-CM codes were created for re-fusions that will provide data that can be used to make further DRG refinements as early as FY 2004 when administrative data using the new codes become available. In FY 2003, new ICD-9-CM procedure codes were added that could lead to additional DRG refinements as early as FY 2005 or add-on payments for new technology (discussed next). These new codes are

- 81.61—360-degree spinal fusion, single incision approach
- 84.51—Insertion of interbody spinal fusion device
- 84.52—Insertion of recombinant bone morphogenetic protein.

Temporary Add-On Payments for New Technology

Reflecting concerns that the PPS did not account for new technology rapidly enough, changes in the Medicare law[18] required that CMS establish a mechanism to recognize the costs of new medical services and technologies under the acute care PPS. The new mechanism applies to a new medical service or technology if the estimated costs for patients receiving the new technology show the DRG payment is inadequate. The payment applies for two to three years until the data with a new ICD-9-CM code can be evaluated. The implementing regulations limit special payments to new technologies that provide substantial improvement in caring for Medicare beneficiaries (because the special payment will create an incentive to use the new technology). CMS uses a federal panel of CMS clinical staff and coding experts to evaluate the new technology using the following criteria:

- The device offers a treatment option for a patient population unresponsive to, or ineligible for, currently available treatments
- The device offers the ability to diagnose a currently undetectable medical condition or diagnose it earlier, and use of the device to make the diagnosis affects patient management
- Use of the device improves clinical outcomes (e.g., morality rate, complication rate, decreased rate of subsequent interventions, hospitalizations or physician visits, and decreased pain, bleeding or recovery time).

To determine if the DRG payment inadequately reflects the cost of the new technology, CMS compares the standardized charges of cases using the device with a threshold set at one standard deviation beyond the geometric mean standardized charge for all cases in the DRG (or the case-weighted average of all relevant DRGs if the technology occurs in multiple DRGs).[19] The payment for a new technology that qualifies for a pass-through is made on a case-by-case basis. If the cost of a new technology case exceeds the DRG payment amount, Medicare pays 50 percent

---

[18]Section 533 of the Benefits Improvement and Protection Act of 2000.

[19]Standardized charges are the charges for an inpatient stay after standardizing for the wage index adjustment and add-on payments for teaching and serving low-income patients. According to CMS, the average standard deviation is 50 percent of the log mean, and on average the new technology must result in average standardized charges of $7,799 above the mean (CMS uses charges rather than costs to establish relative weights). The thresholds are published in the PPS final rule.

of the excess cost (not to exceed 50 percent of the estimated cost of the new technology). The higher payment amount is treated as the base payment in determining outlier payments. Estimated aggregate pass-through payments are to be budget neutral. CMS will adjust the marginal cost factor in future years if the agency estimates that the target limit (1.0 percent of total operating payments) on special payments will be exceeded.[20]

The differences between the Medicare pass-through and the one used by the OMFS are that (1) clinical criteria are used to determine whether the device is eligible for a pass-through, (2) payment is made only if the DRG payment is otherwise insufficient, and (3) the full cost of the device is not passed through, thereby providing a stronger incentive to avoid unnecessary utilization.

Options for Further Consideration

Under current policies, CWCP is paying for the hardware used in back and spinal procedures twice: once through the DRG payment and again in the pass-through payment. Moreover, there is considerable administrative burden involved in establishing the appropriate pass-through amount through pricing of individual claims. Consideration should be given to alternative payment methodologies. In developing potential options, we are mindful of the need to reduce unnecessary expenditures while providing access to medically appropriate hardware. Options 2 and 3 (discussed later in this section) require additional analysis to set an appropriate payment amount. The lack of readily available data on the amounts currently being paid for the hardware on a pass-through basis and on the comparative use of extremely costly hardware by Medicare and CWCP patients precludes a full analysis of options in this study.

Option 1: Incorporate the Costs of the Hardware into the DRG Payment. Based on a comparison of Medicare charges and charges for CWCP patients, Kominski and Gardner (2001) recommended that the pass-through be eliminated. Including the hardware in the DRG payment creates an incentive to eliminate medically unnecessary and costly services. Our analysis of the estimated payment-to-cost ratios for spinal fusion procedures both before and after the DRG refinements are taken into account provides additional support for this recommendation. If this option were adopted, Medicare's temporary add-on for quality-enhancing costly hardware should also become a feature of the OMFS. This would afford additional assurance that high-cost

---

[20]Only one application—for a biotechnology product to treat sepsis—was approved in this first round of applications. An application for an add-on payment for Renew™ Radio Frequency Spinal Cord Stimulation Therapy as a treatment of last resort for chronic intractable pain for DRG 4 was not approved because the DRG relative weights for FY 2003 include any Medicare cases involved in the transplantation of this system. CMS also denied an add-on payment for the InFUSE™ Bone Graft/LT-CAGE™ Lumbar Tapered Fusion Device. The product is applied through use of an absorbable collagen device, which is implanted at the fusion site to promote bone growth. The Food and Drug Administration (FDA) approved the device on July 2, 2002, for single-level fusions; multi-level uses of the technology are off-label. CMS denied the application because the estimated cost for the technology did not meet the cost threshold when used for single-level spinal fusions, and there is no available evidence to determine whether the technology represents a substantial improvement for multi-level uses. Another application for a FY 2004 add-on payment has been submitted for this product.

quality-enhancing new technology is recognized before the higher costs are reflected in the charge data used to establish the DRG relative weights. If desired, a higher percentage of the estimated cost could be paid for technology qualifying for the pass-through.

After the expiration of the pass-through, the high-cost outlier policy provides some protection for hospitals that have a disproportionate share of procedures using high-cost technology. A lower outlier threshold or higher marginal cost factor for these DRGs in general, or when high-cost technology has been used, would increase the financial protection. For example, the DRGs for burn cases have a 90-percent marginal cost factor compared with an 80-percent factor for other DRGs. Relative to the full pass-through, making any additional payments as part of the outlier payment policy retains some incentive to control unnecessary utilization and eliminates additional payments for cases that are not unusually costly. A cautionary note is that hospital markup for devices can be substantially higher than the markup for other services. To reduce abuse, basing the outlier payment on invoice costs rather than applying the cost-to-charge ratio is recommended.

Option 2: Adjust the Medicare DRG Relative Weight for Back and Spinal Procedures to Remove the Estimated Cost of the Hardware and Instrumentation. Duplicate payments for the hardware could be eliminated by reducing the Medicare DRG relative weights for the estimated costs of the hardware and instrumentation. This option addresses concerns that Medicare usage of costly technology is not representative of its use for CWCP patients because it would pay for actual CWCP use of hardware and instrumentation. Determining the correct adjustment requires analysis of Medicare inpatient claims data that contain the revenue center costs for medical devices. The adjustment would need to be periodically updated as technology diffuses to the older population. Unless it is combined with Option 3, Option 2 still leaves open the question of determining an appropriate payment for the hardware costs that does not provide incentives for unnecessary utilization.

Option 3: Establish a Fee Schedule for High-Cost "New Technology" Hardware and Instrumentation. A fee schedule for high-cost technology would reduce ongoing administrative costs and assure the additional payments for state-of-the-art technology are reasonable. Limiting the payment to incremental costs of high-cost technology would eliminate the duplicate payments for incidental or low-cost hardware that is already included in the DRG. Medicare's policies for the temporary add-on for new technology suggests the type of cost and quality considerations that might be taken into account in determining which technologies should qualify for an additional payment. Inappropriate utilization would need to be addressed separately through utilization review or guidelines.

The fee schedule is an attractive alternative if the use of high-cost technology is concentrated in some of the hospitals that perform back and neck procedures. As is the case with the current pass-through, it targets any additional payments on those patients who actually receive the new technology and avoids the high markups that are often associated with expensive new technology. There is, of course, an administrative burden involved in establishing and periodically reviewing the payment amounts. However, using a fixed payment amount in lieu of a pass-through has at least some efficiency incentives relative to cost reimbursement and eliminates the need for pricing of individual bills.

On the other hand, if the use of high-cost technology is more diffuse, a separate fee schedule is not needed, and a methodology that includes the hardware in the DRG rate would be adequate. The PPS assumption is that a hospital will profit on some cases and absorb losses on others but that on average the payment is appropriate for an efficient hospital. Our analysis indicates that the payments are more than adequate to cover the estimated costs of an average stay before adding a multiplier. However, we cannot determine from the OSHPD data whether the payment is adequate when new-technology hardware is used. As indicated earlier, this issue would benefit from an analysis of CWCP inpatient claims data with the amounts billed and paid for hardware costs. In evaluating the merits of the options, the ongoing administrative burden should be considered as well as the cost and access issues.

Payments for Extraordinarily High-Cost Cases

The DRG system is designed to group patients with similar expected costs. However, the cost of treatment may vary widely among the cases in any DRG, and even efficient hospitals may have some cases for which the costs are much higher than the standard DRG payment. The cost outlier payments counter incentives to avoid treating costly patients and protect hospitals from large financial losses. Medicare considers a case to be extraordinarily costly and eligible for an additional payment if its estimated costs exceed the standard DRG payment plus an outlier threshold. The outlier (or fixed stop-loss) threshold is the loss a hospital must absorb before it is eligible for an additional payment. The additional payment equals 80 percent of the difference between the estimated cost of the case and the sum of the standard DRG payment and outlier threshold:

$$\text{Outlier payment}_{ind} = 0.80 \times \text{Estimated cost}_{ind} - (\text{DRG payment}_{ind} + \text{outlier threshold})$$

A hospital's charging practice can affect the cost estimate for the patient stay. At the time a bill is processed, the *charges* for the stay are known but not the actual *costs* of providing the care. A cost-to-charge ratio is applied to the hospital's charges to estimate the costs for the stay. The higher the hospital's markup, the lower the hospital's cost-to-charge ratio:

$$\text{Estimated cost}_{ind} = \text{Billed charges}_{ind} \times \text{cost-to-charge ratio}_{hosp}$$

For example, if a hospital has a cost-to-charge ratio of 0.50 (in other words, costs are 50 percent of charges), the estimated cost of a stay with $100,000 billed charges is $50,000. If the hospital's markup were higher (e.g., the billed charges were $125,000), the estimated costs would still be $50,000 as long as the cost-to-charge ratio is correct (i.e., 0.40). At issue is not the markup *per se* but rather the accuracy of the cost-to-charge ratio. The cost-to-charge ratios are determined from Medicare cost report data and measure the ratio between the hospital's cost of providing

Medicare services and its charges for the services.[21] The intermediary uses the cost-to-charge ratios from each hospital's most recently settled cost report to determine outlier payments.

Hospital charges have been increasing more rapidly than costs. For example, between the cost reporting periods beginning in FY 1999 and FY 2001, the average annual rate of increase in charges per discharge for 152 California hospitals in our analysis file for which data were available for both years was 11.8 percent compared with a 6.7-percent annual inflation in costs per discharge. Greater charge inflation is of particular concern in determining cost outlier payments. When charges increase more rapidly than costs, a hospital's costs in the payment year are a lower percentage of its charges than the percentage reflected in the cost-to-charge ratio used to determine the cost outlier payment. Applying an outdated cost-to-charge ratio to current-year charges will overestimate the hospital's costs in determining the outlier payment.

CWCP has been particularly vulnerable to excessive charge inflation because it is using the cost-to-charge ratios that were published as part of the FY 2001 PPS impact file, and it is using the fixed-loss threshold of $14,500 from FY 2000 compared with the $33,560 used by Medicare in FY 2003. Provision for automatic updates should reduce CWCP vulnerability for making excessive outlier payments. Nevertheless, CWCP will remain vulnerable if some hospitals have excessive charge inflation between the cost reporting period from which the cost-to-charge ratio is derived and the payment year (generally, a time lag of two years or longer). To better understand the potential vulnerabilities, we examined the distribution of two-year increases in hospital markups using Medicare cost report data for cost reporting periods beginning in FY 1999 and FY 2001 (see Table 2.5). We used a matched set of 152 acute care hospitals. The average increase in markup was 6.5 percent. However, 36 hospitals had increases of 15 percent or higher. If cost-to-charge ratios from their cost reporting periods beginning in FY 1999 were used to determine 2001 payments, costs would be overstated from 15 to 74 percent in determining outlier payments.

Table 2.5
Distribution of California Hospitals by Change in Markup over a Two-Year Period

Increase in Markup	Number of Hospitals	Average Change in Markup
Reduction	44	-9.7%
< 5%	25	2.7%
5 to <10%	26	7.4%
10 to <15%	21	12.1%
15 to < 25%	26	19.2%
25 to < 35%	4	27.4%
35 to <75%	6	49.8%

To address higher-than-average change inflation, Medicare recently adopted a policy to adjust retroactively a hospital's outlier payments based on the actual cost-to-charge ratio for the

[21]The Medicare program calculates the cost-to-charge ratio separately for operating and capital-related costs. The California workers' compensation program combines the two ratios for an overall cost-to-charge ratio that is used in this discussion.

payment year's final settled cost report. This option is not feasible for the CWCP, and several other relatively minor actions should be considered instead:

- The cost-to-charge ratios included in the PPS impact file are not computed as part of the update process. Rather, Medicare intermediaries report these values to CMS as the cost-to-charge ratio that they are currently using for payment purposes. The PPS impact file published each August contains the values reported in March. By using these values, CWCP has an additional one-year lag in the cost-to-charge ratios it is using to determine outlier payments. Reported values as of December of the previous year are included in the PPS impact file produced with the notice of proposed rulemaking. For example, the proposed notice for FY 2004 was published in May 2003 and included the cost-to-charge ratios that Medicare intermediaries were using in December 2002. The CWCP lag time could be reduced if the cost-to-charge ratios were automatically updated whenever a PPS impact file is produced as part of the rulemaking process.[22]

- Trends in individual hospital markups can be monitored using OSHPD financial data reported by hospitals on a quarterly basis. Hospitals submit a report within 45 days after the end of each calendar quarter that contains, among other items, total gross patient revenues and total operating expenses that could be used to track the hospital's overall markup. Data are available approximately 105 days after the close of the calendar quarter. Individual cases of excessive charge increases could be dealt with on a case-by-case basis.

Payments for Exempted Services

The Medicare acute care PPS applies to all Medicare beneficiaries who are inpatients in the acute care portion of a hospital. (Patients in a dedicated psychiatric or rehabilitation unit of an acute care hospital are excluded from the PPS.) The OMFS exempts patients in acute care hospitals that are assigned to certain DRGs: Psychiatry (DRGs 424–432); Substance Abuse (DRGs 433–437); Organ Transplants (DRGs 103, 302, 480, 481, and 495); Rehabilitation (DRG 462); Tracheostomy (DRGs 482 and 483); and Burns (DRGs 475 and 504–511). Unlike Medicare, the OMFS exemption does not distinguish between patients who are in the acute care portion of the hospital and those in a dedicated psychiatric or rehabilitation unit. The exempted DRGs account for about 5.5 percent of CWCP hospital stays, of which slightly more than half are in DRG 482, Rehabilitation. In addition, inpatient services provided by a Level 1 or Level 2 trauma center to patients with a life-threatening injury are exempt.

Payment for exempted services is based on rates the payer has negotiated with the hospital or, in the absence of negotiated rates, the amount the payer and hospital are able to agree on for the individual case. In either case, the hospital's charges are likely to be a factor in determining the payment. In hospitals that have a contract with the payer, these high-cost

---

[22]In using the proposed rule, impact files could also be considered for the factors used to make additional payments for teaching and serving low-income patients; however, these adjustments do not pose the same program vulnerabilities, and more frequent updates may pose an unnecessary administrative burden.

services are likely to trigger the contract's stop-loss threshold. When a contract is not in place, the hospital's billed charges are frequently the starting point for determining the payment amount. Thus, the CWCP remains vulnerable to high hospital markups as long as these services remain exempt and, where a contract is not in place, to additional administrative costs for negotiating a payment amount.

The services were exempted when the fee schedule was first implemented and before DWC adopted a cost outlier policy. With the protections against financial loss provided by the cost outlier policy, the exemption may no longer be necessary, particularly if a multiplier is also used. Also, we note that Medicare uses a 90-percent marginal cost factor in paying for high-cost outliers assigned to the Burn DRGs, where 400 of the exempted inpatient stays are concentrated.

In Table 2.6, we summarize information on the number of discharges and patients assigned to each of the exempted DRGs, the estimated costs per discharge, payment-to-cost ratios, and outlier payments. As previously noted, we have not treated patients that might have a life-threatening injury differently from other patients in our payment-to-cost ratios. Except for the Alcohol and Substance Abuse DRGs, the estimated average payment-to-cost ratios are above 1.0, although there are not enough transplant cases to draw any conclusions from this analysis about payment adequacy. At the same time, there is nothing to suggest that with a multiplier and outlier policy the payments for transplant cases would be inadequate.

Under Medicare rules, inpatient stays in psychiatric and rehabilitation units of acute care hospitals are exempt from the acute care prospective payment system. The DRG payments apply only to inpatient stays in the general acute care portion of the hospital. Further analysis of the OSHPD data are needed to determine if some of the stays assigned to the DRGs for Mental Disease (DRGs 424–432) and Rehabilitation (DRG 472) would be exempt under Medicare rules. Even if this is the case, the data do not support continuing to exempt those cases that are subject to the acute care PPS under Medicare's rules.

In FY 2002, Medicare restructured the Alcohol and Substance Abuse DRGs (DRGs 433–437); therefore, the payment-to-cost ratios for stays assigned to these DRGs should improve. An assessment of the actual effect would require using the GROUPER to assign the stays to the new DRGs (see Appendix A), something that is not within the scope of this report. There are relatively few cases assigned to these low-cost DRGs; we believe that paying for them under the PPS should not reduce CWCP patient access to necessary treatment.

Table 2.6

Exempted Stays in Acute Care Hospitals: Distribution by DRG, Estimated Costs, Payment-to-Cost Ratios, and Outlier Payments

DRG	Description	CWCP Stays (N)	% of Total DRG Stays	Average Cost per Case ($)	Average Pay-to-Cost Ratio	Inner-Quartile Range of Pay-to-Cost Ratio: 25th Percentile	Inner-Quartile Range of Pay-to-Cost Ratio: 75th Percentile	Outlier Cases (N)	Average Outlier Payment ($)	Outlier Pay as % Total Pay
TRANSPLANT										
103	HEART TRANSPLANT	2	0.84	78,623	1.79	1.56	2.03	1	9,230	0.0329
302	KIDNEY TRANSPLANT	1	0.066	13,474	1.82	1.82	1.82	0		
480	LIVER TRANSPLANT	1	0.189	111,905	1.03	1.03	1.03	1	57,853	0.5011
481	BONE MARROW TRANSPLANT	1	0.088	45,860	1.40	1.40	1.40	0		
495	LUNG TRANSPLANT	0								
MENTAL DISEASES										
424	OPERATING ROOM PROCEDURE W PRINCIPAL DIAGNOSES OF MENTAL ILLNESS	2	0.548	6,009	2.16	1.77	2.51	0		
425	ACUTE ADJUSTMENT REACTION & DISTURBANCES OF PSYCHOSOCIAL DYSFUNCTION	15	0.466	3,728	1.04	0.74	1.43	0		
426	DEPRESSIVE NEUROSES	14	0.184	1,831	1.88	1.47	5.19	0		
427	NEUROSES EXCEPT DEPRESSIVE	12	0.51	2,277	1.72	1.21	8.27	0		
428	DISORDERS OF PERSONALITY & IMPULSE CONTROL	2	0.2	1,852	2.03	1.39	3.34	0		
429	ORGANIC DISTURBANCES & MENTAL RETARDATION	14	0.284	4,552	1.12	0.82	2.06	0		
430	PSYCHOSES	170	0.193	6,124	1.03	0.84	3.65	14	20,102	0.2629
431	CHILDHOOD MENTAL DISORDERS	0								
432	OTHER MENTAL DISORDER DIAGNOSES	1	0.467	6,523	0.70	0.70	0.70	0		
ALCOHOL AND SUBSTANCE ABUSE										
433	ALCOHOL/DRUG ABUSE OR DEPENDENCE, LEFT AGAINST MEDICAL ADVICE	5	0.211	2,595	0.70	0.58	1.20	0		
434	ALC/DRUG ABUSE OR DEPENDENCE, DETOXIFICATION OR OTHER SYMPTOMATIC TREATMENT W CC	16	0.186	5,345	0.81	0.60	1.46	0		
435	ALC/DRUG ABUSE OR DEPENDENCE, DETOXIFICATION OR OTHER SYMPTOMATIC TREATMENT W/O CC	39	0.364	2,816	0.86	0.68	2.35	0		
436	ALC/DRUG DEPENDENCE W REHABILITATION THERAPY	1	0.193	1,197	3.50	3.50	3.50	0		
437	ALC/DRUG DEPENDENCE, COMBINED REHABILITATION & DETOXIFICATION THERAPY	9	0.282	2,888	1.16	0.91	1.82	0		
REHABILITATION										
462	REHABILITATION	768	1.846	10,731	1.04	0.78	2.55	93	25,149	0.2722
TRACHEOSTOMY										
475	RESPIRATORY SYSTEM DIAGNOSIS WITH VENTILATOR SUPPORT	36	0.169	30,997	1.11	0.85	1.90	11	38,416	0.3402
482	TRACHEOSTOMY FOR FACE, MOUTH & NECK DIAGNOSES	5	0.351	46,000	1.15	0.91	1.69	4	37,171	0.5619
483	TRACHEOSTOMY EXCEPT FOR FACE, MOUTH & NECK DIAGNOSES	62	0.744	130,388	1.24	1.01	1.78	40	86,444	0.3453
BURNS										
504	EXTENSIVE 3RD DEGREE BURNS W SKIN GRAFT	17	11.72	80,375	1.44	1.10	2.16	7	52,107	0.1858
505	EXTENSIVE 3RD DEGREE BURNS W/O SKIN GRAFT	4	5.405	9,970	1.77	1.24	7.75	0		

DRG	Description	CWCP Stays (N)	% of Total DRG Stays	Average Cost per Case ($)	Average Pay-to-Cost Ratio	Inner-Quartile Range of Pay-to-Cost Ratio: 25th Percentile	Inner-Quartile Range of Pay-to-Cost Ratio: 75th Percentile	Outlier Cases (N)	Average Outlier Payment ($)	Outlier Pay as % Total Pay
506	FULL THICKNESS BURN W SKIN GRAFT OR INHALATION INJURY W CC OR SIGNIFICANT TRAUMA	51	12.17	28,959	1.21	0.94	1.94	11	25,983	0.1595
507	FULL THICKNESS BURN W SKIN GRAFT OR INHALATION INJURY W/O CC OR SIGNIFICANT TRAUMA	111	20.15	13,395	1.07	0.71	1.91	17	12,795	0.1363
508	FULL THICKNESS BURN W/O SKIN GRAFT OR INHALATION INJURY W CC OR SIGNIFICANT TRAUMA	15	8.152	10,780	1.35	0.69	2.49	2	27,399	0.2517
509	FULL THICKNESS BURN W/O SKIN GRAFT OR INHALATION INJURY W/O CC OR SIGNIFICANT TRAUMA	25	13.23	4,267	1.40	1.07	4.68	1	161	0.0011
510	NON-EXTENSIVE BURNS W CC OR SIGNIFICANT TRAUMA	25	4.46	13,694	1.08	0.90	5.25	5	21,725	0.2941
511	NON-EXTENSIVE BURNS W/O CC	152	12.07	5,797	1.23	1.11	3.51	14	12,254	0.1577

Special Payment Protections for Sole Community Hospitals

Medicare has special payment protections for hospitals that represent the sole source of care reasonably available to Medicare beneficiaries residing in the communities the hospitals serve. The qualifying criteria are based on distance to the next nearest hospital and other considerations such as travel time and market share. Thirty-one California hospitals have received this designation. Their Medicare payment rates are based on the higher of a hospital-specific rate or the standard PPS rate (equivalent to the OMFS composite factor). The PPS impact file includes the applicable hospital-specific rates. This makes it feasible to apply this test as part of the process of issuing the composite factors. In estimating payment-to-cost ratios, we did not take this provision into account and would expect the rural payment-to-cost ratio to improve if it were implemented as part of the OMFS.

Payments to Medicare-Exempt Hospitals

The Medicare PPS for general acute care hospitals does not apply to children's hospitals, designated cancer hospitals, long-term care hospitals, psychiatric hospitals and psychiatric units of acute care hospitals, and rehabilitation hospitals and rehabilitation units of acute care hospitals. Table 2.7 shows the number of CWCP patient stays in these facilities in 2000. The information provides a sense of the magnitude of program vulnerabilities in continuing to exempt these facilities from the OMFS. The far-right column summarizes Medicare's current payment system for services provided by these facilities. For small-volume facilities, it may not be worth the administrative burden of determining amounts that would be payable by Medicare. Given the differences between the Medicare and CWCP populations, some analysis of the appropriateness of using the Medicare payment system to pay for CWCP patients would be advisable before per-discharge prospective payment systems are adopted.

Acute Care Hospitals

Medicare exempts two designated cancer hospitals and children's hospitals from the PPS for acute care hospitals. With respect to cancer hospitals, the concern is that they have systematically higher costs than acute care hospitals for patients assigned to the same DRG. For children's hospitals, the concern is that the DRGs and relative weights are based on an elderly population and do not reflect the resources required for a child. There are only a handful of CWCP patients who received care at these hospitals in 2000; therefore, we are unable to assess whether Medicare DRG payments would be sufficient to cover the costs of care provided to CWCP patients.

Table 2.7
Summary of CWCP Utilization of Medicare-Exempt Hospitals and Medicare Payment Methodology

	Inpatient Services Provided to CWCP Patients in 2000			
Type of Hospital	Facilities (N)	Discharges (N)	Total Charges ($)	Medicare Payment Methodology
Children's	4	1	6,393	Cost subject to a hospital-specific limit on the rate of increase in average costs per discharge
Cancer	2	11	265,012	Cost subject to a hospital-specific limit on the rate of increase in average costs per discharge
Long-term care	3	24	2,249,875	Long-term care DRG–based PPS
Rehabilitation	8	190	4,670,522	PPS based on impairment and functional status
Psychiatric	21	141	2,148,875	Cost subject to a hospital-specific limit on the rate of increase in average costs per discharge; PPS to be implemented

Medicare also exempts critical access hospitals from the acute PPS. These are small facilities in rural areas that are unable to support a full-service hospital. Qualifying facilities (no more than 15 beds and an average length of stay of less than 96 hours) are paid on a reasonable cost basis. As of September 2002, Medicare has certified 12 critical access hospitals in California. These facilities were included in our analysis because all but one was a Medicare-certified acute care hospital in 2000. Given their small claims volume and provider vulnerability, exemption under the OMFS is also appropriate.

Long-Term Care Hospitals

Medicare defines long-term care hospitals (LTCHs) as having an average inpatient length of stay of greater than 25 days.[23] Effective October 1, 2002, a prospective payment system replaced the reasonable cost-based payment system under which these facilities were paid. The new payment system is being phased in over a five-year transition period; however, DWC could adopt the prospective payment rates from the outset if determined to be appropriate. Given the differences in patient characteristics, however, we do not believe that it would be advisable to do so without some examination of the characteristics of the CWCP stays in long-term care hospitals and the amounts that Medicare would pay for the stays. Because there were only a few CWCP stays, it may not be worth the administrative burden to maintain the fee schedule. However, if further analysis does indicate that the Medicare LTCH-PPS payments would be reasonable and equitable maximum allowable payments for CWCP patients, the LTCH-PPS is no more complicated than the acute care PPS.

[23]Two California cancer hospitals are exempt from the Medicare PPS: City of Hope in Los Angeles and the USC Kevin Norris Cancer Hospital.

For each long-term care DRG (LTC-DRG), payment is made at a predetermined, per-discharge amount. Similar to the acute care system, the payment covers all inpatient costs of furnishing covered services other than certain pass-through costs such as direct medical education and blood clotting factors. The basic formula for determining LTC-DRG payment is:

Prospective payment = LTC-DRG relative weight X standard federal rate X wage adjustment

The LTC-DRGs are based on the DRGs used under the acute care hospital inpatient PPS but are weighted to reflect the resources required to care for the medically complex patients treated at long-term care hospitals. Case-level adjustments are made for short-stay cases, interrupted stays for acute care hospitalization, cases discharged and readmitted to co-located providers, and high-cost outlier cases. Unlike the PPS for acute care hospitals, no additional payments are made for teaching and serving a disproportionate share of low-income patients.

Updates to the prospective payment rates for each federal fiscal year are published in a Federal Register Notice. CMS moved the annual update effective date to July 1 as of 2003. With this change, the final rule is scheduled for publication by June 1 each year. However, because the LTC-DRGs are tied to the acute care DRGs, the DRG changes will remain effective on a federal fiscal year basis.

Rehabilitation Hospitals

The majority of CWCP patient stays in exempted hospitals were for inpatients of freestanding rehabilitation hospitals. We assume that at least some of the DRG 472, Rehabilitation, stays in the OSHPD acute care hospital records were in dedicated rehabilitation units that are also exempt for the acute care PPS. Medicare pays for stays in freestanding rehabilitation hospitals and rehabilitation units of acute care hospitals using a predetermined prospective payment per discharge (inpatient rehabilitation facility [IRF] PPS). Patients are assigned to a case mix group (CMG) based on the underlying reason for rehabilitation (e.g., trauma), functional status (cognitive and motor), and age. Payment takes into account the relative weight for the CMG and is further adjusted by a hospital wage index, location in a rural area, and serving low-income patients. Additional payments are made for certain complications and comorbidities and for high-cost outlier stays. Special rules apply to short stays, interrupted stays for acute care hospitalization, and transfer cases.

Given the volume of inpatient rehabilitative care provided to CWCP patients, some type of fee schedule would be appropriate to ensure reasonable payments. However, because the Medicare and CWCP populations are quite different, and because the payment is on a per-discharge basis, it would be advisable to assess the appropriateness of Medicare per-discharge payments for the services provided to CWCP patients before linking the OMFS to the IRF PPS. If the Medicare system were adopted, facilities would need to complete a functional assessment instrument for CWCP patients and submit that information along with the claim. Medicare does not require that the form be completed for all patients, although many rehabilitation facilities do so for quality monitoring and care planning. The functional status information is also needed to model the estimated impact of linking the OMFS to the IRF PPS.

Psychiatric Hospitals

Freestanding psychiatric hospitals and dedicated psychiatric units in acute care hospitals are exempt from the Medicare PPS for acute care hospital services. CMS is required to implement a per diem prospective payment system for these services. A report to the U.S. Congress concerning the research efforts to develop an adequate patient classification system indicates that the new system will use currently available facility and patient-specific variables, and that additional patient assessment data will not be needed. The proposed rule was expected to be published in July 2003 with implementation in 2004 (CMS, 2003). The proposed rule for the new PPS should contain sufficient information to determine whether it would be an appropriate payment system for the CWCP to consider.

Until the PPS is implemented for psychiatric facilities, Medicare pays for services furnished by the exempted hospitals based on the estimated costs of providing services to Medicare beneficiaries. The costs are determined retroactively based on Medicare cost report information and are subject to a rate of increase limit on Medicare costs per discharge. It is not practical to adopt a reasonable cost reimbursement system for the CWCP patients because final payment is not known when the patient's bill is processed. An alternative would be to establish a payment rate based on discounted customary charges. The latter approach could utilize recent OSHPD data to determine an appropriate discount rate on a hospital-specific basis. For example, if the hospital's cost-to-charge ratio is 0.30, a payment based on 36 percent of billed charges would produce an estimated payment-to-cost ratio of 1.20 (1.2 x 0.30 = 0.36), which is in line with the payment-to-cost ratio for acute care hospitals before consideration of a multiplier.

An alternative existing fee schedule is the per diem system used by the Department of Defense's (DoD's) TRICARE program for active duty military and retirees (DoD, 2003). This system uses two sets of per diems:

- Hospitals that have at least 25 or more TRICARE discharges are paid a hospital-specific rate.
- Hospitals with fewer than 25 TRICARE discharges are paid using a regional per diem with adjustments for area wage differences and medical education.

The patient population served by the DoD may utilize mental health benefits that are more like those provided to CWCP patients than those provided by the Medicare program.

Other Hospitals Exempted from the OMFS

The OMFS also exempts any acute care hospital that is not included in the Medicare PPS impact file for the rate year used to establish the OMFS maximum allowable amounts. Different circumstances lead to situations in which a general acute care hospital may not be listed on the impact file. For example, we identified two different situations in which hospitals operating on different campuses under the same ownership had a single Medicare provider number but two OSHPD numbers. Under DWC rules, only the main hospital is subject to the OMFS, and the second hospital is exempt. Another circumstance is a new hospital that had no claims data for the year used in the PPS impact files (the second year preceding the payment year). In lieu of exempting these two types of hospitals, consideration should be given to assigning an appropriate composite rate factor based on their geographic location and using the cost-to-charge ratio and other payment parameters of the main hospital, or the statewide cost-to-charge ratio in the case of a new hospital.

Summary of Findings

The OMFS for inpatient hospital services demonstrates that the Medicare fee schedules can be modified for the CWCP if there is flexibility for DWC to make modifications as the fee schedules are updated in the future. Building in 60 days to allow for understanding the annual Medicare changes and their implications for the CWCP and for notifying affected parties of the changes and providing those parties with any clarifications would help prevent unintended consequences from linking the OMFS to Medicare's fee schedules. Modifications to the fee schedule involve trade-offs between administrative burden and payment accuracy. Given DWC's limited resources and the administrative rulemaking requirements, any modifications should be constructed in a way that they can be automatically carried over when Medicare rates are updated.

Potential inflation measures that would be independent of Medicare policy adjustments are the rate of increase in the hospital market basket (an input price index) or the Producer Price Index for hospital services. The hospital market basket has the advantage of being an integral part of Medicare's annual update and involves less of an administrative burden. More-frequent updating of the cost-to-charge ratios used to determine cost outlier payments would reduce potential abuse from excessive charge escalation.

Our analysis of the OSHPD data indicates that Medicare payment rates without any modifications result in an estimated payment-to-cost ratio of 1.19. This is somewhat higher than the national payment-to-cost ratio for private payer payments to hospitals (MedPAC, 2003). However, the range in DRG-specific payment-to-cost ratios is substantial and, consistent with the current OMFS, adjustments may be appropriate for some DRGs. Other OMFS modifications that have been made to the Medicare inpatient payment system should be reexamined:

- Consideration should be given to either incorporating the hardware and instrumentation into the DRG payments for back and neck procedures or to reducing the DRG relative weight for the estimated costs that are covered by the DRG payment.
- Similarly, consideration should be given to eliminating the exemption for certain types of care provided by acute care hospitals. The payment-to-cost ratios indicate on average the payment for these cases will cover the costs of care. The cost outlier policy will provide

additional protection against financial loss. These changes would both reduce the administrative burden and the program's vulnerability to making excessive payments.

- Payment-to-cost ratios for rural hospitals are relatively low, and consideration should be given to adopting Medicare's added protection for hospitals that are the sole source of care reasonably available to beneficiaries within a community.

Medicare exempts certain classes of hospitals from the prospective payment system for general acute care hospitals. Those hospitals include critical access hospitals, rehabilitation hospitals and units of acute care hospitals, psychiatric hospitals and units of acute care hospitals, long-term hospitals, children's hospitals, and cancer hospitals. Prospective payment systems are in place for rehabilitation facilities and long-term hospitals. The volume of services provided by Medicare-exempt hospitals is relatively small and, if consideration is being given to adopting these fee schedules, further analysis is advisable to determine whether Medicare's new payment systems for these facilities are also appropriate for the CWCP population. Two options that might entail less administrative burden than adapting the Medicare fee schedules would be to either (1) continue to exempt these facilities and leave the payment determination to negotiations between the hospital and payer or (2) establish a payment rate based on discounted customary charges. The latter approach could utilize recent OSHPD data to determine an appropriate discount rate on a hospital-specific basis. For example, if the hospital's cost-to-charge ratio is 0.30, a payment based on 36 percent of billed charges would produce an estimated payment-to-cost ratio of 1.20 ($1.2 \times 0.30 = 0.36$), which is in line with the overall payment-to-cost ratio for acute care hospitals before addition of a multiplier.

3. Physician and Other Professional Services

This chapter details specific aspects of the Medicare fee schedule that should be considered in tying the CWCP medical fee schedule to the Medicare RB-RVS fee schedule. Table 3.1 compares features of CWCP's current OMFS with those of the Medicare physician fee schedule. In keeping with the scope of this study, we have concentrated on differences in existing CWCP and Medicare policies and generally do not explore other alternatives that have been adopted for RV-RBS fee schedules used by other workers' compensation programs.[24]

Overview of Medicare RB-RVS Fee Schedule

The Medicare RB-RVS fee schedule has three basic elements:[25]

- The first element consists of relative value units (RVUs) for each medical service based on the resources associated with the physician's work (the time and skill required for the procedure), practice expenses (the staff time and costs of maintaining an office), and malpractice expenses. For some procedures, the RVUs for practice expenses vary based on whether the procedure is performed in the physician's office or at a facility. The RVUs compare the resources required for one service to those required for other services. The RB-RVS tends to provide lower relative values for surgical procedures and higher relative values for evaluation and management (E&M) services than relative value scales based on historical charging practices (such as the current OMFS).

---

[24]Appendix C lists high-volume workers' compensation procedure codes established by the Health Care Financing Administration (the HCFA Common Procedure Coding System, or HCPCS) with their associated relative value units (RVUs) and other relevant payment information. These procedure codes are taken from a "market basket" of services furnished to workers' compensation patients that the WCRI created from those codes. These high-volume codes, which were identified from workers' compensation medical expenditure data, accounted for 77 percent of total medical expenditures in aggregate data from six states. These codes can be used to illustrate certain issues that should be considered in adopting the Medicare physician fee schedule.

[25]The Medicare law governing the RB-RVS fee schedule is Section 1833 of the Social Security Act. The regulations can be found in *Code of Federal Regulations* (CFR), Title 42, Vol. 2, Public Health, Human Services, Part 414, "Payment for Part B Medical and Other Health Services" (42CFR414), revised as of October 1, 2002. Proposed and final rules dealing with physician services are published each year in the *Federal Register.* The citations for the most recent updates to the Medicare laws as of this writing are listed in the References to this report under U.S. Department of Health and Human Services. Additional instructions are contained in CMS carrier manuals and program memoranda pertaining to fee schedule payment issues and can be accessed at the CMS Web site at http://cms.hhs.gov/.

Table 3.1
Comparison of Key Features of the Medicare Physician Fee Schedule and the Current OMFS

Fee Schedule Feature	Current California OMFS	Medicare Fee Schedule	Comments/Issues
Applicability	Applies to all covered services provided, referred, or prescribed by physicians regardless of type of facility in which the services are performed. Separate facility fees for hospital emergency room or for operating room are allowed.	Applies to services provided by physicians, dentists, optometrists, podiatrists, chiropractors, and certain limited license practitioners and services "incident to" their services; non-hospital radiology services (including magnetic resonance imaging [MRI]) and other diagnostic tests (other than clinical laboratory); outpatient rehabilitation services.	Decision needed on whether non-emergency hospital outpatient therapeutic and diagnostic services should be paid under the physician fee schedule or the fee schedule for hospital outpatient services.
Non-physician practitioners	Pays for acupuncture and services provided by family therapists that are not covered under Medicare. Non-physician practitioners receive same payment as physicians for same procedure.	Reduced fees are payable to physician assistants, nurse practitioners, and clinical nurse specialists. No RVUs for acupuncture.	Process needed to establish and refine codes for acupuncture. Decision needed on whether to adopt any payment differentials for non-physician practitioners.
Procedure codes	Primarily uses 1997 *Current Procedural Terminology* (CPT) codes with some CWCP-specific codes or definitions; 1994 CPT used for anesthesia services and physical medicine.	HCFA Common Procedure Coding System (HCPCS) contains codes for more than 7,000 distinct services—Level 1: the American Medical Association's (AMA's) CPT codes; Level 2: CMS-established G codes; Level 3: Carrier-established with CMS permission. Codes updated annually.	Decisions needed on which CWCP-specific codes or unique definitions are still needed and which Medicare G-codes or carrier-established codes may be used for CWCP patients.
Relative value units	Medicode RVUs from 1993 to 1997 derived from charge data except American Society of Anesthesiologists (ASA) 1993 *Relative Value Guide* used for anesthesia.	Resource-based RVUs take into account resources for three components: physician work, practice expense, and malpractice expenses. Developed with input from physician specialties. Limited review annually and full review and update every five years. Uses 1998 ASA *Relative Value Guide* for anesthesia and American College of Radiology work RVUs.	Need RVUs for codes for which Medicare does not pay or that Medicare defines differently through G-codes.
Geographic adjustment	No geographic adjustment.	Nine California payment areas: Anaheim/Santa Ana, Los Angeles, Marin/Napa/Solano, Oakland/Berkeley, San Francisco, San Mateo, Santa Clara, Ventura, rest of California. Adjustment reviewed at least every three years.	The adjustment for geographic cost differences aligns payments with the costs of providing services.
Conversion factor	Separate conversion factors by type of service.	Uniform conversion factor for all specialties; separate fee schedule and conversion factor for anesthesiology.	Uniform conversion factor is consistent with aligning payments with costs but will involve significant payment reductions for surgery and anesthesia.

Fee Schedule Feature	Current California OMFS	Medicare Fee Schedule	Comments/Issues
Update process	No established process for regular review and updates subject to California administrative policies for rulemaking.	Annual formal rulemaking process. Annual updates in codes, selected RVUs and conversion factor; review and update of all RVUs at least every five years; review of geographic indices at least every three years.	Major advantage of linking to the Medicare fee schedule is having an established process for refining and updating payment parameters.
Update factor	Not applicable.	Established by law based on a sustainable growth rate system that updates the prior year conversion factor using a formula that takes into account inflation and growth in Medicare program expenditures.	Consideration should be given to establishing an automatic update for inflation only.
Site-of-service differential	Same payment applies to services furnished in office and facility settings.	Lower practice expense RVUs generally apply if a separate facility payment is made.	Site of service differential aligns payments with costs and avoids duplicate payments for facility component; eliminates incentives to furnish services in office settings.
Surgery	Discounting for multiple procedures performed on the same day; global fee periods based on Medicare; physician assistant-at-surgery payments are 20 percent of surgeon's fee.	Discounting for multiple procedures are more liberal; updated global fee periods; physician assistant-at-surgery paid 16 percent of applicable global fee amount.	Although policies are comparable, they differ in particulars. Decisions need to be made on whether to continue OMFS policies or adopt Medicare policies.
Pathology and clinical laboratory tests	Pays both pathologist and laboratory using RVUs with technical and professional components specified for each procedure.	Physician fee schedule applies only to physician pathology services: surgical pathology, certain clinical consultative services, and specific cytopathology, and hematology and blood-banking services. Outpatient clinical laboratory tests paid under separate fee schedule.	There is the assumption that the OMFS will link to the Medicare clinical laboratory fee schedule for services that do not have a professional component.
Anesthesia services	Uses 1993 ASA *Relative Value Guide* for base units, 15-minute time increments for first four hours and 10-minute increments thereafter. Additional units for patient status modifiers and conditions.	Uses 1998 ASA *Relative Value Guide* for base units and 15-minute time increments. No units allowed for patient status modifiers.	Decision needs to be made on whether to adopt Medicare RB-RVS policies and relative conversion factor or to continue current OMFS for anesthesia.

- The second element of the fee schedule is the conversion factor (CF) that converts the RVUs into a Medicare payment amount for the procedure. The conversion factor determines overall fee schedule payment levels. The Medicare program uses a single conversion factor for all services except anesthesia.

- The third element is a GAF that adjusts for geographic differences in the costs of maintaining a physician practice. Separate geographic practice cost indices (GPCIs) apply to the RVUs for the three components comprising the service: physician work, malpractice expense, and practice expense. There are adjustment factors for nine geographic areas in California.

The general formula for determining a payment amount under the fee schedule is:

Payment = ([RVU work x GPCI work] + [RVU practice expense x GPCI practice expense] + [RVU malpractice expense x GPCI malpractice expense]) x CF

The RB-RVS fee schedule applies to Medicare-covered services furnished by physicians (defined as allopathic and osteopathic physicians, optometrists, podiatrists, and chiropractors), radiology services, diagnostic tests other than clinical laboratory tests, and outpatient rehabilitation therapy services. Non-physician practitioners furnishing Medicare-covered services within their scope of practice are paid certain percentages of the fee schedule amount (e.g., physician assistants and nurse practitioners receive 85 percent of physician fees). Payment modifiers are used for atypical services (e.g., an assistant-at-surgery or multiple surgical procedures) that require payment adjustments. A separate fee schedule applies to anesthesia services furnished by anesthesiologists and certified nurse anesthetists.[26] Medicare uses the American Medical Association's *Physicians' Current Procedural Terminology*, 4th Edition (CPT-4) to describe most services covered by the fee schedule; the program has established additional codes (HCPCS Level II or G-codes) to accommodate Medicare-specific coverage and payment policies. The fee schedule is normally updated annually each January 1. The update includes new procedure codes and interim RVUs for those procedures, refinements to the RVUs for selected procedures, an adjustment in the conversion factor based on a formula that accounts for inflation but is also intended to keep physician spending consistent with growth in the national economy, and policy changes. The RVUs and GPCIs are reviewed and updated as needed and at least every five and three years, respectively.

Geographic Adjustment Factor

Unlike Medicare, the CWCP OMFS does not vary the maximum payment amount by geographic area. The Medicare fee schedule adjusts the uniform national conversion factor to account for geographic differences in the costs of physician work, practice expenses, and malpractice expenses relative to the national average for each component. The GAF is a

---

[26]Physicians furnishing services in Health Professional Shortage Areas (HPSAs) receive a 10 percent incentive payment.

composite of separate GPCIs for each of the three components of the physician fee schedule (U.S. Department of Health and Human Services [DHHS], 2000c):

- The *work index* (54.5 percent) is based on geographic differences in the median hourly earnings in six professional specialty occupations.[27] By law, the index reflects only one-quarter of the relative wage differences in the payment area relative to the national average.
- The *practice expense index* (42.3 percent) measures the full relative cost differences for employee wages, rent, and other office expenses. The measure for employee wages (16.8 percent) is based on median hourly earnings of clerical workers, registered nurses, licensed practical nurses, and health technicians. The rent measure (11.6 percent) is based on Department of Housing and Urban Development (HUD) fair market rents. Miscellaneous expenses (13.9 percent) are assumed not to vary substantially across payment areas and carry a weight of 1.0.
- The *malpractice expense index* (3.2 percent) is based on premiums paid for mature "claims made" policies for physicians in different risk classes.

The same expense categories are used in the Medicare Economic Index (MEI), which measures changes in the costs of maintaining a physician's office (the MEI is discussed later in this chapter).

The Medicare fee schedule has nine payment areas or localities for California (see Table 3.2). The current payment areas were developed from historic carrier localities using county-level composite indices. Separate payment areas were established where a higher cost area's composite cost index was more than 5 percent higher than the weighted average indices for the remaining areas in the state (DHHS, 1998a). Columns A through C of the table show the GPCI for the three fee schedule service components by the nine payment areas, and Column D shows the weighted composite GAF indices. The GAF is highest for San Francisco (1.221) and lowest for those counties that do not constitute a separate payment area (1.010 for counties in the "rest of California" category). Column E shows the premium in the GAF for the eight county-defined payment areas relative to the GAF for the rest of California (payment area [GAF/rest of California GAF] – 1.00). Using the Anaheim/Santa Ana area (Orange County) as an example, Medicare's payments to providers with practices located in Orange County are 8.6 percent higher than payments to providers located in the remaining areas of the state.

The Medicare law requires that CMS review and adjust the GPCIs if necessary at least every three years. If more than one year has elapsed since the last revision, the adjustment is phased in over two years. The last revisions to the GPCIs were implemented in 2001. Thus, a review of the current factors will occur in connection with the 2004 update to the physician fee

---

[27]The specialties are engineers, surveyors and architects; natural scientists and mathematicians; teachers, counselors and librarians; social scientists, social workers, and lawyers; registered nurses and pharmacists; and writers, artists, and editors. Physician hourly earnings are not included because physicians' fees are largely determinate of their earnings.

schedule. As is the case with other changes, any revisions will be proposed for public comment before the final rule is issued.

Table 3.2
2003 Geographic Practice Cost Indices by Medicare Locality

Payment Area	A. Work GPCI	B. Practice Expense GPCI	C. Malpractice Expense GPCI	D. GAF	E. % Higher Than "Rest of California" (Area GAF/1.010)
Anaheim/Santa Ana[a]	1.037	1.184	0.955	1.097	8.6
Los Angeles	1.056	1.139	0.955	1.088	7.7
Marin/Napa/Solano	1.015	1.248	0.687	1.104	9.3
Oakland/Berkeley[b]	1.041	1.235	0.687	1.113	10.2
San Francisco	1.068	1.458	0.687	1.221	20.9
San Mateo	1.048	1.432	0.687	1.199	18.7
Santa Clara	1.063	1.380	0.639	1.184	17.2
Ventura	1.028	1.125	0.783	1.062	5.1
Rest of California	1.007	1.034	0.748	1.010	–

SOURCE: DHHS (2002c).
[a]Orange County
[b]Alameda and Contra Costa Counties

The differences in GPCI values across the California payment areas reflect measured differences in the resources involved in operating a private medical practice. (The work GPCI reflects only one-quarter of the difference). Although each index is based on cost differences relative to the national average, the indices also reflect relative cost differences across California payment areas. Adoption of the GAF as part of the CWCP maximum fee schedule is consistent with a policy objective of aligning payments with the costs of providing services. At the same time, it adds a level of administrative complexity to the payment system that does not exist under the current fee schedule and results in payment redistributions. Studies examining RB-RVS–related fee schedule issues for the CWCP have not modeled the implications of using a geographic adjustment factor.[28] The decision whether to incorporate the GAF into the OMFS impacts the determination of a budget-neutral conversion factor (further discussed later in this chapter).

Site-of-Service Differential

Physicians furnish services in a variety of settings, including private offices and clinics, hospitals, ambulatory surgical centers, and patient homes. The OMFS pays the same amount for a

---

[28]At the request of the Industrial Medical Council (IMC), the Lewin Group (2002) in its RB-RVS study did not incorporate a claim-by-claim geographic adjustment factor into the payment simulation. Instead, a one-time adjustment was made to the RVUs to reflect the geographic distribution of services so that procedures that are disproportionately furnished in higher-cost areas have higher RVUs than procedures that are more evenly distributed across geographic areas. However, a physician performing the procedure in a low-cost area received the same payment as a physician in a high-cost area, according to the Lewin Group analysis.

physician service regardless of where the service in furnished. In contrast, Medicare varies the practice expense component of the payment for many services based on whether it is furnished in a facility or non-facility setting.

The practice expense component is intended to compensate for the practice or overhead costs associated with delivering services, including nursing and administrative staff salaries, medical supplies, and office space. Practice expenses are higher when the services are provided in the office setting than in a facility setting because the facility assumes some of the costs. Accordingly, the Medicare fee schedule generally establishes two levels of practice expense RVUs per code:

- The lower practice expense RVUs apply when the service is furnished in a facility for which Medicare makes a facility payment. This includes services furnished in a hospital or in an ASC when the service is on the list of Medicare-approved procedures for which a facility fee is paid.

- The higher practice expense RVUs apply when the service is furnished in a physician's office, a patient's home, or other institution for which no facility payment is made for the physician's expenses, including ASC services that are not on the list of Medicare-approved ASC procedures.

For certain services, including the following, there is only one set of practice expense RVUs:

- Services such as diagnostic tests that have only a technical or practice expense component and no professional component

- Certain evaluation and management services, such as hospital visits, that are performed exclusively in one setting

- Major surgical procedures that are performed only in a facility setting.

The list of high-volume procedure codes in Appendix C includes information on whether Medicare applies the site-of-service differential to the procedure code, i.e., whether there are different practice expense RVUs for services furnished in non-facility versus facility settings. Table 3.3 shows the total RVUs for a small set of procedures for illustrative purposes. The total RVUs are the sum of the work, malpractice expense, and practice expense RVUs for the procedure code. Any differences between the total non-facility RVUs and the facility RVUs are attributable to how the site-of-service differential is applied.

Table 3.3
Non-Facility and Facility Total RVUs for Selected Procedures, 2003

Type of Service	CPT Code	Description	Non-Facility Total RVUs	Facility Total RVUs
Minor surgery	12001	Repair superficial wounds	3.99	2.77
Minor surgery	20610	Drain/inject, joint or bursa	1.84	1.29
Major surgery	64721	Carpal tunnel surgery	10.85	10.52
Major surgery	63047	Lumbar laminectomy	–	27.45
Radiology	72100	X-ray examine of lower spine–total	1.02	–
	72100	Professional component only	0.32	0.32
	72100	Technical component only	0.70	N/A
General medicine	95851	Range of motion measurements	0.74	0.25
Physical therapy	97110	Therapeutic Exercises	0.76	N/A
E&M	99214	Office/outpatient visit; established patient	2.17	1.54

SOURCE: DHHS (2002c).
N/A= Not applicable.

In reviewing the RVUs in Table 3.3, it is important to keep in mind that separate and additional payments are made to a facility for the costs it incurs when services are provided in a Medicare-covered facility setting (generally, a hospital, skilled nursing facility, or ambulatory surgery center). For example, for a minor surgical procedure such as CPT-12001, Medicare's average payment to a California physician would be $155.57 if the service were provided in a non-facility setting and $108.00 if it were provided in a hospital outpatient clinic.[29] However, in the outpatient clinic, Medicare makes an additional payment to the hospital for its facility costs ($117.27 before taking into account beneficiary coinsurance).[30] The small difference between non-facility and facility total RVUs for carpal tunnel surgery is an anomaly of the method used to allocate overhead expenses when a small number of procedures typically performed only in a facility setting are provided in an office setting (which may be an ASC that is not certified by Medicare). There are no non-facility RVUs for lumbar laminectomy because this is a major surgical procedure that is always performed in facility settings.

The total RVUs for an X-ray of the lower spine illustrate Medicare's payment approach to radiological diagnostic tests. The OMFS tests are divided into two parts: a technical component that represents the resources required to take the X-ray and the professional component that represents the resources required for the physician to interpret the results.[31] Medicare pays for the total procedure only when the X-ray is taken and interpreted in a physician's office or freestanding radiology diagnostic center. Because neither setting qualifies for a separate facility fee, there are no facility-setting RVUs for the total procedure. Similarly, there are no facility-

---

[29]The payment amounts are based on the Medicare conversion factor of $36.7856 and on an average California GAF of 1.06. The GAF adjustment is based on a Lewin Group estimate that the average California conversion factor for CWCP would be 6 percent higher than the national conversion factor (The Lewin Group, 2002).

[30]The payment is based on a $96.52 standard payment and an average hospital wage index adjustment of 1.215.

[31]The RVUs for the technical component are set to equal the difference between the RVUs for the total procedure and the RVUs for the professional component.

setting RVUs for the technical component only because the RB-RVS fee schedule does not apply to hospitals and other providers receiving a facility fee.

Outpatient rehabilitation services (physical, speech-language pathology, and occupational therapy) are an exception to the general rule that separate payments are made for professional and facility costs when services covered by the RB-RVS schedule are furnished in a facility setting. Medicare's payment does not vary according to where the outpatient rehabilitation service is furnished, i.e., no separate facility fee is payable when the services are furnished in a hospital outpatient department or other facility setting. If the services are covered as facility services, the payment is made to the facility; otherwise, the payment is made to the therapist in independent practice or physician furnishing the service.

Medicare's site-of-service differential represents a significant policy difference in the way services are currently paid under the OMFS. The current fee schedule does not contain a site-of-service differential. Per California code, the OMFS applies to "all covered medical services provided, referred, or prescribed by physicians, regardless of the type of facility in which medical services are performed, including clinic and hospital-based physicians working on a contract basis." The OMFS has an exception allowing a hospital or ambulatory surgical center to charge and collect a facility fee for the use of the emergency room or operating room of the facility.[32] Thus, the same fee schedule applies regardless of whether a facility payment is also made for the service but, except for emergency room and surgical procedures requiring an operating room, a separate facility payment is not expressly allowed.

RAND believes that there are three basic payment policy options to consider in adopting the Medicare fee schedule (see Table 3.4). The decision regarding the site-of-service differential has implications for CWCP expenditures and/or the conversion factor. Further analysis is needed to understand the financial implications of the three options. In particular, it is important to understand the types of surgical and non-emergency medical services that are being paid a facility fee under the OMFS and how payments would change if the site-of-service differential were adopted along with the Medicare fee schedules for hospital outpatient and ASC services.

Option 1: Adopt the Medicare Fee Schedule Policies for All Services

This option applies Medicare policies so that, in general, physician payment is lower if the service is furnished in a facility that is eligible for separate payments under Medicare fee schedules (e.g., hospitals and ASCs). The option eliminates potential duplicate payments when a facility fee is payable in addition to the physician service; however, it increases total payments for those services provided in a facility setting that are currently not eligible for a facility payment under the OMFS. As a result, this option eliminates incentives under the current system to furnish these services in the office setting and is likely to increase payments over time. For providers, the option has the administrative simplicity of following known Medicare rules

[32]CA Code of Regulations, Section 9791, 1999.

without modifications. It also avoids disputes over whether there should be a facility payment in addition to the physician payment.

Table 3.4
Payment Policy Options for Procedures Performed in Different Ambulatory Settings

	RB-RVS Payment Policy	Facility Fee Payment Policy
Option 1: Adopt the Medicare fee schedule policies for all services	Different practice expense RVUs for physician services performed in facility and office settings; office setting RVUs apply to ASC procedures not on approved list	Payable for all hospital outpatient procedures and ASC procedures on approved list
Option 2: Adopt the Medicare fee schedule policies only for services for which facility fees are payable under the OMFS	Different practice expense RVUs for surgical and physician emergency room services; same payment for office-based and non-emergency hospital outpatient medical and diagnostic services	Payable only for surgical procedures and emergency room services
Option 3: Continue current OMFS policy	Same practice expense RVUs regardless of where procedure is performed; same payment for office-based and non-emergency hospital outpatient medical and diagnostic services	Payable only for surgical procedures and emergency room services

Option 2: Adopt the Medicare Fee Schedule Policies Only for Services for Which Facility Fees Are Payable Under the OMFS

This hybrid option relies on current OMFS policies to determine when facility fees are payable (i.e., emergency room and surgical procedures). It assumes that facility fees are payable only in the limited circumstances expressly authorized by the OMFS and are not payable when non-operating procedures are involved (e.g., diagnostic and clinic services). This option applies the Medicare facility RVUs when OMFS facility fees are payable and applies the non-facility RVUs in the remaining situations. The option has the advantage of eliminating duplicate payments for facility costs while retaining the policy of paying similar amounts for the facility component across different settings for many services. A disadvantage is that it may entail some additional administrative burden for the DWC in clarifying the rules regarding which procedures qualify for a facility fee and periodically updating the policies. It also poses an additional administrative burden on providers by requiring them to adhere to CWCP-specific billing rules instead of Medicare rules.

Option 3: Continue Current OMFS Policy

Option 3 continues the current OMFS policy to pay the same amount regardless of where the service is furnished. From a policy perspective, this option has the advantage of creating the same total payment for physician and facility costs across sites of service except for those procedures for which a separate facility fee is payable. While there is an incentive to furnish procedures that are eligible for a facility fee in a facility setting, the current incentives to furnish non-surgical procedures in an office are retained. It avoids an issue that the Medicare program is currently struggling with—namely, the extent to which different payments for the facility cost component across hospital outpatient departments, ambulatory surgery centers, and physician offices are appropriate. (This issue is discussed in greater detail in Chapter 4.)

Major disadvantages emerge when deciding which practice expense RVUs should be used to implement this option. The Lewin Group (2002), for example, determined average practice expense RVUs for each procedure weighted by the relative frequency with which the procedure was performed in facility versus non-facility settings. This solution imposes an administrative burden to redetermine practice expense RVUs each time the fee schedule is updated and negates some of the administrative simplicity that would be gained in tying CWCP payments to the Medicare fee schedule. It also runs counter to the objective of an RB-RVS. The average-practice-expense RVUs underpay when the service is furnished in the physician's office and overpay when it is furnished in a facility setting.

An administratively simpler solution would be to apply the "non-facility RVUs" to all services, including those for which a facility fee is payable. However, this solution also runs counter to the RB-RVS objective of aligning payments with the costs of providing services. While payment for office-based procedures would be appropriate, the facility component of minor surgical services would be paid twice (once in the practice expense component of the RB-RVS schedule and again in the hospital or ASC facility fee), and this option increases the incentive to furnish minor surgical services in a facility setting. The extent to which this is a problem depends on the surgical services for which a facility fee is paid. As seen in the comparison between the RVUs for services performed in non-facility and facility settings (see Table 3.3), the financial implications of this option are greater for minor surgical procedures than for major procedures. If only emergency room and surgical procedures requiring an operating room are paid a facility fee, the potential for duplicate payments is minimal because the RVUs for both major surgical procedures and emergency department visits assume that the services are provided in a facility.

Anesthesia Services

Both the OMFS and Medicare fee schedule pay for anesthesia procedures using fixed-base RVUs that depend on the type of anesthesia procedure performed and time units that depend on the length of the actual procedure. The OMFS uses 1994 CPT-4 codes and 1993 relative values established by the American Society of Anesthesiologists (ASA). Medicare's 2003 fee schedule uses 1988 ASA relative values and does not allow modifier units for patient health status, risk, age, or unusual circumstances (see Table 3.5).[33]

---

[33]An exception is made for two procedures: four base units are recognized for anesthesia services furnished during cataract or iridectomy surgery (Code *of Federal Regulations*, Title 42, Part 414, "Payment for Part B Medical and Other Services," Section 414.46, "Additional Rules for Payment of Anesthesia Services," 42 [CFR414.46], revised October 1, 2002).

Table 3.5
Comparison of Policies for Anesthesia Services

	Medicare RB-RVS	OMFS
Anesthesia time units	One unit per 15 minutes. Fractions of units counted for fractions of time.	One unit per 15 minutes or at least 5 additional minutes for first four hours and thereafter one unit per 10 minutes or at least 5 additional minutes. By report (BR) after eight hours.
Modifier units	Not allowed	Allowed for selected patient status modifiers and qualifying circumstances
Medical direction of certified registered nurse anesthetist (CRNA) or anesthesia assistant (AA)	Each receives 50 percent of payment. No more than four concurrent procedures. If there are more than four, physician receives base units only.	Anesthesiologist receives basic units plus one unit per hour or fraction thereof. Total payment to both not to exceed listed value if performed by anesthesiologist.
Multiple anesthesia procedures for same patient	If same operative session, payment is based on the anesthesia procedure having the highest base units and the total time for all procedures.	If done in same operative session *or* on same day, payment based on anesthesia procedure having the highest base units and the total time for all procedures.

There are only a few differences between the base units used by Medicare and the current OMFS. The Lewin Group (2002) found that only 0.43 percent of the procedures and 0.64 percent of payments correspond to codes with different base values. Thus, the decision regarding whether to adopt the Medicare RVUs for anesthesia services is largely a question of whether the Medicare policies or current OMFS policies on time and modifier units should be used. A separate issue discussed later in this chapter is whether the existing OMFS conversion factor ($34.50) or the Medicare conversion factor ($17.05) should apply.[34]

The Medicare conversion factor for anesthesia services was established in a manner to assure that the payments for anesthesia services are consistent with the RB-RVS payments for other services. As with other services, physician work, practice expenses, and malpractice are taken into account in establishing the national conversion factor, and the geographic adjustment factor applies. Because there are no work values for specific procedure codes, refinements and adjustments for physician work and practice expenses are made to the anesthesia conversion factor, and all anesthesia services are affected. The 2003 Medicare fee schedule update included a 2.1 percent increase in the anesthesia conversion factor to reflect the results of the five-year review of anesthesia RVUs.[35]

The choice of conversion factor for anesthesia services largely depends on the policy goals for tying the OMFS to the Medicare fee schedule. Administrative simplification does not require a change in the anesthesia conversion factor. However, if another important goal is to

---

[34]In this regard, we note that the Lewin Group maintained the current level of payments for anesthesia services and did not model the impact of the different time/modifier policies or the impact of relating the conversion factor to payment levels for other services.

[35]A corresponding reduction was made in the conversion factor for all other physician services to maintain budget neutrality in the RVU refinement process.

relate payments to the resource requirements and to value anesthesiologist work effort consistent with other physician specialties, the anesthesia conversion factor should be set in a manner that is comparable to that for other services. Tying the conversion factor to the Medicare conversion factor for anesthesia accomplishes this goal by changing from a charge-based conversion to a resource-based conversion factor.

Conversion Factor

The conversion factor is a dollar amount that converts the RVUs for a service into a payment amount. Medicare uses a single conversion factor that applies to all physician services without regard to specialty. The 2003 Medicare physician fee schedule conversion factor is $36.7856.[36] The conversion factor for anesthesia services is $17.05.

Medicare's initial conversion factor was "budget-neutral" to total physician payments being made under the reasonable charge methodology that was replaced by the RB-RVS fee schedule. Conversion factors for subsequent years have been determined by applying an update formula to the conversion factor for the preceding year (the current update factor methodology is discussed later in this chapter).[37] The transition from reasonable charges to the RB-RVS occurred in separate stages for the physician work, practice expense, and malpractice expense components of the fee schedule, and full implementation of resource-based relative values did not occur until 2002. The purpose of the transition policies was to soften the re-distributional effects of moving in a "budget-neutral" manner from a charge-based to resource-based payment system.

Three key decisions need to be made in tying the OMFS to the Medicare fee schedule: (1) the level at which the conversion factor(s) should be set, (2) whether there should be a uniform conversion factor or separate conversion factors by type of service, and (3) whether the payment changes should be phased in. These issues are interrelated and have important access and cost implications for the CWCP. The impact of major payment reductions can be softened through transition policies or eliminated through differential conversion factors. If "cost-neutral" conversion factors are implemented by type of service, there may be no need to phase in the payment changes. (Cost-neutral conversion factors are estimated to result in total payments under the new fee schedule that are equal to the total payments that would have been made under the current OMFS.) On the other hand, a multi-year transition may be needed if a national uniform conversion factor is adopted, even if it is cost-neutral to current CWCP expenditures under the OMFS.

---

[36]This conversion factor was effective as of March 1, 2003. The regularly scheduled update that would have occurred January 1 was delayed to provide time for the Congress to make a technical correction in the formula used to determine the update factor.

[37]The update formula created separate conversion factors until a single conversion factor and revised update formula were implemented in 1998.

Establishing the Level of the Conversion Factor

Ideally, payment levels should be sufficiently high to assure that workers' compensation patients have access to high-quality medically appropriate care without making excessive expenditures and creating incentives for inefficient and unnecessary care. Unfortunately, there is no "gold standard" for determining the appropriate payment level, and the decision should take into account a number of factors: whether there is adequate access to care, current maximum allowable fees, the relationship between Medicare and private-payer fee levels in California, and available information on the cost of providing specific services. A multiplier can be applied to the Medicare conversion factor to establish an overall payment level that is adequate to provide access to high-quality care. Setting the rate too low may create access problems, while setting the rate too high may encourage unnecessary utilization and result in excessive program expenditures.

Medicare payment levels are frequently used to benchmark other payment systems. Only two states out of 40 included in a recent Workers' Compensation Research Institute (WCRI) study (Eccleston et al., 2002) had overall payment levels below Medicare fee levels (Massachusetts[38] and Florida). The study found that most workers' compensation programs provide higher fees than Medicare does. The average premium is about 40–50 percent; California ranked sixth from the bottom of those 40 states in 2001 with an overall payment level that was 12-percent higher than Medicare fee levels.[39] However, in the WCRI study the relationship between state workers' compensation fees and Medicare fees varied across types of service (see Table 3.6), ranging from a 59-percent premium for general medicine to a 10-percent discount for evaluation and management services. The high premium for surgical services and relatively low payment levels for evaluation and management services are characteristic of charge-based fee schedules such as the OMFS.

Table 3.6
OMFS Fee Schedule Premiums: Percentage Greater or Less Than Medicare Fees

Overall	Surgery	Radiology	General Medicine	Physical Medicine	Evaluation and Management
12%	36%	14%	59%	–1%	–10%

SOURCE: Eccleston et al. (2002).

MedPAC's recent report to Congress concluded that Medicare payment levels are adequate to assure access for Medicare program beneficiaries (MedPAC, 2003). However, the report's assessment also painted a mixed picture. The number of physicians billing Medicare has increased, but there is anecdotal information regarding access problems in some geographic areas

[38]Effective December 2002, the Massachusetts workers' compensation fee schedule was set at 100 percent of the Medicare payment rates.

[39]The relationship between CWCP fee levels and Medicare was determined by comparing the amounts that would be payable for a standard market basket of procedures under the two fee schedules; it was not determined through claims analysis of the actual distribution of CWCP claims. We estimate that the California 12-percent premium will have increased to about 15 percent since 2001 because Medicare's conversion factor has decreased 3.8 percent while California's fee levels have remained unchanged.

and specialties. A national MedPAC-commissioned survey suggests that physicians are becoming more selective about accepting new Medicare patients, but this trend also applies to Medicaid and private HMO patients (Schoenman and Feldman, 2002). With reference to private-payer fee levels, another common benchmark for assessing the adequacy of fee levels, MedPAC-sponsored research estimated that Medicare 2002 fee levels were about 77–79 percent of private rates. However, the relationship varied by type of service (a lower percentage for anesthesia and procedure-oriented services than for evaluation and management services) and geography (a higher percentage for large cities with higher geographic adjustment factors than for rural areas and smaller cities) (MedPAC, 2003).

WCRI's report (Eccleston et al., 2002) suggests that a premium over and above Medicare payments may be needed to assure workers' compensation patients have access to medically appropriate care. WCRI gives two reasons for this need. First, workers' compensation patients may have more administrative requirements and other complicating issues that might require more time and expertise to treat. Second, Medicare payment levels have been affected by federal budgetary constraints that should not apply to state workers' compensation programs (see the discussion later in this chapter on the update factor).

To the extent that a premium is needed to assure access, it could be provided through adjustments in the relative values for specific services, or through the conversion factor, or through both. An adjustment to the relative values has the advantage of targeting those procedures for which there is evidence that workers' compensation patients require more resources than do Medicare patients. It is generally thought that this is most likely to be the case with evaluation and management services. The Lewin Group study commissioned by the Industrial Medical Council examined this issue using a methodology patterned after the approach used to establish the Medicare RB-RVS values. The study found that workers' compensation patients require relative value units that are on average 28 percent higher than those Medicare uses for evaluation and management services (The Lewin Group, 2002).

As can be seen from the following formula for determining total OMFS physician payments, the decisions regarding other features (such as a geographic adjustment factor, modifications in the RVUs for workers' compensation patients, site-of-service differentials, inclusion of anesthesia services, and other such features) also play a role in determining aggregate payment levels and changes in those levels for specific groups of physicians or types of services. Assuming for the moment that the policies determining the RVUs and GAFs are established, a decision to target total payments at a specific level will determine the overall conversion factor, whereas a decision to establish the conversion factor(s) at a specified level will determine aggregate expenditures.

$$\text{Total OMFS physician payments} = \sum \left(RVU_{PROCi} \times CF_{SPi} \times GAF_{PAi}\right) + \left(RVU_{PROCii} \times CF_{SPii} \times GAF_{PAii}\right) + \left(RVU_{PROCiii} \times CF_{SPiii} \times GAF_{PAiii}\right),$$

Where:

PROC = CPT-4 procedure code for the service

SP = the specialty of the provider furnishing the service

PA = the payment area in which the service is provided

Basic options for establishing the conversion factor are presented next. We did not have the detailed claim information for physician and other practitioner services that would have enabled us to model the implications of the different choices. Therefore, we drew on work done by The Lewin Group for the IMC to illustrate the options and discuss the broad impacts by service category that are likely to occur (see Table 3.7).[40] The estimated impacts assume all services are paid under the OMFS whereas in actuality some percentage is paid under contractual arrangements.

Table 3.7
Payments Using Medicare RB-RVUs Compared to Total Payments Under OMFS

		Option 1A: Cost-Neutral CF Excluding Anesthesia ($44.73)		Option 1B: Cost-Neutral CF Including Anesthesia and Excluding Pathology and Laboratory ($45.36)	
OMFS Service Category	Total Payments Under OMFS	Total Payments	% Change	Total Payments	% Change
Anesthesia	$6,145,869	$6,145,869	0	$3,745,770	-39.1
E&M	$40,935,969	$50,316,739	22.9	$51,028,617	24.7
Surgery	$42,098,904	$35,432,041	-15.8	$35,933,331	-14.6
Radiology	$24,523,624	$24,341,127	-0.7	$24,685,504	0.7
Pathology and laboratory	$1,818,870	$2,188,852	20.3	$1,818,870	0.0
Medicine	$13,155,808	$12,375,410	-5.9	$12,550,497	-4.6
Physical medicine	$75,053,599	$73,271,755	-2.4	$74,308,399	-1.0
Special services	$11,845,046	$11,505,896	-2.9	$11,506,701	-2.9
Subject to RBRVS	$396,042	$ 56,892	-85.6	$ 57,697	-85.4
Pass-throughs	$11,449,004	$11,449,004	0.0	$11,449,004	0.0
Total	$215,577,690	$215,577,689		$215,577,689	

Option 1: Determine a Budget-Neutral Single Conversion Factor

The first option for establishing a conversion factor makes the total payments under the RB-RVS fee schedule cost-neutral to current estimated payments. With a cost-neutral conversion factor, total program payments are estimated to remain the same, but there are redistributions across specialties and types of services. Determining the cost-neutral conversion factor involves modeling the policy decisions that are made in adopting the Medicare RB-RVS fee schedule.

---

[40]In keeping with our general approach of not considering alternatives to the Medicare fee schedule, we have modeled our options for the conversion factor and transition policies using the Medicare RVUs. We have not reviewed the details of the Lewin methodology. Refining the Medicare RVUs to reflect the added resources required to treat workers' compensation would improve the alignment of payments with treatment costs. However, it would also add an administrative burden because the CWCP would need to periodically review and refine the RVUs. Using the RVUs from the Lewin study, we estimate that the cost-neutral conversion factor for Option 1B in Table 3.7 for evaluation and management services would be $41.95.

Using a sample of bills for care provided to CWCP patients representing approximately 40 percent of the workers' compensation premium in 2000, The Lewin Group simulated payments allowed under the current OMFS and the Medicare RB-RVS to determine the conversion factor that would be cost-neutral to the maximum allowed amounts under the OMFS. The cost-neutral conversion factor was estimated to be $44.73 in 2001 if anesthesia services remained outside the RB-RVS. Clinical laboratory services were included in the estimate by converting the Medicare national fee schedule amounts into relative values. No differentials were incorporated into the conversion factors for limited license practitioners. The estimate took into account the average geographic conversion factor that would be applicable to a given procedure as well as the relative proportions of time the procedure is furnished in an office versus a facility setting.[41] The model that The Lewin Group used in its study made a one-time adjustment for the geographic adjustment factor and site-of-service differential and simulated the impact of paying the average adjustments for procedures regardless of actual geographic location or site of service. While this approach should not affect the cost-neutral conversion factor, the specialty and geographic impacts would be different if claim-by-claim adjustments were applied instead of the average adjustments. The results of The Lewin Group simulation are shown as Option 1A in Table 3.7.

Further analysis of claims data would be required to determine the actual cost-neutral conversion factor that reflects the policies that are adopted for the OMFS and to model the redistributions that would occur across specialties and geographic areas. We used the information generated by The Lewin Group study to estimate the impact of incorporating anesthesia services and excluding pathology and clinical laboratory tests (Option 1B). In doing so, we assumed that the Medicare relationship between the anesthesia conversion factor and the factor for all other services would be preserved.[42] We excluded all pathology and clinical laboratory tests because we did not have information on the pathology services (professional component only) that would be paid under the RB-RVS. The resulting cost-neutrality conversion factors are $21.03 for anesthesia and $45.36 for other services. The conversion factors include an average geographic factor of 1.06. This geographic factor may understate the adjustment factor for anesthesia services because a disproportionately higher percentage of surgical services are likely to be performed in high-cost areas.

The impact on anesthesia services is notably large (–39.1 percent). A reduction of this magnitude could reduce access unless it is accompanied by a multi-year transition (see the next section for a discussion of transition options). Total anesthesia payments will be further reduced if Medicare policies on time and modifier units are adopted.

---

[41]Because the site of service was not available in the CWCP data, The Lewin Group based the average RVUs for practice expense on Medicare data.

[42]In other words, we assumed that the anesthesia conversion factor would be 46.3 percent of the conversion factor applicable to other services. Given data limitations, the estimate also assumes that the OMFS time and modifier policies continue so that there is no change in the total anesthesia RVUs.

Option 2 : Apply a Single Multiplier to the Medicare Conversion Factor

A multiplier could be applied to the Medicare conversion factor to approximate the conversion factor needed to achieve specific policy objectives. Assuming that a geographic adjustment factor is adopted in tying OMFS payments to the Medicare fee schedule, existing analyses suggest a multiplier in the 1.15 range would be cost-neutral:

- The WCRI estimate (Eccleston et al., 2002) that overall California OMFS professional fee payments were 12 percent higher than Medicare payments in 2001 (see Table 3.6) supports a 1.15 multiplier after taking the reduction in the Medicare conversion factor between 2001 and 2003 into account.
- The $44.73 cost-neutral conversion factor estimated by The Lewin Group (2002) is 1.15 times the 2003 Medicare conversion factor after the average GAF is taken into account.
- Our $45.36 cost-neutral estimate for including anesthesia and paying for clinical laboratory tests under the separate fee schedule is 1.16 times the 2003 Medicare conversion factor after the average GAF is taken into account.

Depending on the decision for anesthesia services, the impact of adopting a 1.15 multiplier is similar to that shown for either Option 1A or 1B. If there is no geographic adjustment factor, a higher multiplier is needed to account for the generally higher cost of providing physician services in California relative to the national average cost. For example, the $44.73 cost-neutral conversion factor is 1.22 times the unadjusted Medicare national conversion factor.

The MedPAC finding, mentioned earlier in this section, that Medicare fee levels are about 77–79 percent of private-payer fee levels would result in a 1.3 multiplier based on the national data. However, MedPAC also found that there is considerable variability across geographic areas and types of services. If the conversion factor is to take comparability to private-payer rates into account, California-specific data on private-payer fee levels should be examined to determine the actual differentials between Medicare and private payers in California by service category and geographic area.

Option 3: Develop Cost-Neutral Conversion Factors by Type of Service

The previous two options assume that a single conversion factor would apply to physician services and that the policy decisions regarding differentials, if any, for non-physician practitioners would be considered in determining the appropriate conversion factor. Option 3 is intended to maintain current payment levels by type of service and to reduce the redistributions that would occur in adopting the Medicare RB-RVS. This option is *not* consistent with the goal of aligning payments with resource requirements. Because it would perpetuate the existing discrepancies between payments and the costs of providing services, it is not recommended as a long-term policy option. As discussed later in this chapter, it could be part of a transition payment methodology.

We have not suggested that specialty-specific cost-neutral conversion factors be considered because implementation of a policy that would employ those factors would be problematic for several reasons:

- A substantial proportion of services are billed by multi-specialty clinics or hospitals.
- There is no commonly accepted definition of "physician specialist." Most payer designations of specialists include both board-certified physicians and self-designated physicians.
- Physicians who provide a different mix of services than other physicians in the same specialty could receive substantially higher or lower payments than those at the current levels.

In contrast, the current OMFS is a precedent for differential conversion factors by type of service and should not impose a substantial administrative burden after the initial cost-neutral conversion factors are determined. However, there may still be a significant impact on program payments to an individual physician if the relative values for the procedures within the service category provided by the physician have substantially larger increases or decreases than the average change for the service category.

The current OMFS conversion factors cannot be used to establish cost-neutral conversion factors because of the change to resource-based relative values. However, the WCRI (Eccleston et al., 2002) and The Lewin Group studies provide rough estimates of the conversion factors that would be applicable (see Table 3.8). The WCRI results are taken from their analysis of California differentials for a market basket of services. From The Lewin Group study, we estimated the multiplier by dividing estimated OMFS payments for the type of service by the estimated total Medicare RB-RVUs and comparing the result to the Medicare conversion factor. This estimate accounts for the proportion of time a procedure is furnished in office versus facility settings and the average GAF adjustment. The multipliers are quite similar for evaluation and management services, surgery, and radiology. Further analysis is needed to confirm the reasons for the large differences for general medicine and physical medicine; however, we believe it is largely attributable to definitional differences. The Lewin Group used the types of service as defined by the OMFS, which includes chiropractic manipulative treatments as a subcategory under medicine. WCRI included chiropractic services in physical medicine. The Lewin Group multipliers for medicine and physical medicine are more consistent with the current structure of the OMFS.

Table 3.8
Estimated Cost-Neutral Multipliers to the Medicare Conversion Factor by Type of Service

	Anesthesia	Evaluation and Management	Surgery	Radiology	Medicine	Physical Medicine
WCRI study	N/A	0.90	1.36	1.14	1.59	0.99
Lewin Group study	1.91	0.93	1.36	1.16	1.22	1.18

SOURCE: RAND estimates based on Eccleston et al. (2002) and The Lewin Group (2002).
N/A = not available.

Transitional Payment Policies

The impact of significant increases or decreases in payment levels can be softened through transitional payment policies that limit the annual amount of change in payment. Next, various policies are identified that have been used by Medicare and/or other workers' compensation programs to phase in the payment changes. The first three options are based on a comparison of the service-specific conversion factors with the conversion factor under the new payment systems. These options involve less administrative burden than the fourth option, which would make payment comparisons on a procedure-specific basis. These options eliminate the need to crosswalk obsolete OMFS codes to new procedure codes and to maintain both the old and new payment amounts for each procedure. The major shortcoming of these options is that they are based on the average payment change within the service category and do not take into account the actual mix of services provided by an individual physician. A physician with an atypically high proportion of services with above-average payment reductions will not receive as much protection as under a comparable policy applied on a procedure-specific basis.

We have used the estimated current expenditures and Medicare RB-RVS RVUs from The Lewin Group analyses to estimate the length of the transition and the impact on program expenditures of the first three options. For each option, we assumed that the OMFS conversion factor is set for 2003 by applying a 1.15 multiplier to the Medicare conversion factor. We estimated that the conversion factor is $44.84 and assumed that it is updated in subsequent years based on the CMS Office of the Actuary's forecasted rates of change in the Medicare Economic Index.[43] Comparable estimates for procedure-specific transition policies require additional simulations using claims data that are not within the scope of this report.

Option 1: Establish Floors and Ceilings on Maximum Annual Changes in Service-Specific Conversion Factors

Option 1 limits the maximum percentage increase or decrease in the conversion factor in any given year, e.g., the policy might be such that the conversion factor cannot increase or decrease by more than 10 percent each year. This option involves making an annual comparison between the prior-year conversion factor and the current-year conversion factor before applying the transition policy. If the change threshold is set at 10 percent and there is more than a 10-percent increase or decrease, the current-year conversion factor is set at 110 percent or 90 percent of the prior-year conversion factor, as appropriate. The choice of a change threshold is a policy decision and it could be higher or lower than 10 percent.

Table 3.9 illustrates the effect of this policy on estimated annual changes in payment rates and CFs assuming a 2003, 2004, and 2005 1.15 multiplier to the Medicare conversion factor. It also illustrates a two-year hold-harmless policy applied in conjunction with this option (which is discussed under Option 3 below). Table 3.9 assumes a 10-percent change threshold is used for

---

[43]The conversion factor is equal to 1.15 x 36.7856 x 1.06 (the average GAF adjustment). The forecasted changes in the MEI are: for 2004, 2.0 percent; for 2005, 2.2 percent; and for 2006, 1.8 percent.

both increases and decreases in the conversion factor. The RB-RVS conversion factor ($44.84) would apply to radiology, medicine, and physical medicine in 2003 and increase for inflation in subsequent years. The cost-neutral conversion factor for evaluation and management services ($36.39) would increase 10 percent annually the first two years and would increase 6.2 percent in 2005 and thereafter for inflation. The cost-neutral conversion factor for surgery ($53.15) would decrease 10 percent the first two years and thereafter increase by the inflation adjustment.

We estimate the anesthesia conversion factor ($34.50) would be reduced 10 percent annually until 2008 when the updated 1.15 Medicare conversion factor would apply. Relative to adopting the $44.84 conversion factor for all services in 2003, this particular transition policy would reduce the maximum allowable amounts under the RB-RVS by about 0.4 and 0.1 percent in 2003 and 2004, respectively, and increase payments by 0.5 percent in 2005. In the first two years, the phased-in payment increases for evaluation and management services more than offset the estimated cost for phasing in the reductions for anesthesia services and surgery.

Option 2: Use Blended CFs with Progressively Decreasing Percentage of Cost-Neutral Service-Specific CF and Progressively Increasing Percentage of New CF

Option 2 applies the transition policy to all service categories regardless of the amount of dollar change. Generally, it spreads the absolute payment change in each service category over the years in the transition period. Because the length of the transition is the same for all service categories, the annual percentage change varies across service categories. Policy decisions regarding the length of the transition as well as the blend percentage for each year typically take into consideration the magnitude of the changes. Common transition policies using blended rates are shown in Table 3.10.

The blended conversion factor allows some room for fine-tuning in the payment policies over the transition period before all payments are based on the RB-RVS. If desired, Option 2 also provides a mechanism to maintain cost neutrality in the first year by using a blend of the cost-neutral conversion factors by type of service with the cost-neutral conversion factor for all services (by definition, if new payments are cost-neutral to old payments, paying a fixed percentage of each will also be cost-neutral). Cost neutrality to the new conversion factor can be maintained in the remaining transition years by increasing the old conversion factor by the same inflation factor as the new conversion factor.

Table 3.11 illustrates Option 2 assuming that a three-year transition policy is used and the inflation adjustment is applied to both the cost-neutral conversion factor for the service category and the RB-RVS conversion factor. The percentage reductions relative to the prior year payment exceed 10 percent per year for anesthesia services, e.g., –15.9 percent in 2003, –17.3 percent in 2004, and –21.5 percent in 2005. The blended conversion factors for all other categories change by less than 10 percent a year. The conversion factor for evaluation and management services increases more slowly relative to Option 1: 7.7 percent in 2003, 9.3 percent in 2004, and 9.0 percent in 2005.

Table 3.9

Illustration of a Transition Policy (Option 1) Using Floors and Ceilings on Maximum Annual Changes Assuming a 10-Percent Payment Change Threshold and OMFS New Conversion Factor of 1.15 Times the Medicare Conversion Factor

OMFS Service Category	Estimated Service-Specific 2003 Cost-Neutral CF	Estimated % Payment Change Using 2003 1.15 Multiplier[a]	2003 Transition Conversion Factor	Estimated Additional 2003 Expenditures	Estimated % Payment Change Using 2004 1.15 Multiplier[b]	2004 Transition Conversion Factor	Estimated Additional 2004 Expenditures	Estimated % Payment Change Using 2005 1.15 Multiplier[c]	2005 Conversion Factor	Estimated Additional 2005 Expenditures
Anesthesia	$34.50	-47.6	$31.05	$2,311,740	-40.6	$27.95	$1,694,221	-32.6	$25.15	$1,124,159
E & M	$36.39	23.2	$40.03	($5,412,764)	14.3	$44.03	($1,918,654)	6.2	$46.74	
Surgery	$53.15	-15.6	$47.83	$2,368,534	-4.4	$45.74		2.2	$46.74	
Radiology	$45.07	-0.5	$44.84		2.0	$45.74		2.2	$46.74	
Medicine	$47.55	-5.7	$44.84		2.0	$45.74		2.2	$46.74	
Physical Medicine	$45.82	--2.1	$44.84		2.0	$45.74		2.2	$46.74	
Total				($732,490)			($224,433)			$1,124,159
Total Payments Using 1.15 Multiplier				$199,445,175			$203,434,079			$207,909,629
Cost as % of Total Payments Using 1.15 multiplier				-0.37%			-0.11%			0.54%
Illustration of Two-Year Hold-Harmless Policy Applied In Conjunction with Option 1 for Phasing in Payment Changes										
Radiology	$45.07	-0.5	$45.07	$124,265.24	1.5	$45.74	$0	2.2	$46.74	
Physical Medicine	$45.82	-2.1	$45.82	$1,598,957.18	-0.2	$45.82	$129,864.34	2.0	$46.74	
Additional Cost of Hold-Harmless Policy				$ 1,723,222.41			$129,864.34			
Additional Cost as % of Total Payments Using 1.15 Multiplier				0.86%			0.06%			

[a]The GAF-adjusted conversion factor is $18.07 for anesthesia services and $44.84 for other services.

[b]Assumes MEI increases 2.0%. Conversion factor is $18.43 for anesthesia and $45.74 for other services.

[c]Assumes MEI increases 2.2%. Conversion factor is $18.84 for anesthesia and $46.74 for other services.

Table 3.10
Examples of Transition Policy Option 2 Using Blended Rates

Length of Transition	Year 1		Year 2		Year 3		Year 4		Year 5	
	% Old Rates	% New Rates	% Old Rates	% New Rates	% Old Rates	% New Rates	% Old Rates	% New Rates	% Old Rates	% New Rates
5 years	80	20	60	40	40	60	20	80	0	100
4 years	75	25	50	50	25	75	0	100	–	–
3 years	66.7	33.3	33.3	66.7	0	100	–	–	–	–

Option 3: Establish a Hold-Harmless Policy for Conversion Factor Estimated to Exceed the Cost-Neutral Conversion Factor Within a Specified Period

If the payment reductions are relatively small, the general transition policy can produce a reduction in the first year or two that is followed by an increase in subsequent years. This occurs in the Option 1 (see Table 3.9) and Option 2 (see Table 3.11) transition models. For example, the physical medicine conversion factor under Option 1 would decrease 2.1 percent in 2003 only to increase 2.2 percent in 2004. Under Option 2, it would decrease 0.7 percent in 2003 and increase 1.3 percent in 2004. One way to eliminate this type of fluctuation is to *hold harmless* (or in other words, make no payment reductions) in service-specific conversion factors that are estimated to be less than the uniform conversion factor within a few years. If a hold-harmless policy were used, the service-specific conversion factor for physical medicine would apply in 2003; beginning in 2004, the updated RB-RVS conversion factor would apply under Option 1 and the updated blended conversion factor under Option 2. We estimate that this hold-harmless option would increase 2002 CWCP payments (exclusive of payments for pathology and clinical laboratory tests and special reports) about 0 .9 percent under Option 1 and about 0.4 percent under Option 2. Longer hold-harmless policies are, of course, an option but would further increase program expenditures.

Update Factor

The update factor is an annual adjustment to the conversion factor that accounts for inflation. The choice of an appropriate inflation index should take into consideration the underlying purpose for the adjustment. It could be to recognize (1) differences in the costs of maintaining a physician office, (2) changes in the market prices for physician services, or (3) changes in economy-wide earnings. To some extent, there are interrelationships between indices measuring the different types of inflation rates. For example, changes in physician prices in part reflect changes in practice costs, which in turn are impacted by changes in prevailing wage levels for nurses and administrative staff. Other considerations that should guide the selection of the appropriate indicator include the degree to which the adjustment is "self-implementing" and the availability of information forecasting future changes in the index.

Table 3.11
Illustration of a Three-Year Transition Policy Using a Blend of a Cost-Neutral Service-Specific Conversion Factor and a Conversion Factor of 1.15 Times the Medicare Conversion Factor

	A. Estimated Medicare RB-RVUs	B. Estimated Service-Specific 2003 Cost-Neutral Conversion Factor	C. 1.15 Medicare 2003 Conversion Factor (with GAF)	D. 2003 Conversion Factor	E. % Change from Prior Year	F. Estimated Additional 2003 Payments	G. 2004 Conversion Factor	H. % Change from Prior Year	I. Estimated Additional 2004 Payments	J. 2005 Conversion Factor	K. % Change from Prior Year
				0.667B + 0.333CB	(D–B)/B	(D–C) x A	(0.333B + 0.667C) x 1.02	(F–D)/D	(F–C x 1.02) x A	C x 1.02 x 1.022	(I–F)/F
OMFS Service Category											
Anesthesia	178,141	$34.50	$18.07	$29.03	–15.9%	$1,951,860	$24.01	–17.3%	$993,956	$18.84	–21.5%
E + M	1,124,899	$36.39	$44.84	$39.20	7.7%	$(6,340,743)	$42.87	9.3%	$(3,228,931)	$46.74	9.0%
Surgery	792,131	$53.15	$44.84	$50.38	–5.2%	$4,387,809	$48.56	–3.6%	$2,234,428	$46.74	–3.7%
Radiology	544,179	$45.07	$44.84	$44.99	–0.2%	$81,201	$45.81	1.8%	$41,351	$46.74	2.0%
Medicine	276,669	$47.55	$44.84	$46.65	–1.9%	$499,922	$46.66	0.0%	$254,578	$46.74	0.2%
Physical Medicine	1,638,090	$45.82	$44.84	$45.49	–0.7%	$1,066,504	$46.07	1.3%	$543,102	$46.74	1.5%
Estimated Cost of Transition Policy							$580,050			$295,382	
Total Estimated Payments Based on 1.15 Multiplier							$199,445,175			$203,434,079	
Cost as % of Total Estimated Payments							0.29%			0.15%	
Illustration of Option 3: Hold Harmless Policy Applied with Option 2 For 3-Year Transition											
							Greater of B or (0.333B + 0.667C)				
Radiology	544,179	$45.07	$44.84	$45.07	0.0%	$40,540	$45.81	1.7%	N/A	46.74	2.0%
Medicine	276,669	$47.55	$44.84	$47.55	0.0%	$249,586	$47.55	0.0%	$246,614	46.74	–1.7%
Physical Medicine	1,638,090	$45.82	$44.84	$45.82	0.0%	$532,453	$46.07	0.6%	N/A	46.74	1.5%
Additional Cost of Hold Harmless Transition Policy							$822,579			$246,614	
Additional Cost as % of Total Estimated Payments Based on 1.15 Multiplier							0.41%			0.12%	

NOTES: The formulas for determining the values for D through K are shown in the first row. The letters in the formulas refer to the items in the column heads.
N/A = Not applicable.

Next, two national price indices are discussed that could be used to determine the update factor: the Medicare Economic Index, which measures changes in the costs of maintaining a physician's office, and the Producer Price Index for physicians' offices. The latter measures changes in the prices that are paid for physician services by purchasers. A state-specific measure being used by several other workers' compensation programs is also discussed: the average increase in statewide weekly wages (SWW).

Option 1 to Determine the Update Factor: Medicare Economic Index

The MEI is an input price index that measures the weighted average of price changes for the costs of maintaining a private practice. The expense categories and weights are consistent with those used for the geographic adjustment factor and include physician work (54.5 percent) and practice expense categories (45.5 percent including professional liability expenses).

The MEI is most appropriate as an inflation measure if, in keeping with the concept of linking payments with the resources required to produce services, the update factor is intended to recognize changes in the costs of maintaining a physician's practice.[44] The MEI has several other advantages:

- It is an integral part of the Medicare RB-RVS. Changes in the MEI are published annually as part of the update process for the Medicare fee schedule.
- Forecasted rates of increase that can be used for budgeting and establishing premiums are available from the CMS Office of the Actuary.[45] The forecasted MEI could also be used to set the update for the coming year (see the next section for more information).
- A productivity adjustment is included to avoid double counting productivity gains. Without this adjustment for economy-wide multifactor productivity, gains from increases in service intensity and volume would be included in both the MEI and the additional procedures that physicians bill. The calendar year (CY) 2003 productivity adjustment is 0.8 percent.

Although the MEI theoretically is different from the CPI, Figure 3.1 indicates that the MEI's pattern of growth has been quite similar to that of the CPI over the period 1997 through 2002 for physician services.

---

[44]We do not believe it would be appropriate to use the annual percentage increase in the Medicare conversion factor to update the CWCP conversion factor. This is because Medicare's annual update to the prior year's conversion factor is also affected by a sustainable growth rate (SGR) target for prior years that is intended to control growth in aggregate Medicare expenditures for physicians' services. Actual physician expenditures in prior years are compared with the SGR target for those years. If actual expenditures exceed allowed expenditures under the SGR, the update is reduced. If actual expenditures are less than allowed SGR expenditures, the update is increased. Thus, the annual update factors adjust for changes in Medicare utilization as well as inflation.

[45]The Office of the Actuary may be contacted through the Centers for Medicare and Medicaid Services, 7500 Security Boulevard, Baltimore, MD 21244-1850, 877-267-2323.

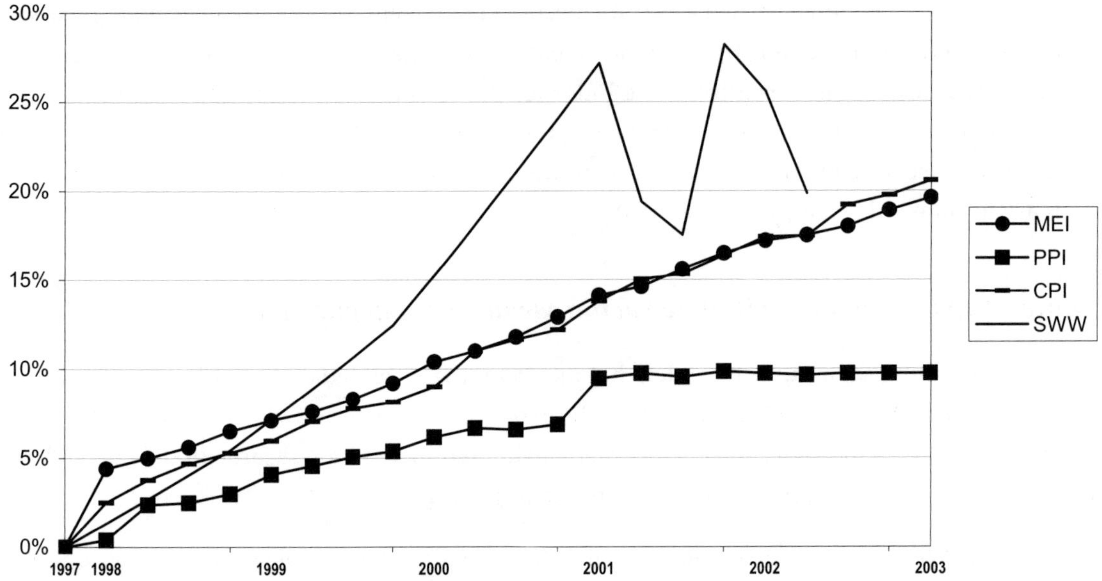

Figure 3.1—Cumulative Percentage Change in Inflation Measures for Physician Services

The Medicare update methodology takes into account historical increases in the MEI, e.g., the CY 2003 update is based on historical data on input price indices through the second quarter of 2002.[46] MedPAC has recommended that CMS instead use a measure of forecasted input price increases over the coming year (MedPAC, 2001a). (This forecast is required by Congress and readily available from the CMS Office of the Actuary.[47]) If CWCP decided to use the projected MEI increase as the update factor, it could link automatic future updates to the projected increase for the year, as announced in Medicare's annual trustees' report. In determining the update for the coming year, an adjustment for the prior year's forecast error would be appropriate. For example, the projected rate of increase for CY 2003 is 2.0 percent (The Boards of Trustees, 2003). If the CY 2003 actual rate of increase turns out to be 3.0 percent, an additional 1.0 percentage point could be added to the CY 2005 update to take into account the underestimation of the CY 2003 factor. Conversely, if the increase turned out to be 1.5 percent, 0.5 percentage point could be subtracted from the CY 2005 update.

---

[46]The CMS policy rationale is that increases in the MEI should not lead current measures of inflation but rather follow them.

[47]A two-year forecast is maintained on the CMS Web site (http://www.cms.gov/statistics/health-indicators/t13.asp). The annual Trustees report contains a multiyear forecast and is also available on the Web site (http://www.cms.gov/publications/trusteesreport/).

Option 2 to Determine the Update Factor: Producer Price Index

The PPI would be an appropriate inflation measure if the main intent of the update factor is to keep CWCP payments in line with market changes for physician services. The index measures growth in prices received by producers from public and private payers. There is both a general health services index and an index specific to physician's offices and clinics. Monthly changes are reported in the middle of the month following the reference month. Forecasts of future changes in the PPI are not available from the federal government. The flatter rate of growth for the PPI, as compared with the MEI and CPI, over the 1997–2003 period (see Figure 3.1) reflects the growth of enrollment in managed care health plans and more aggressive price discounting by managed care organizations.

Option 3 to Determine the Update Factor: Statewide Average Weekly Wages

Several workers' compensation programs base their update factors on the rate of increase in the statewide average weekly wage (Kominski, Pourat, and Black, 1999). The SWW series measures quarterly changes in the average weekly wages for workers covered by state and local unemployment insurance. Average weekly wages are computed by dividing the total quarterly payroll for covered workers by the average monthly number of these employees and further dividing the result by 13 (the number of weeks in the quarter). Self-employed workers are not included in the data. State-specific series are available by type of industry, type of employer (federal, state, private), and establishment size. Industry classifications changed in 2000 so that the current industry-level series is available only from 2001 on and is not comparable to the industry-level data for earlier years (U.S. Department of Labor, Bureau of Labor Statistics [BLS], 2003).

SWW is an attractive basis for an inflation factor adjustment that is intended to keep physicians' payments in line with changes in prevailing California wage levels. However, it is not as good as the MEI if the update factor is intended to account for changes in the costs of providing services. Measuring general increases in wage levels may not capture differences in physician practice costs, and there is no adjustment for productivity gains. Moreover, Figure 3.1 indicates that the SWW changes are more volatile than those of the other measures and are subject to temporary market conditions. The pre-2001 data used to create Figure 3.1 are based on annual rates of change and may mask quarterly fluctuations evident in the quarterly data for 2001 and later.

Update and Refinement Process

The preceding sections and those that follow discuss a number of issues that need to be addressed in linking OMFS payments for physicians and practitioners to the Medicare RB-RVS. After the necessary decisions are made through the legislative or administrative process, the RB-RVS provides a mechanism to shift the ongoing burden of updating and refining the payment system on an ongoing basis to CMS. As discussed next, CMS has processes in place to ensure that affected parties have input into the refinement process.

Dates

The Medicare law provides for annual updates in the RB-RVS fee schedule effective January 1 of each year. Generally, a proposed notice of rulemaking setting out the proposed policy and rate changes for the coming year is published sometime around June with a 60-day comment period. The final rule is scheduled for publication by November 1 but is typically late. The CY 2003 final rule was not published until December 31, 2002, and changes in the payment amounts were delayed until March 1 to allow the Congress time to fix technical problems with the update factor.

Refinement Process

By law, relative value units are reviewed and updated at least every five years. In the intervening years, refinements are made on an as-needed basis. CMS takes into account the recommendations of two advisory committees in making refinements. The American Medical Association's (AMA's) Relative (Value) Update Committee (RUC) reviews data submitted by specialty societies and other professional organizations and makes recommendations on revisions to the physician work RVUs. The AMA's Practice Expense Advisory Committee (PEAC) makes recommendations on the refinement process and values for the practice expense RVUs. The law requires that the aggregate adjustments in the RVUs not change program expenditures more that $20 million. If CMS estimates the changes will have more than a $20 million impact, an across-the-board cost-neutrality adjustment is made to the RVUs. This adjustment keeps changes in relative values from affecting aggregate expenditures and preserves the conversion factor as the determinant of overall program expenditures.

Because the mix of services for CWCP patients is different from that for Medicare patients, the impact of the RVU changes over time on CWCP patients should be monitored to determine whether overall expenditures have been affected. The law also requires that the geographic adjustment factors be reviewed at least every three years. If more than one year has elapsed since the last revision, the adjustment is phased in over two years. Thus, any redistribution changes from updates in the GAF will be spread out over a two-year period. The proposed revisions for CY 2004 were scheduled to be published in the proposed CY 2004 rule sometime around August 2003 and would affect the determination of an OMFS cost-neutral conversion factor that is effective in 2004.

Operational Issues

The unpredictability of when the Medicare RB-RVS final rule will actually be published in a given year suggests that some leeway should be built into the effective date of an OMFS automatic update, e.g., changes could be effective 60 days after publication of any changes. This would allow time for DWC review and for systems changes to be made. Medicare sends a "Dear Doctor" letter to all physicians providing services to Medicare patients in connection with the participating physician program. The letter serves as a useful summary of payment and policy changes and would enable DWC's notices to concentrate on specific items that are unique to CWCP, such as the conversion update factor. This would reduce the administrative burden of notifying affected parties of the changes.

Carrier-level files produced in conjunction with the final rule contain all the procedure code information needed to determine Medicare's payment for an individual claim. The files are available for public use on the CMS Web site (http://cms.hhs.gov/). We believe they could be modified relatively easily to incorporate any CWCP-specific relative values, e.g., for services for which Medicare does not have RVUs.

Other Issues

This section covers other issues pertaining to tying the CWCP medical fee schedule to the Medicare RB-RVS fee schedule, including issues surrounding fee schedule payments for services furnished by non-physician practitioners, specific rules to determine the payment for surgical procedures, rules for determining the maximum allowable amounts for physical medicine, separately reimbursed items used during medical procedures, and program-specific procedure codes.

Payments for Non-Physician Practitioners

Medicare's definition of physician includes optometrists, podiatrists, and chiropractors and pays them at the same rate as MDs and doctors of osteopathy for Medicare-covered services.[48] Fee schedule payments for services furnished by other non-physician practitioners depends on whether the services are billed directly by the practitioners or are "incident to" a physician's service and included in the physician's bill.

"Incident to" services are performed in a physician's office by an employee working under the physician's direct supervision. The services are billed by the physician and are paid at 100 percent of the fee schedule amount. When the services are billed directly by non-physician practitioners providing services within their scope of practice, the following percentages of physician fees are payable:

- Physician assistants: 85 percent. Payment is made only to the employer.
- Nurse practitioners and clinical nurse specialists: 85 percent.

---

[48]Chiropractic services are covered only for manual manipulation of the spine to treat a subluxation. Medicare does not cover routine foot or eye care.

- Certified nurse anesthetists: 100 percent if not medically directed; 50 percent if medically directed (in which case the anesthesiologist providing medical direction also receives 50 percent).
- Physical therapists and occupational therapists: 100 percent. (Speech language pathology services are covered only as "incident to" services.)
- Clinical psychologists: 100 percent.
- Clinical social workers: 75 percent.

CWCP has a broader definition of physician that includes psychologists and acupuncturists along with the practitioners included within the Medicare definition. Medicare does not cover the services of acupuncturists and defines chiropractors as physicians for the limited purpose of manipulation of the spine to correct a subluxation. CWCP's definition of non-physician practitioner explicitly includes practitioners that are not permitted to bill Medicare directly (e.g., marriage, family, and child counselors). The OMFS applies the same conversion factors to covered services furnished by physicians and non-physician practitioners.

One issue in adopting the fee schedule is whether the Medicare differentials for non-physician practitioners should be used. In a recent report examining the question of whether the Medicare differentials should be eliminated (MedPAC, 2002a), the Medicare Payment Advisory Commission concluded that it was unable to judge whether non-physician practitioners are delivering a different product than are physicians that would warrant the lower payment levels. MedPAC found that studies have shown that outcomes of services delivered by physicians and non-physicians are comparable, but that imprecise billing codes may not be capturing subtle differences between the services delivered by physicians and non-physician practitioners. While MedPAC determined that additional study would be needed before it could assess whether the payment differential should be eliminated, its findings also do not provide support for adopting differentials where they do not already exist. Further, retaining current OMFS policies avoids the administrative burden associated with determining whether services provided by a limited-license practitioner are furnished independently or incident to a physician's service.

Another issue is whether the procedure codes and relative values used by the Medicare RB-RVS need to be expanded to include the broader range of services covered by CWCP, e.g., codes for chiropractic manipulative treatments and acupuncturists. This issue is discussed later in the section on CWCP-specific procedure codes.

Surgery

Both the OMFS and the Medicare fee schedule have specific rules to determine the payment for surgical procedures. In general, the policies are similar; however, they vary in particulars that should be given attention in tying the OMFS to the Medicare fee schedule. We discuss these policies in the subsections that follow.

Assistant-at-Surgery and Multiple Surgeons. Medicare pays for an assistant-at-surgery only when the assistant actively assists in the actual performance of the surgical procedure and the services are not otherwise covered in a payment to the facility where the procedure is performed. As shown in Table 3.12, a physician assistant-at-surgery receives 16 percent of the surgeon's payment for the procedure while nurse practitioners and physician assistants receive 13.6 percent of the payment (i.e., 85 percent of the 16 percent consistent with the payment differential for their services). In comparison, the OMFS sets the maximum amount for a physician assistant-at-surgery at 20 percent of the surgeon's payment[49] and the amount for nurse practitioners and physician assistants at 10 percent. For these practitioners, the issue is whether current OMFS payment policies should be continued or whether Medicare's policies should be adopted. In addition, there may be some payments that are currently being made under the OMFS (e.g., for surgical technologists acting within their scope of practice) that are also covered by the Medicare DRG payment for inpatient services or the facility payment for ambulatory surgical procedures. For these practitioners, at issue is a more fundamental question of whether the separate billing should be continued because payment for their services is included in the facility fee. This issue does not apply to residents because their services are not included in the facility fees.

Table 3.12
Comparison of Policies on Multiple Surgeons and Assistants-at-Surgery

	Medicare RB-RVS	OMFS
Two surgeons	Each receives 62.5%	Add 25% to payment; divide according to physician agreed-upon distribution and in accordance with medical ethics.
Assistant physician	16%	If modifier = –80 or –82 : 20%; if modifier = –81 : 1.1 RVUs
Nurse practitioner/physician assistant/clinical Nurse specialist	13.6% (0.85 x 16%)	10%
Resident	Not separately payable; included in payments for graduate medical education	Use modifier –80: 20%
Registered nurse/surgical technologist	Not separately payable; included in facility fee	If licensed and acting within scope of practice and in lieu of physician assistant: 10%

When two surgeons are involved in a procedure, Medicare pays each surgeon 62.5 percent of the fee that would be payable if only one surgeon were involved. While the total payment (125 percent of the standard fee) is the same, the OMFS divides the payment as agreed upon by the surgeons and in accordance with medical ethics. This is one example of several situations in which Medicare uses a formula to divide the payment while the OMFS divides according to the physicians' agreement. Depending on the administrative burden entailed in dividing the payments on a claim-by-claim basis, the Medicare policies might be an easier and more equitable way to make the division.

---

[49]When modifier –81(minimum assistant surgeon) is used, 1.1 base units are paid under the OMFS.

Multiple Surgical Services. There are also minor differences in the Medicare and OMFS policies for the third and fourth surgical procedures that are performed on the same day (see Table 3.13). As with other policies, the issue is whether there are administrative benefits for the CWCP, the payers, and the providers alike in adopting the current Medicare rules.

Table 3.13
Comparison of Policies on Multiple Procedures

	Medicare RB-RVS	OMFS
Bi-lateral procedures	50%	50%
Major (highest-value) procedure	100%	100%
Second-highest-value procedure	50%	50%
Third-highest-value procedure	50%	25%
Fourth-highest-value procedure	50%	By report
Five or more procedures	By report	By report
Selected arthroscopic procedures on same joint	Same policies as other multiple procedures apply	Primary at 100%; remainder at 10% unless justified by report

Global Fees. The Medicare fee schedule has separate global fee policies for major surgeries, minor surgeries, and "non-incisional" procedures (e.g., trigger point injections). The global period during which related pre- and post-operative services are built into the relative values for the surgical procedure may be 0 days, 10 days, or 90 days. For major surgeries, the pre-operative period is 1 day and the post-operative period is 90 days.

The OMFS already uses the 1997 Medicare fee schedule global billing periods. Thus, linking to the current Medicare fee schedule should not be problematic. It would automatically establish the global billing periods for new procedure codes and incorporate any other Medicare revisions that have occurred since 1997.

On occasion, a physician other than the surgeon may provide the pre- or post-operative care that is covered by the global fee. These services are identified under both the Medicare fee schedule and the OMFS by the use of modifier codes[50] (–54, –55, and –56). Medicare uses the pre-operative, surgical procedure only and post-operative relative values to determine how to divide the global fee between the surgeon and the physician providing the pre- and/or post-operative care. Current OMFS policy is to divide the payment between the physicians by agreement and in accordance with medical ethics. Adopting Medicare's policy would provide an equitable distribution and should reduce the administrative burden.

Physical Medicine

The OMFS has several rules for determining the maximum allowable amounts for physical medicine that do not have counterparts in the Medicare fee schedule.

First, multiple procedures and modalities furnished during the same visit are subject to discounting:

---

[50]Modifiers are codes that are used to describe special circumstances related to a procedure. They are part of CPT-4.

- Major (highest-value procedure or modality): 100 percent.
- Second-highest-value procedure or modality: 75 percent.
- Third-highest-value procedure or modality: 50 percent.
- Fourth-highest-value procedure or modality: 25 percent.

(Physical therapist assessment and evaluation codes and test and measurement codes, group exercises, and education are not included in the multiple procedures discount.)

Second, OMFS values for the physical medicine and acupuncture treatment codes include follow-up evaluation and management services for the routine assessment of established patients and the value of an office visit. As a result, these services are generally not separately payable. Also, if a physical therapy assessment or tests and measurements are billed on the same day as an evaluation by the same provider, 2.4 relative value units are subtracted from the combined total.

Medicare does not have the comparable rules for multiple procedures and follow-up evaluation and management services. In addition, there are differences in the instructions regarding when certain codes, e.g., group therapy, should be used and how time should be counted. If the OMFS is tied to the Medicare fee schedule, it will be important to decide whether the current rules should continue and, if so, whether adjustments are needed in the Medicare RVUs.

Items and Supplies Furnished in Conjunction with Procedures

The RVUs for the procedures in the OMFS include supplies and materials generally necessary to perform the service. Exceptions are made for certain items (e.g., cast and strapping materials, sterile trays, applied dressings beyond simple wound occlusion, taping supplies for sprains, and other such supplies).[51] Payment for the separately reimbursed items is by report and is based on cost plus 20 percent up to a maximum of cost plus $15.

The separately reimbursed items used during the procedure are items that Medicare generally includes in the practice-expense RVUs for office-based procedures or in the facility payment for facility-based procedures. In tying the OMFS to the Medicare fee schedules, consideration should be given to adopting the Medicare bundled payment policies. Otherwise, payment will be made for the same items twice—once through the separate payment and again in the practice expense/facility component of the payment.

---

[51]Exceptions are also made for dispensed items such as crutches, ACE bandages, and braces. Medicare's payment for these items is discussed in Chapter 5.

Program-Specific Procedure Codes

The CWCP covers a broader range of services than does the Medicare program. As a result, the OMFS currently uses certain CPT-4 codes for which Medicare has not established relative values as well as some CWCP-established codes for specific programmatic needs. Similarly, Medicare has established a set of G-codes to meet program-specific needs. Below, we discuss by type of service the general issues that will need to be considered in tying CWCP to the Medicare fee schedule.

Evaluation and Management. There are a number of evaluation and management services that do not have Medicare RVUs for which the current OMFS has relative values. These services include prolonged evaluation and management, physician standby services, team conferences, telephone consultations, and basic life and disability examinations. Medicare does not cover basic life and disability examinations. Medicare's policy is that the other services are either included in the pre- and post-work values for reimbursable services or in the facility payment (physician standby). If the OMFS is to continue to pay for these services separately, a process is needed to develop and periodically review the RB-RVS values for the codes.

Surgery. With few exceptions (e.g., certain eye and ear procedures), Medicare has established RVUs for all surgical procedures regardless of whether the services are covered by the program.

Medicine. Medicare has established HCPCS G-codes that provide the specificity the program needs to apply its coverage rules for positron emission tomography (PET) scans but may be unnecessary for the CWCP. However, RVUs have been established only for the professional component for these services. Regardless of whether a decision is made to adopt the G-codes or use CPT-4 codes, the Medicare RVUs are for the professional component only (modifier–26) services. Medicare carriers price the technical component for PET scans. Consideration should be given to either using California carrier-established policies or the amounts that are paid for PET scans under the fee schedule for hospital outpatient services to establish the RVUs for these services. Using existing payment levels to set the fee for the technical component should be less burdensome than claim-by-claim pricing.

Physical Medicine. Most CWCP-specific codes may no longer be required to describe services because the CPT now includes a number of codes for physical therapy procedures. However, certain CWCP-specific codes may still be needed to implement program coverage and utilization policies. Medicare has not established RVUs for acupuncture and, at a minimum, a process will be needed to develop and periodically review the RB-RVS values for acupuncture.

Special Services and Reports. Medicare has assigned RVUs to only a handful of these procedure codes. Payments for specimen collection are made under the separate fee schedule for clinical laboratory services. Generally, Medicare does not make additional payments for after-hour services, travel, and special circumstances for anesthesia. If payments are to continue under the OMFS for these services, a process will be needed to develop appropriate RVUs. Moreover, some of the reports may be more extensive than those defined by CPT-4 and may warrant establishing codes specific to CWCP.

There are several ways the relative values could be established for procedure codes that will be retained under the OMFS but for which there are no Medicare RVUs:

- *RVUs for similar procedures.* These could be either RVUs Medicare has established for procedures that require comparable resources or RVUs that have been established by other workers' compensation programs that use an RB-RVS (including the federal workers' compensation program).
- *The RVUs established by The Lewin Group for evaluation and management services specific to the workers' compensation population.* Unless the Lewin RVUs (The Lewin Group, 2002) for other evaluation and management services are also adopted, an adjustment might be needed to preserve the appropriate relationship between these services and the remaining evaluation and management services for which Medicare has established RVUs.
- *Current payment levels for the procedures.* A resource-based relative value could be determined by adjusting the current payment level for the procedures by the average change in payments across all procedures within the same type of service. Dividing the result by the conversion factor provides a revised relative value that approximates the effects of taking resource requirements into account.

The same methodology may not be appropriate for all services for which resource-based relative values are needed. Administrative burden is minimized if the values can be tied to comparable procedures in the Medicare fee schedule (in which case any refinements could be automatically incorporated). This consideration might also apply to tying the procedure codes with missing values to the federal workers' compensation fee schedule or to the program of another state. A mechanism would need to be established to periodically review and refine relative values developed from The Lewin Group study or current payment amounts.

Summary of Findings

The structure of the Medicare RB-RVS differs from the current OMFS in a number of ways that require policy choices to be made before the OMFS is linked to the Medicare fee schedule. Some of the most important of those policy decisions are

- the level at which the conversion factor should be initially established
- the index measure that should be used to update the conversion factor in the future
- whether a geographic adjustment factor should apply
- whether the site-of-service differential for the practice expense component should be adopted
- whether anesthesia should be included.

Using the results from The Lewin Group (2002) analysis of the impact of adopting the RB-RVS, we determined that a 1.15–1.16 multiplier (depending on the decision with respect to anesthesia) to the Medicare conversion factor would be cost-neutral to the maximum allowable fees under the current OMFS. A higher multiplier may be needed to reflect overall fee levels paid by private payers.

Potential inflation measures that would be independent of Medicare policy adjustments are the Medicare Economic Index and the Producer Price Index for physicians' offices and clinics. The MEI would relate payment changes to changes in the costs of maintaining a physician's practice. The MEI is consistent with the RB-RVS concept and has the added advantage of being an integral part of the annual Medicare update to the physician fee schedule. The PPI would account for market changes in the amounts paid for physicians' services.

Medicare's geographic adjustment factors and site-of-service differentials are designed to improve the match between payments and the resources required to provide the services but would involve additional payment redistributions.

Bringing anesthesia under the RB-RVS is also consistent with the goal of relating payments to resources, but assuming a cost-neutral multiplier of 1.16, it would reduce payments for anesthesia services approximately 39 percent. A cost-neutral change from a charge-based to resource-based fee schedule would involve significant payment redistributions for other services as well—evaluation and management (plus 25 percent), surgery (minus 15 percent), and medicine (minus 5 percent). The change for radiology and physical medicine would be less than 1 percent. While the actual impact of these changes will depend on the multiplier that is selected, a transition should be considered to soften the impact of adopting the RB-RVS on anesthesia and surgery.

4. Hospital Outpatient and Ambulatory Surgery Center Facility Services

Payments for the facility component of hospital outpatient department (HOPD) and ambulatory surgical center services represent about 16 percent of total CWCP medical costs (CHSWC, 2003). Generally, HOPDs are an integral part of a hospital and are subject to the health and safety standards and licensure requirements that are applicable to hospitals. ASCs are freestanding surgical centers that are either participating in the Medicare program or have been licensed by the State of California. The OMFS allows facility fees for either entity for ambulatory surgery and for emergency room services provided by HOPDs. The facility fees are not subject to a fee schedule. The negotiated or contracted rates that are used to pay for these services are often based on discounted charges. Where a contract is not in place, the facility's charges are the starting point for determining payment for workers' compensation patients. Under Medicare, different fee schedules apply to services provided in HOPDs and in ASCs.

Assembly Bill (AB) 749[52] authorized the establishment of a fee schedule for ambulatory surgical services but imposed a number of requirements that must be met before the fee schedule is implemented. In this chapter, we explore both the administrative burden and issues that need to be addressed in fulfilling the AB 749 mandates as well as the policy issues that should be considered in adopting Medicare's fee schedules in lieu of establishing one designed solely for CWCP patients.

Using the existing Medicare fee schedules offers several benefits:

- The payment systems are already established and could be adapted if needed for CWCP-unique needs with fewer resources and in a much shorter timeframe than developing a fee schedule from CWCP-specific data would require.
- The administrative burden of maintaining and updating the systems is shifted to CMS. MedPAC and a Medicare advisory panel on ambulatory payment classification (APC) groups provide regular input into the fee schedule refinement process.
- Updates to the fee schedules are regular and predictable. Annual changes proceed through an established rulemaking process that provides an opportunity for public comment.
- Standard product definitions enable cost comparisons with other programs and payers for comparable services and facilitate quality and utilization monitoring.

The major disadvantages—which must be considered with any Medicare fee schedule adopted by the OMFS—are that the fees would not be based on CWCP-specific data on the

[52]The State of California (2002). The effective date for the provisions of AB 749 was January 1, 2003.

charges and costs of providing services to workers' compensation patients, and that the structure of the Medicare fee schedules raises a number of issues that would need to be addressed.

This chapter begins with a discussion of the AB 749 requirements and follows with an overview of Medicare's hospital outpatient prospective payment system (OPPS) and ASC fee schedule. The remaining subsections deal with specific issues that would need to be considered in adopting the Medicare fee schedules and providing for automatic updates. Modeling the implications of policy choices would be desirable but is not within the scope of this study.

AB 749 Requirements

Section 5307.21 of AB 749 gives the Administrative Director (AD) of the California DWC authority to establish an outpatient surgery facility fee schedule for services not performed under contract providing certain requirements are met. The fee schedule requirements (per the language of AB 749) are listed below in bold type. Each requirement is followed by our assessment of whether it might be satisfied by the Medicare fee schedules.

1. **Include all facility fees for outpatient surgery performed in any facility authorized by law to perform the surgery.** Physician fees are not included. Both the Medicare OPPS and ASC rates cover facility services only and should satisfy this requirement.

2. **Promote payment predictability and minimize administrative costs. Review and revision of the fees is to occur at least every two years.** Linking the OMFS fee schedule to the Medicare fee schedules would provide regular and predicable payment. The administrative burden would be reduced by eliminating the need for negotiation on individual bills and by shifting to CMS the major burden of maintaining and updating the system. Both the OPPS and ASC fees are updated annually (although the ASC payment groups have not been updated regularly).

3. **Provide access to quality care and payments that are sufficient to cover the cost of each surgical procedure.** As with other fee schedules, payment levels must be adequate to provide access to quality care without creating incentives for unnecessary care. Payments are generally regarded as sufficient when they cover the costs of an efficient provider in furnishing the service to a typical patient. The Medicare fee schedules are intended to do this for the Medicare population; modifications for specific procedures or in the overall fee level may be needed for the CWCP patient population. The modifications can be built into the OMFS fee schedule without eliminating the administrative benefits of linking to the Medicare fee schedules.

A fee schedule need not cover the cost of a procedure *each* time that procedure is furnished. A fee schedule establishes a predetermined price for a service and is not based on the actual costs incurred in providing that service to a particular patient. Knowing the payment in advance provides incentives to deliver services efficiently. A fee schedule assumes that some patients will require more services than will others, but that on average the payments are sufficient to cover the costs of an efficient provider furnishing care to a typical patient. Providers are protected through the payment adjustments for systematic cost differences that are beyond the provider's control, such as geographic differences in wage levels. Moreover, additional payments can be made, as they are under the Medicare OPPS, to protect providers from incurring large financial losses on extremely costly cases. However, only a charge or cost reimbursement payment system covers the costs of a procedure each time it is furnished. Such systems are not fee schedules, and they provide no incentives for providers to control costs and deliver services efficiently.

AB 749 also sets out a number of process requirements for developing the outpatient surgery fee schedule. As a prerequisite for establishing the fee schedule, AB 749 requires the DWC to consider the following data:

- One year of published data collected pursuant to Section 128737 of the Health and Safety Code.
- Any published data collected from providers of outpatient surgery services.
- Payment data including, but not limited to, type of payer and amount charged.
- Cost data including actual expenses for labor, supplies, equipment, implants, anesthesia, overhead, and administration.
- Outcome data including, but not limited to, expected level of rehabilitation, expected coverage timeframe, and incidence of infection.
- Access data including, but not limited to, date of injury, date of surgery recommendation, and date of procedure.
- Other data that are mutually agreed upon by the OSHPD and the AD.

The requirement that the fee schedule take into consideration formal analysis of ambulatory surgery data collected by OSHPD will postpone a fee schedule based on CWCP for several years. OSHPD's reporting requirements have been delayed until 2004, which means that a year's worth of data will not become available for analysis until mid-2005 at the earliest. Neither the OSHPD nor the DWC currently collect the detailed cost and outcome data required by AB 749.

While California-specific data on all ambulatory surgery claims are very desirable to have and should be collected on an ongoing basis for a number of purposes, we believe that with the other available data and the existing fee schedules used by Medicare and other programs, these data do not need to be prerequisites to establishing an appropriate fee schedule. A suitable substitute for the type of information that OSHPD is to collect might be the State Ambulatory Surgery Databases (SASD) for 15 participating states that are available through the federal Agency for Healthcare Quality Research (AHQR).

The SASD capture surgeries performed on the same day in which patients are admitted and released. The SASD might offer even more powerful data than California-specific data to explore some of the analyses specified by AB 749. SASD data are available for the years 1997–2000, and through the Hospital Cost and Utilization Project of the AHQR, those data can be linked with inpatient data in some states. All participating states obtain data from hospital-affiliated ambulatory surgery sites and some states include records from freestanding surgery centers as well. The SASD contain a core set of clinical and non-clinical information on all patients, regardless of payer, including persons covered by Medicare, Medicaid, private insurance, and the uninsured. Information on the expected payer, as collected by the state, is preserved in the data so that workers' compensation patients can be identified in the SASD records from some states. In addition to these sources, Medicare and MediCal administrative data can be examined for state-specific issues, albeit only for Medicare and Medicaid patients, and databases covering all payers are commercially available. The SASD provide information on the amount charged for ambulatory surgery services but not the amounts paid. Information on payment schedules used by other workers' compensation programs has already been collected for other studies (CHSWC, 2003; Kominski and Gardner, 2001; The Lewin Group, 2002) examining this issue for CWCP, and information on other public programs is generally available.

Medicare cost report data provide a mechanism to convert charge information into cost information for specific surgical procedures performed in HOPDs by applying a cost-to-charge ratio to the charges in the administrative data. CMS has already used Medicare administrative data to do this in developing its relative weights for the APCs. Because CMS rules require that charges be uniformly imposed on all patients, we would not expect the standardized costs for specific procedures to vary for workers' compensation patients unless there are major differences in the related services based on patient characteristics. This is a question that could be answered through comparative analyses of Medicare and worker's compensation charge data for a sample of patients.

CMS also used cost-to-charge ratios to estimate the costs and relative weights for specific procedures performed in ASCs. In contrast to the OPPS for which the relative weights are updated annually, the procedure-specific cost information used to establish the ASC payment groups is based on a 1986 survey of ASCs.[53] CMS is required by law to conduct a survey of ASC costs and charges every five years but has not done so since 1994. Thus, CMS does not have current information on the costs of procedures performed in ASCs. In the past, the survey has collected detailed expenditure information by procedure similar to that specified in AB 749.

In addition to considering cost and charge data, AB 749 requires consideration of outcome and access data. These data should be collected in an ongoing monitoring system to

---

[53]Unfortunately, it also appears that OSHPD's annual *Utilization Report of Specialty Clinics* cannot be used to develop cost estimates. The reporting form collects information on net patient revenues and total operating expenses, but it does not collect total gross patient revenues that could be used to establish recent cost-to-charge ratios. If this annual report were modified to include aggregate gross charges and if the Medical Information Reporting for California (MIRCal) system collected procedure-specific charges, it would be possible to estimate procedure-specific costs in the future.

assure that the fee schedule does not have unintended consequences on access, quality, and outcomes. The outcome data would also provide information on whether quality of care differs across alternative ambulatory settings for surgical procedures and whether patient characteristics affect where care is delivered. This information would be useful in making policy decisions regarding site-of-service differentials for the facility component of ambulatory procedures and whether coverage of certain procedures should be restricted to particular settings (discussed further in the next section). The SASD files or those from a commercial vendor offer a mechanism for examining outcomes across hospital outpatient departments and ambulatory sites in the absence of existing data for California workers' compensation patients.

Overview of Medicare Payment Systems

Medicare uses separate payment systems to pay for the facility component of services furnished in HOPDs and in ASCs. The payment systems have evolved over time from various legacy payment methodologies and, as shown in Table 4.1, differ in many important aspects. This section provides an overview of each system. Particular aspects of the systems that should be considered in linking OMFS to Medicare fee schedules are described in greater detail in the sections that follow. (A schedule of payments for high-volume workers' compensation procedures is in Appendix E.)

Hospital Outpatient PPS

Medicare's prospective payment for hospital outpatient services was first implemented in 2000 and, as a result, is not as mature a payment system as the PPS for acute care hospital inpatient services (Medicare's inpatient PPS [IPPS], discussed in Chapter 2). OPPS applies to medical and surgical services furnished by hospital outpatient departments other than outpatient rehabilitation services and clinical laboratory diagnostic tests. These services are paid for under the RB-RVS and laboratory fee schedules, respectively. In addition to general acute care hospitals, the system applies to specialty facilities that are excluded from the IPPS. Small rural critical-access hospitals are excluded from the system.

Table 4.1
Comparison of Key Features of Medicare's Hospital Outpatient PPS and ASC Fee Schedule

Feature	Hospital Outpatient PPS	ASC Fee Schedule
Applicability	Applies to medical and surgical services furnished in an HOPD. Does not apply to outpatient rehabilitation services or clinical diagnostic lab tests.	Applies to surgical procedures on Medicare's approved list. Other service paid under RB-RVS fee schedule.
Units of payment	570 procedure groupings based on clinical coherency and estimated cost (ambulatory payment classification groups [APCs]). More than one APC may be billed for a single inpatient encounter. RB-RVS discounting for multiple surgical procedures.	9 procedure groups based on estimated cost. Same discounting for multiple surgical procedures.
Coding system	CPT-4	CPT-4
Source of rates	Updated 1996 HOPD charges converted to cost	Updated 1986 survey of ASC charges converted to cost
Update factor	Hospital market basket	CPI-U
Geographic adjustment	Hospital wage index applies to 60% of payment	Hospital wage index applies to 34.45% of payment
Other adjustments	High-cost outlier policy; new technology pass-through	None
Product definition	Services integral to the procedure are packaged with the primary procedure, including, for surgical procedures: anesthesia, use of recovery rooms, surgical and medical supplies, and most drugs. Separate payment for blood, blood products, and plasma-based and recombinant therapy. With certain exceptions, hospital is required to bill for all services furnished through referral or outside suppliers in connection with an outpatient encounter.	Same packaging as OPPS for approved surgical procedures; otherwise, RB-RVS rules apply.

Payment is based on grouping outpatient services into clinically coherent groups that require comparable resources (i.e., APC groups). The payment rate for an APC group is based on the median estimated cost of all the procedures assigned to the group.[54] A hospital may bill for more than one APC during an outpatient encounter; however, the RB-RVS discounting policy applies when multiple surgical procedures are involved. A relative weight is developed for each APC based on the median cost for the procedures assigned to that group compared with the median cost across all groups. A conversion factor converts the relative weight into an unadjusted payment rate. The labor-related share of the standard payment rate (60 percent) is adjusted by the hospital wage index. The WI in effect for IPPS on October 1 is used to adjust

[54]To estimate the cost of an individual bill, CMS developed departmental cost-to-charge ratios from Medicare cost report data and applied them to the hospital's bills for services provided to Medicare patients. Single-procedure bills were used because the charges applicable to each procedure when multiple procedures are billed on a single line item cannot be determined.

OPPS rates in the following calendar year.[55] The general formula for determining the adjusted payment rate is:

$$\text{Adjusted Rate}_{proc} = \text{Relative weight}_{proc} \times \text{conversion factor} \times (0.60 \times WI_{hosp} + 0.40)$$

The relative weights and average California payment rate for high-volume workers' compensation procedures are shown in Appendix E. In determining the average California payment, we adjusted the 2003 national conversion factor ($52.15) by a wage index value of 1.21. This is our estimate of the average hospital wage index value that would be applicable to workers' compensation claims. Because we do not have access to outpatient hospital data for CWCP patients, we used the OSHPD inpatient hospital data to compute an average hospital wage index adjustment factor weighted by the number of CWCP inpatients at each hospital. We determined that the average adjustment was 1.21 and used this value as the geographic adjustment factor for both the OPPS adjusted rates and ASC rates included in Appendix D.

Special APCs have been created for new technology services. These groupings do not take into account the clinical aspects of the services that are assigned to the groups, only their costs. In addition, temporary pass-through payments are made for new drugs, biologicals, and devices where the cost of the item is significant in relation to the OPPS payment amounts.

Additional payments are made to protect hospitals from financial losses on extraordinarily high-cost patients.[56] The outlier payment is determined on a service-by-service basis based on a comparison of the estimated cost for the individual service with the total payment (including new technology pass-throughs). The outlier policy is revised annually so that estimated outlier payments equal 2.0 percent of estimated total payments. For 2003, if the estimated cost for the service exceeds 2.75 times the OPPS payment, the outlier payment is calculated as 45 percent of the difference. The formula for computing the outlier payment is:

$$\text{Outlier pay}_{ind} = \text{Billed charges}_{ind} \times \text{cost-to-charge ratio}_{hosp} - (2.75 \times \text{total payment}_{ind}) \times 0.45$$

In the case of cancer hospitals, Medicare's payments are increased to ensure that the OPPS amount is no lower than the proportion of costs received before OPPS.

ASC Fee Schedule

Medicare's payment under the ASC fee schedule is limited to an approved list of procedures that are commonly performed in an inpatient setting but can be safely performed in an outpatient setting. To prevent the shift of services from physicians' offices, procedures that are commonly performed in physicians' offices are excluded and paid under the RB-RVS only.

---

[55]Medicare's actual payment takes beneficiary liability into account. Because workers' compensation patients do not have cost-sharing liabilities, this report does not include a discussion of the coinsurance calculation nor are the applicable coinsurance rates shown in the procedure listing in Appendix D.

[56]Transitional payment corridors are also in effect through 2003 to ensure that hospitals do not experience a significant loss of payments in the initial years of the payment system.

Typically, the approved procedures require less than 90 minutes operating time and less than four hours of recovery time and are not emergent or life threatening. By law, an update in the list of approved procedures is to occur every two years in consultation with appropriate medical organizations. However, with the exception of updating for coding changes, the list of procedures was not modified from 1995 to 2003.

Approved procedures are assigned to nine payment groups based on the median estimated cost of the procedure. The payment rate for the group is based on the median estimated cost of the procedures assigned to the group. The labor-related share of the rate (34.45 percent) is adjusted by the hospital wage index. The established inflation adjustment factor is the rate of change in the Consumer Price Index: All-Urban Consumers (CPI-U). However, actual updates were limited from FY 1998–2002 to the CPI-U minus 2 percentage points (but not less than 0). The FY 2003 standard payment rates range from $333 to $1,339 for the nine payment groups.

CMS is required to conduct a survey of ASC costs and charges every five years. The estimated cost used to establish the current ASC procedure groupings is based on a 1986 survey of costs and charges from a sample of ASCs. A more recent survey was conducted in 1994 but has not been used to establish updated payment groupings and rates. Thus, the cost information on which the rates are based is quite dated and may not represent current procedure costs. Some workers' compensation programs are using the 1994 survey to establish their ASC rates (CHSWC, 2003), but even these data are outdated given technological advances over the past decade.

The ASC payment covers diagnostic or therapeutic facility services or items directly related to providing the surgical procedure, such as overhead expense items, surgical supplies, medical equipment and drugs, biologicals and pharmaceuticals, anesthesia materials, and splints, casts, pins, wires, and other supplies to reduce fractures and dislocations. A separate amount is payable when the descriptor for a CPT code specifies "with or without" some kind of imaging, guidance, or other diagnostic test, and the services fall outside the scope of ASC facility services. "Waived" tests under the *Clinical Laboratory Improvement Act* that are performed as part of preparing the patient for surgery on the day of the surgery are included.

Approved Procedures

Technological advances such as improved anesthesia and pain management coupled with health care financing changes have produced a shift in services from inpatient to outpatient services and increased the volume and complexity of procedures provided in ambulatory settings. Very little is known about the quality of care implications of the shift from inpatient to ambulatory care and the choice of ambulatory setting. Medicare's different payment amounts for the facility component of ambulatory procedures (that is, the prospective payments for hospital outpatient services [APCs], the ASC facility rate, and the practice expense component of the physicians' fee schedule) raise concerns that financial incentives could influence the choice of ambulatory setting and affect workers' compensation patient access and quality of care as well as CWCP program expenditures.

In implementing the OPPS, Medicare identified a group of procedures that are typically performed for Medicare beneficiaries in an inpatient setting only and determined that it would not pay for the procedure if it were performed in an HOPD.[57] In subsequent rules, the agency has established the following criteria (any one of which would apply) for removing a procedure from that list:

- Most outpatient departments are equipped to provide the service to the Medicare population.
- The simplest procedure described by the code may be performed in most outpatient settings.
- The procedure is being performed in numerous hospitals on an outpatient basis.
- The procedure can be appropriately and safely performed in an ASC.

The "inpatient-only" list generated considerable public comment during the CY 2003 rulemaking process. The advisory panel on APC Groups noted that while no facility fee is payable for these procedures, the physician performing the procedure is still paid. The panel believed that the physician should determine what procedure to perform and that both the hospital and physician should receive payment for the procedure (DHHS, 2003a). This position was strongly endorsed during the public comment period by hospital and surgical associations that argued the list interferes with the practice of medicine and should be eliminated.

Medicare recently updated its list of approved ASC procedures effective July 2003. The procedures on the revised list generally meet the following clinical and safety criteria:

- The time needed to perform the procedure should not exceed 90 minutes of surgery time or four hours of recovery time. Anesthesia time should be less than 90 minutes.
- The procedure should *not* generally result in extensive blood loss, require major or prolonged invasion of body categories, directly involve major blood vessels, or be generally emergent or life threatening.

Procedures that would otherwise meet the criteria for inclusion but would be significantly overpaid in the lowest ASC payment group are excluded from the list to avoid creating an incentive to provide these procedures to an ASC setting.

We examined CMS's current listings of approved procedures as they relate to the WCRI high-volume surgical procedures (see Appendix D). The inpatient-only list includes certain spinal fusion procedures, insertions of spinal fixation devices, spinal bone autografts, neck spine disc surgery, and total knee arthroplasty. We do not have the data to determine whether these

---

[57]Hospitals can receive payment under certain conditions for procedures on the inpatient list that are performed on an emergency basis for an outpatient.

procedures are being performed on an outpatient basis for workers' compensation patients.[58] Of the surgical codes in WCRI's market basket, only 56 procedures are on the current ASC approved list; two additional codes will be added effective July 2003. When Kominski and Gardner (2001) examined sample CWCP payment records involving facility fees, they were able to crosswalk only 65 percent of the records with approved ASC procedure codes. The study did not indicate whether the non-matched procedures had been furnished in the hospital outpatient department or in an ASC. Nevertheless, it is clear that if the ASC fee schedule is utilized, a significant issue will be how procedures that are not on the approved list should be treated.

The list of inpatient-only procedures and ASC procedures raises several issues for consideration in linking the OMFS to Medicare payment systems. Medicare's list of inpatient-only procedures is intended to ensure that Medicare beneficiaries receive care in a setting appropriate for their needs. The ASC list is intended to serve this purpose but also serves to protect the program from shifts in sites of service from physicians' offices to ASCs. (The latter issue relates to the site-of-service differentials and is discussed in the next section.) From a quality of care perspective, a basic issue is whether CWCP wants to restrict payment for certain procedures based on the setting in which they are performed or whether the choice of setting should be left to the physician based on the patient's condition. In this regard, Medicare's list is based on the program's judgment regarding where a procedure can be safely performed for its elderly population but that may not be appropriate for a younger patient population. If a list of approved procedures is used, modifications in Medicare's lists may be appropriate and a process for making these determinations will be needed. If CWCP adopts a less restrictive policy, payment rates will be needed for those procedures that Medicare does not pay for. For example, Medicare does not classify an inpatient-only procedure into an APC until it is removed from the list. The classification decision at that time takes into consideration which APCs have procedures that are similar in both clinical characteristics and costs; this type of decisionmaking process will be needed for any hospital outpatient and ASC procedures that CWCP pays for and that Medicare does not.

Site-of-Service Differentials

Medicare's differing payment amounts for the facility component of ambulatory procedures (that is, the APC payment for hospital outpatient services, the ASC facility fee, and the practice expense component of the physician's fee schedule) raise concerns that financial incentives could influence the choice of ambulatory setting and affect workers' compensation patient access and quality of care as well as CPWC program expenditures. High-volume services with large site-of-service differentials are of particular concern. (Appendix D contains a comparison of Medicare's facility component payments for procedures in the WCRI market basket of high-volume workers' compensation procedures.)

---

[58] Kominski and Gardner (2001) reported the high-volume procedures that matched with either ASC or OPPS fee schedule rates. They did not report procedure-specific information on ambulatory surgery codes for CWCP that Medicare does not pay for. Similarly, we cannot discern the relative distribution of procedures between hospital outpatient departments and ambulatory surgical centers.

Table 4.2 compares average CWCP payments with Medicare payment rates for the facility component of high-volume ambulatory services. Each payment rate has been adjusted for the average California geographic adjustment factor.[59] We defined the facility component of the RB-RVS fee schedule as the non-facility practice expense RVUs minus the facility setting practice expense RVUs. The difference represents the additional payment that is made to the physician when the procedure is furnished in the office. The results for selected high-volume procedures identified by Kominski and Gardner (2001) using sample bill data for CWCP patients are shown in the table.

Table 4.2

Comparison of Average CWCP Payments in 2000 with Medicare 2003 Geographically Adjusted Payment Rates for Facility Component of High-Volume Ambulatory Services

Procedure	Medicare Service Description	Average CWCP Payment[a]	OPPS Payment Rate	ASC Payment Rate	RB-RVS Differential
12001	Repair superficial wound(s)	$252	$97	N/A	$67
20550	Inj tendon sheath/ligament	$292	$106	N/A	$20
20610	Drain/inject, joint/bursa	$770	$106	N/A	$21
20680	Removal of support implant	$1,658	$907	$547	N/A
23420	Repair of shoulder	$2,846	$2,126	$1,067	N/A
29826	Shoulder arthroscopy/surgery	$2,571	$2,137	$547	N/A
29881	Knee arthroscopy/surgery	$2,538	$1,362	$676	N/A
49505	Prp i/hern init reduc > 5 yr	$2,123	$1,342	$ 676	$18
64510	N block, stellate ganglion	$ 630	$301	$357	$110
64520	N block, lumbar/thoracic	$842	$301	$357	$161
64721	Carpal tunnel surgery	$1,495	$825	$478	$ 13

[a]SOURCE: Kominski and Gardner (2001).

NOTES: The entries in this table under the Medicare Service Description column are as they appear in the source data files. N/A = Not applicable.

The first three procedures listed in Table 4.2 are commonly performed in physicians' offices and are not on the list of ASC-approved procedures. Under Medicare policies, the physician would be paid the non-facility setting RB-RVS RVUs for these procedures, and no separate facility payment would be made. If the same procedure were furnished in a hospital outpatient department, an APC payment would be made in addition to the physician payment.

The surgical procedure codes with no RB-RVS facility differentials are furnished to Medicare patients exclusively in facility settings. Procedure codes 49505 and 64721 (see Table 4.2) are essentially facility-setting procedures as well; the small differential is an anomaly of the allocation methodology for indirect practice costs when a few facility-based procedures have

[59]For services furnished in a hospital outpatient department, the standard payment amount is adjusted for the estimated average hospital wage index, i.e., the standard rate is multiplied by a factor equal to (0.60 x 1.21 + 0.40). Similarly, the standard rate for a procedure furnished in an ASC is adjusted for wage differences by multiplying the payment rate for the group to which the procedure is assigned by a factor equal to (0.3445 x 1.21 + 0.6555). For the RB-RVS, the difference between the non-facility and facility RVUs is multiplied by the Medicare conversion factor ($38.99) and the estimated average California geographic adjustment factor (1.06). These adjustments to the standard payment amounts are needed for comparative purposes because each fee schedule uses a different methodology to adjust for geographic cost differences.

been provided in physicians' offices (which could be ASCs that are not Medicare-certified). The site-of-service differentials for the high-volume procedures raise some concerns about the appropriate payment amount for these services. If payment is too high, incentives are created to shift services to that setting; if payment is too low, access to appropriate care can be affected. MedPAC has noted that Medicare's relatively low payment rates for interventional pain services furnished in physicians' offices may be contributing to a shift in the location of these services from physicians' offices to facility settings. For example, 72.1 percent of facet joint blocks for Medicare beneficiaries were performed in physicians' offices in 1995, and only 23.4 percent of such procedures were performed in physicians' offices in 1998 (MedPAC, 2001b).

Earlier in this discussion, the question was raised of whether the Medicare fee schedules might increase facility fee payments under the OMFS for minor surgical services. The high-volume procedures identified by Kominski and Gardner (2001) suggest that facility fee payments are already being made in addition to the OMFS physician payment and that adopting a fee schedule(s) for these services would reduce program expenditures significantly. Kominski and Gardner did not report the relative distribution of payments between hospital outpatient departments and ASCs. This is important because, under Medicare rules, a minor surgical service does not qualify for a facility fee when it is performed in an ASC but does qualify for a facility fee if it is performed in an HOPD. However, even if a significant percentage of minor surgical services is performed in an HOPD, the potential savings are quite large.

The site-of-service differentials across facility settings raise an issue regarding whether CWCP should (1) follow Medicare's policies and apply the OPPS rates to HOPDs and the ASC fee schedule to ASCs or (2) apply one fee schedule to procedures performed in either setting. An evaluation of this issue is complicated by the lack of current cost information for ASC procedures and data on the relative distribution of CWCP volume across the two settings. Further, little has been published regarding the quality and cost implications of performing procedures in different ambulatory settings. Questions regarding the type of patients receiving care, the quality of care provided, and patient outcomes in different outpatient settings remain unanswered. It is difficult to assess whether the payment system provides appropriate incentives without adequate evidence on which to base a judgment regarding whether one ambulatory setting is more appropriate than another for ambulatory surgical procedures. However, we believe that these are long-term research questions that do not need to be addressed in the initial implementation of a fee schedule. Initially, the fee schedule should provide payment that is adequate to cover the estimated costs of providing services in that setting to a typical patient. Subsequent refinements to the fee schedules can be made (and are likely to be made by the Medicare program in the future) as experience is gained under the new payment system and more is learned about the quality of care in different settings. Ongoing monitoring is also important to determine if

- there are increases in the proportion of procedures furnished in the most-expensive ambulatory sites. This would suggest that the higher payment might be influencing where care is provided. Reducing or eliminating the payment differential in the future would be a potential way to address the problem.

- there is evidence that patients can receive appropriate medical care in the least costly setting. This would suggest that the payment rate be set at the cost levels of the most-efficient setting.

Thus far, this section has concentrated on ambulatory surgical services. The site-of-service differential issue also applies to other medical and diagnostic services furnished by HOPDs. Except for emergency room services, the current OMFS does not expressly authorize separate payment for the facility fee for these services. In contrast, Medicare's OPPS has APCs for outpatient clinic services as well as emergency room care. The OMFS fee schedule pays the same amount for the technical component of diagnostic tests across ambulatory settings, whereas the OPPS APCs for these procedures differ from the amounts payable under the RB-RVS to freestanding diagnostic treatment centers and physicians' offices. The payment policy differences are illustrated in Table 4.3.

Table 4.3
Comparison of OMFS Payments with Geographically Adjusted Medicare Payments for the Technical Component of Selected High-Volume Diagnostic Tests and Evaluation and Management Services

Procedure	Description	OMFS Payment	RB-RVS Payment	OPPS APC Payment	Total Medicare Payment
Payments for Technical Component of Diagnostic Tests					
71020	Chest X-ray	$28.50	$25.34	$44.95	N/A
72052	X-ray exam of neck spine	$57.75	$45.62	$75.68	N/A
72148	MRI lumbar spine w/o dye	$512.00	$503.75	$387.49	N/A
95900	Motor nerve conduction test	$16.97	$37.04	$59.17	N/A
Payments for E&M Clinic Service					
99204	Office/outpatient visit, new	$109.65	$109.95	$85.91	$195.87
99214	Office/outpatient visit, established	$72.25	$60.04	$85.91	$145.96

N/A = Not applicable.

- For diagnostic procedures, the comparison is between the OMFS payment for the technical component of the test and Medicare's RB-RVS and APC payments. Medicare's payment for a two-view chest X-ray (Procedure 71020) is $25.34 when it is furnished in a physician's office or freestanding diagnostic treatment center and $44.95 when it is furnished to a hospital outpatient.. The latter payment is higher than the maximum allowable amount under the OMFS for all ambulatory settings.

- For evaluation and management non-emergency room services, the comparison is between the OMFS payment and the sum of Medicare's RB-RVS payment to the physician for facility-based services and the APC payment to the hospital (there are some definitional differences in the code that might affect the comparison, but they are minor compared with the overall effect). Medicare's APC payment for the facility component of E&M clinic services is the same for both new and established visits, while the RB-RVS payment is higher for new patients. When combined, the APC and RB-RVS payments are considerably higher than the OMFS maximum allowed amount. For purposes of comparison, Medicare's RB-RVS payments for 99204 and 99214 are $139.97 and $84.61, respectively, when the same codes are furnished in a physician's office.

There are two basic options that CWCP might wish to consider with respect to site-of-service differentials for facility fees:

- Use Medicare's policies for determining when facility fees are payable. This option would allow facility payments to HOPDs for both medical and surgical services. It could either incorporate Medicare's different payments to HOPDs and ASCs for surgical procedures or provide a uniform facility fee.

- Retain current OMFS policies regarding when facility fees are payable (surgical procedures and emergency room only). When a facility fee is not payable for an HOPD service, limit the total payment (HOPD and physician) to the non-facility setting to the RB-RVS amounts (i.e., the same total payment that would be made for an office-based service). The facility fee schedule could either incorporate Medicare's different payments to HOPDs and ASCs for surgical procedures or provide a uniform facility fee.

The limited amount of readily available data on hospital outpatient services precludes an analysis of the financial impact of the two options. However, we believe that the administrative benefits of linking the OMFS to existing Medicare fee schedules will be diluted if the program's basic payment policies are not adopted at the same time. Regardless of the decision, it will be important to monitor where ambulatory care is being delivered in the future.

New Technology

In deciding whether to link the OMFS to Medicare fee schedules, one consideration is whether the Medicare fee schedules will provide CWCP patients with sufficient access to quality-enhancing technology. Relative to the IPPS, in which the DRG payment covers all services furnished during the inpatient stay, APCs are procedure-specific and the cost of technology can be a substantially higher proportion of the service covered by the OPPS payment. For example, 53 percent of the cost of APC 222, Implantation of Pain Management Device, and 81 percent of the cost of APC 225, Implantation of Neurostimulator Electrodes, are attributable to the cost of the device (DHHS, 2002b). Thus, appropriate payment for quality-enhancing new technology is an important aspect of the payment system.

The OPPS accounts for new technology in the annual refinement of the APC groups and recalibration of the relative weights. In addition, there are two mechanisms designed to assure that Medicare beneficiaries have access to costly new technologies: (1) pass-through payments for drugs, biologicals, and devices whose costs are not reflected in the applicable APC to which the service is assigned, and (2) new technology APCs for new services that are not adequately described by existing APCs and do not qualify for the pass-through payment.

Similar to the inpatient prospective payment system, the OPPS provides for transitional pass-through payments for high-cost new technologies whose costs are not reflected in the cost data used to establish the APC relative weights. The pass-through payments are budget-neutral and are limited to no more than 2.5 percent of total OPPS payments. For devices, clinical criteria are used to determine whether the technology will substantially improve the diagnosis and treatment of beneficiaries relative to the technologies whose costs are reflected in the data. A quality-enhancing high-cost new device is eligible for a transitional pass-through for two to three years until its costs are reflected in the cost data used to refine the APCs. The amount of the pass-through payment equals the estimated cost of the device (determined by applying the hospital's cost-to-charge ratio to the charge for the device) less the amount in the APC payment for the device and is made without regard to the total costs of the service. Clinical criteria are not used to determine whether new high-cost drugs and biologicals are eligible for a pass-though; the transitional payment is based on 95 percent of the average wholesale price of the product.

CMS has also established 20 APCs to assign to a technology that is a new service or a procedure that is not adequately described by existing APCs. It must be a new Medicare-covered service that does not meet the requirements for a pass-through payment. For example, PET scans are currently assigned to a new technology APC. The APCs are determined by cost groupings, ranging from less than $50 for Level I procedures to $20,000 for Level XX procedures. The new procedure is assigned to a new technology APC based on its estimated costs. Currently, there are 75 new technologies that are assigned to these APCs. Unlike the pass-through payments, there are no budget-neutrality constraints. MedPAC (2003) estimates that new technology services accounted for about 1 percent of Medicare OPPS payments in 2001.

For Medicare beneficiaries, high-cost new technology is generally used in providing hospital services. Except for technologically advanced intra-ocular lenses (for which an additional payment is provided), the ASC fee schedule does not have special provisions for high-cost technology.

Deciding on a Conversion Factor

This section addresses decisions to be made regarding an appropriate conversion factor if the Medicare OPPS payment methodology and ASC fee schedules are adopted for CWCP patient services.

OPPS for HOPD Services

The Medicare OPPS was not designed to cover the full accounting costs of furnishing services to Medicare beneficiaries. The original system was intended to be budget-neutral to the prior payment system, which paid approximately 82 percent of amounts reported on the Medicare cost report. This means that the original conversion factor was set to provide an 18-percent discount below reported cost for each APC grouping. To some extent, these costs are overstated because the PPS for inpatient services encouraged cost-shifting to outpatient services. Nevertheless, in keeping with the intent of AB 749 that the payments be sufficient to cover the cost of the procedure, a 1.22 multiplier is needed to cover estimated costs. A somewhat higher multiplier is needed to also provide an efficient hospital with a margin on outpatient services (e.g., 1.28 would provide a 5 percent margin). To be comparable with the rates paid by private payers, i.e., an estimated payment-to-cost ratio of 1.125, the multiplier would need to be as high as 1.37 (1.125 x 1.22).

The impact of applying a multiplier to the Medicare conversion factor on aggregate CWCP payments for HOPD services would need to be modeled after decisions are made regarding whether the APCs will also be used to pay for non-emergent medical treatment and diagnostic services. Having sample paid claims data for hospital outpatient services would allow a comparison between current payments and payments using the OPPS methodology and indicate whether a transition policy is needed to soften the immediate effects of moving to fee schedules. Because there are not pre-existing fee schedules, a feasible transition policy would be to set a higher multiplier initially and decrease it over time to the desired level.

ASC Facilities Services

Current cost data are not available to assess the adequacy of Medicare's current payment levels for ASC services. MedPAC recently reviewed this issue and concluded that ASC payments were more than adequate and that the FY 2004 update should be eliminated.[60] MedPAC also expressed concern that some ASC payment rates exceeded the OPPS amounts for the same procedures and should be reduced. Medicare beneficiaries use a different mix of ASC services than do CWCP patients; therefore, an analysis of paid claims data would be needed to assess how alternative payment levels using either the ASC or OPPS payment methodologies would impact program expenditures and payments to ASCs. Overall, California ASCs reported high patient margins to OSHPD in 2000, the most recent year for which data are available. Of the 324 facilities reporting net patient care revenues and total operating expenses, the overall payment-to-cost ratio was 1.37. In other words, net patient care revenues were 37 percent higher than costs. If the OPPS payment methodology is adopted for ASC facility services, available information suggests ASCs do not need as high a conversion factor as hospitals:

- MedPAC concluded that hospital outpatient departments probably have higher cost structures than ASCs because they must meet higher regulatory requirements, such as the *Emergency Medical Treatment and Active Labor Act*, and stricter Medicare certification and state licensure requirements (MedPAC, 2003).
- MedPAC also found that hospitals were more likely than ASCs to perform procedures on Medicare patients at higher risk than the Medicare patients receiving the same procedures in ASCs.

---

[60]In reaching its conclusion, MedPAC cited several market indications of payment adequacy, including a steady growth in the number of Medicare-certified ASCs and in the volume of services furnished to Medicare beneficiaries. Rapid growth in both independently owned and investor-owned chains of ASCs suggests that they have adequate access to capital. Companies that manage and invest in ASCs have had strong revenue and earnings growth. MedPAC also found no evidence that the payment rates have presented barriers to the use of new technology. Assuming that ASC facility productivity growth in FY 2004 is comparable to the estimated growth in multifactor productivity in the national economy, MedPAC found that the current payments are sufficient to cover inflation for that year.

- In addition, hospitals offer a broader range of services than do ASCs, they do not have the efficiencies and productivity gains associated with specialization in certain services (e.g., orthopedic procedures), and they have higher uncompensated care costs.

Until CMS conducts a new cost survey or OSHPD collects this information, the empirical data needed to inform a decision regarding the appropriate conversion factor will be limited. We assume that an analysis of paid claims data will show ASCs will experience significant payment reductions under a fee schedule. One option is to phase in the payment reductions by setting the initial conversion factor at a relatively high level and reducing it over time. In the interim, monitoring for changes in where care is delivered and analyzing the cost and quality implications of care furnished in alternative ambulatory settings can be undertaken to better inform this issue.

Deciding on an Update Factor

Medicare uses different measures of inflation to update the OPPS and ASC rates:

- OPPS rates are updated by the estimated rate of increase in the hospital market basket for inpatient services. The update factor for 2003 was 3.5 percent.
- The ASC rates are updated by the increase in the CPI for all urban consumers. The FY 2003 rates were updated by 3.0 percent.

As is the case with inpatient prospective payments, other adjustments are made to the OPPS conversion factor during the annual update process. Most notably, an adjustment is made to account for changes in the estimated cost of pass-through payments for new drugs and devices. Presumably, the pass-through payments would also be allowed under the OMFS if the OPPS is adopted; however, the use of devices might be quite different for CWCP patients. If the update is linked to increases in the Medicare conversion factor, DWC should evaluate the actual adjustments made by the Medicare program in any given year, including potential changes stemming from federal budgetary considerations and the level of pass-through payments for CWCP patients. It would be administratively easier to link the OMFS update directly to an inflation measure, such as the hospital market basket or the PPI. These measures were discussed in Chapter 2.

Update Process

This section addresses issues regarding the OPPS update process and updates to ASC fee schedules.

OPPS

The law requires CMS to review the components of the OPPS at least annually and to revise the payment groups and related payment factors to take into account changes in medical practice, new technology and services, and more recent cost data. CMS is required to consult with the advisory panel on APC groups in refining the payment groups.

The rulemaking process is used to make annual changes that are effective on a calendar year basis. A proposed rule with a 60-day public comment period typically precedes the final rule in early August. The final rule is scheduled for publication by November 1. This would give CWCP 60 days to review and implement the changes to payment groups and payment factors if they are to be effective on a calendar year basis; a longer period may be needed if modifications are made to tailor the OPPS to CWCP's needs. In addition, quarterly updates are made as the HCFA Common Procedure Coding System (HCPCS) G-level procedure codes are created to describe services newly covered by Medicare. A review of these codes may reveal that they are not needed for CWCP patients.

ASC Fee Schedule

As previously noted, the law requires CMS to review the list of ASC approved procedures at least every two years and to conduct a cost and charge survey for a sample of ASCs every five years. The last proposal to update the ASC rates based on the 1994 cost survey was in 1998. Competing computer system priorities prevented the proposal from being issued as a final rule. The law now requires CMS to conduct a cost survey before making modifications in the payment groups. CMS has not yet initiated another survey and has issued updates in the payment amounts as program instructions. Thus, unlike the other fee schedules discussed in this report, there has been no ongoing refinement process for the ASC fee schedule. A revised list of ASC procedures is effective as of July 2003.

Summary of Findings

AB 749 imposes a number of requirements that will postpone a fee schedule for ambulatory surgery for a number of years. While California-specific data on workers' compensation claims for ambulatory surgery should be collected on an ongoing basis in the future to support monitoring activities, data are currently available that could be used to establish a fee schedule for ambulatory surgery, including the Medicare facility fee schedules for ambulatory services.

Several policy issues should be considered in adapting the Medicare fee schedules to pay for ambulatory surgery services. The most basic issue is whether the Medicare payment scheme of paying for surgery furnished in hospital outpatient departments using one payment system and paying for surgery performed in freestanding ambulatory surgical centers with a different fee schedule should be adopted or whether the same fee schedule, perhaps with different conversion factors, should be used for both settings.

There are two reasons the hospital outpatient fee schedule should be considered in lieu of the ASC fee schedule. The first is that Medicare has a relatively narrow list of Medicare-approved procedures that are covered in an ASC that does not include some procedures that are currently paid for in an ASC under the OMFS. The list of approved procedures includes only procedures that can be safely performed in an ASC for Medicare patients and may be more restrictive than necessary for the younger and less frail workers' compensation population. In addition, the list does not include procedures that are commonly performed in physicians' offices to discourage a shift of these procedures from those offices to ASCs. Procedures that are not on the approved list are paid under the RB-RVS as if they were furnished in a physician's office (i.e., no separate facility fee is payable). It appears that ASCs are already paid a facility fee for minor surgical services under the OMFS; therefore, adopting the hospital outpatient fee schedule would not create a new incentive to shift services from physicians' offices to ASCs. The second reason for using the hospital outpatient fee schedule is that the information used to establish the costs of procedures performed in ASCs is outdated and may not reflect the current costs of performing those procedures.

The shortcomings of the current ASC fee schedule suggest that it might be less burdensome to simply use the hospital outpatient prospective payment system to pay for services in either setting. This raises the question of the appropriate level for the conversion factor and whether the same conversion factor should be used for both settings. The Medicare payment system for hospital outpatient services was not designed to cover the full accounting costs of furnishing services to Medicare beneficiaries. The original conversion factor was set to provide an 18 percent discount below reported cost. Thus, a somewhat higher than 1.22 multiplier is needed to cover estimated costs and provide an efficient hospital with a positive margin on outpatient services (e.g., 1.27 would provide a 5-percent margin, which is the average hospital margin on patient care services). To be comparable with the rates paid by private payers, i.e., an estimated payment-to-cost ratio of 1.125, the multiplier would need to be as high as 1.37 (1.125 x 1.22).

In the absence of current cost data, the empirical data needed to inform a decision regarding the appropriate conversion factor for ASC services is limited. Available information suggests ASCs do not need as high a conversion factor as hospitals for ambulatory surgery. Hospital outpatient departments have higher cost structures than ASCs because they must meet higher regulatory requirements, such as the *Emergency Medical Treatment and Active Labor Act*, and stricter Medicare certification and state licensure requirements (MedPAC, 2003), and they are more likely to incur uncompensated care costs. ASCs are also likely to have higher productivity because they specialize in particular procedures whereas most hospitals perform the full array of surgical procedures. An examination of Medicare beneficiary characteristics found that hospitals were more likely than ASCs to perform procedures on patients at higher risk than the patients receiving the same procedures in an ASC (MedPAC, 2003). Setting the conversion factor at an unnecessarily high level would provide incentives for unnecessary utilization. However, available information also indicates that ASCs will experience significant payment reductions under a fee schedule. One option is to phase in the payment reductions by setting the initial conversion factor at a relatively high level and reducing it over time. In the interim, monitoring for changes in the settings where care is delivered, analyzing the cost and quality implications of care furnished in alternative ambulatory settings, and analyzing the amounts paid by private payers can be done to better inform this issue.

Another important issue is whether Medicare's fee schedule for hospital outpatient services should also be used to pay for other medical and diagnostic services furnished by hospital outpatient departments. Except for emergency room services, the current OMFS does not expressly authorize separate payment for the facility fee for these services. In contrast, Medicare pays a facility fee for clinic as well as emergency room care. The OMFS fee schedule pays the same amount for the technical component of diagnostic tests across ambulatory settings, whereas the Medicare payments for these procedures in a hospital outpatient department differ from the amounts payable under the RB-RVS to freestanding diagnostic treatment centers and physician offices. There are two basic policy choices concerning medical and diagnostic services furnished in hospital outpatient departments:

- Use Medicare's policies for determining when facility fees are payable. This option would allow facility fees for both medical and surgical services and would create site-of-service differentials for radiology and other diagnostic tests.
- Retain current OMFS policies regarding when facility fees are payable (surgical procedures and emergency room only). When a facility fee is not payable, the total payment (hospital and physician) would be limited to the same total payment that would be made for an office-based service.

Overall, we believe that the administrative benefits of linking the OMFS to existing Medicare fee schedules will be diluted if the program's basic payment policies are not adopted at the same time. The limited amount of readily available data on hospital outpatient services precludes an analysis of the financial impact of the alternative policies. Regardless of the decision, it will be important to monitor where ambulatory care is being delivered in the future.

5. Other Items and Services

Diagnostic Clinical Laboratory Tests

Currently, the OMFS uses a relative value fee schedule to pay for laboratory tests. Medicare pays the lowest of the actual charge billed for the test, a locally determined fee schedule amount, or a national limitation amount (NLA). For most tests, the NLA is 74 percent of the median of the local fees and is typically the controlling payment amount. As with other fee schedules, CMS has an established process for updating the fee schedule on an annual basis.

The law requires CMS to solicit public comment on determining the payment amount for new codes, which the agency obtains through a public meeting and written comments. Two different approaches are used in pricing new codes (DHHS, 2002c):

- Some laboratory tests are "crosswalked" to a comparable existing test and assigned its local fee schedule amount and NLA.
- If there are no comparable tests, carriers "gap-fill" the payment amount using available data on charges and discounted charges for the tests, amounts paid by other payers, resources required for similar tests, and other pertinent factors. These amounts may change during the course of the year as more information becomes available and the payment amount is refined. CMS considers the gap-filled prices in setting the succeeding year's fee schedule amounts.

The default annual update in the laboratory fee schedule is the rate of change in the CPI-U. For 2003, the increase was 1.1 percent. However, the fee schedule has been frozen several times since it was first established, most recently between 1998 and 2002. If the OMFS is linked to the Medicare fee schedule, one issue will be whether to adopt the Medicare inflation factor or to establish an independent adjustment for inflation.

Another issue is how G-codes should be treated. For example, the CPT-4 2003 revisions changed the definitions for specimen collection, but CMS is continuing to use a G-code (G0001) for this service. Another issue is whether to exempt the "gap-fill" codes or to obtain the price information from the California carriers on locally priced codes.

CMS issues a program memorandum each year outlining in considerable detail the upcoming changes in the laboratory fee schedule. Around the same time, a data file is made publicly available on the CMS Web site (at http://www.cms.gov/payment). Generally, the changes are released in early November to allow Medicare carriers enough time to make the necessary systems updates. The provider community is also notified of the changes through a "Dear Doctor" letter that is released as part of the participating physician program.

Durable Medical Equipment, Prosthetics, Orthotics, and Supplies

For the Medicare beneficiary, durable medical equipment (DME) is defined as equipment that can withstand repeated use, that serves a generally medical purpose, and that is intended for use in the home. DME, prosthetics, orthotics, and supplies (DMEPOS) are paid on a fee schedule reflecting local and regional prices for the following six categories of items that are updated annually based on the rate of change in the CPI-U:

- Payment for inexpensive or routinely purchased items is made on a rental or lump-sum basis using the lower of the actual charge or the fee schedule amount.
- Equipment requiring frequent servicing is reimbursed as a rental.
- Oxygen and oxygen equipment is paid a monthly fee schedule amount with an added payment for portable oxygen equipment.
- Carrier discretion is allowed for customized DME.
- Prosthetics and orthotics are generally reimbursed on a lump-sum payment basis.
- Certain rental items (e.g., hospital beds and wheelchairs) are paid at national rates based on the lesser of actual charges or 10 percent of the allowable purchase price for the first three months and then 7.5 percent each month for up to 15 months of continuous use. Thereafter, suppliers must furnish the item at no charge other than maintenance and servicing.

One issue in linking the OMFS to the Medicare DMEPOS fee schedule is whether the range of equipment covered by CWCP is broader than the range of equipment covered under Medicare such that there are items and equipment that do not have Medicare prices. A second issue is whether the rules concerning rental versus purchase and other special policies should be adopted at the same time. For example, Medicare makes a payment equal to 10 percent of the fee schedule amount for the purchase of a transcutaneous electrical nerve stimulator (TENS) for the first two months of usage. The two months is a trial period prior to purchase that permits an attending physician to determine whether the purchase of a TENS is medically appropriate. If it is medically appropriate, the full purchase price is then paid without an adjustment for the two monthly rental payments.

The DMEPOS fee schedules are updated on a quarterly basis in order to implement fee schedule amounts for new codes and to revise any fee schedule amounts for existing codes that were calculated in error. A program memorandum is issued and electronic files containing the fee schedule amounts, floors, and ceilings, and the payment categories for procedure codes subject to the DMEPOS fee schedule payment methodology are available on the CMS Web site (http://www.cms.gov/payment). While the necessary information to make the changes is readily available, the frequency of the updates may pose an administrative challenge. An annual update with new services excluded from the fee schedule for up to nine months may be sufficient for purposes of the OMFS.

Skilled Nursing Services

Medicare pays for short-term skilled nursing facility care following a three-day qualifying hospital stay using a per diem prospective payment rate. An SNF level of care is provided if the patient needs skilled care or skilled rehabilitative care on a daily basis (five times per week for therapy) that as a practical matter can be provided only on an inpatient basis. Custodial care[61] is not covered under the Medicare program. Thus, one issue that needs to be reviewed in linking the OMFS fee schedule to the Medicare fee schedule is whether Medicare's payment for skilled nursing care is appropriate for the levels of care covered by CWCP.

Patients are assigned to one of 44 resource utilization groups based on periodic assessments of a patient's service needs and expected resource requirements. The per diem for each group is the sum of a fixed amount for routine (room and board) services, a variable amount reflecting nursing intensity, and a variable amount reflecting intensity of therapy services. Separate rates apply to urban and rural areas, and there is a geographic adjustment factor (based on the hospital wage index). Concerns over the adequacy of payment for 12 complex care groups led Congress to provide for a temporary 20-percent increase in the payments for those groups until case mix refinements are adopted. CMS conditions of participation for SNFs require that a patient assessment instrument be completed for all patients. Information needed to make resource utilization group (RUG) assignments is gathered as part of the assessment. Thus, the information needed to determine payment is already being collected and should be available if the OMFS adopts Medicare's SNF per diem payment rates.

Medicare's rates are all-inclusive and cover all medically necessary services provided by the SNF. The SNF is required to bill directly for all services (whether they are provided by the SNF or by an outside supplier under arrangements with the SNF) that are not expressly excluded from the provision.[62] A comparable rule would be needed to ensure that CWCP does not pay for services twice: once through the per diem rate and again through an outside supplier (e.g., a physical therapist or pharmacy).

SNF payment rates are updated annually through the rulemaking process. The update factor is based on the projected increase in the SNF market basket, which is conceptually similar to the hospital market basket but is weighted to reflect the goods and services SNFs purchase to provide care. The updates are effective each October 1. The final rule implementing the changes should be published no later than 60 days in advance (i.e., by August 2). The rulemaking documents and program instructions are readily available on the CMS Web site (http://www.cms.gov/payment).

---

[61]Medicare defines *custodial care* as follows: Treatment or services that could be rendered safely and easily by a person not medically skilled, or that are designed mainly to help the patient with activities of daily living.

[62]The excluded services include the professional component of physician services (but not the technical component) and other professional services covered under Medicare Part B, certain hospital outpatient and dialysis-related services, ambulance services, and hospice care related to the beneficiary's terminal condition.

Home Health Agency Services

Medicare makes a prospective payment covering all services other than DME during a 60-day episode of care provided by a home health agency. The payment is adjusted for clinical severity, functional severity, and service utilization. However, it also reflects the nature of the Medicare home health benefit. To be eligible for home health care, a Medicare beneficiary must be homebound and need intermittent skilled nursing care or therapy services. Eligible beneficiaries may receive

- part-time or intermittent skilled nursing and home health aide services
- physical therapy, speech language pathology, and occupational therapy
- medical social services
- medical supplies and durable medical equipment.

For coverage purposes, the skilled nursing and home health aide services may be furnished on any number of days provided that together they are furnished less than 8 hours per day and 28 or fewer hours per week (or, subject to case review, 35 or fewer hours per week).

The per-episode payment reflects the typical mix of Medicare-covered services provided during the 60-day episode and may not reflect the types and duration of home care needed by CWCP patients. Further analysis of the home care services provided to CWCP patients is advisable. If the episodic payment is not appropriate, another feature of the payment system might be. If fewer than five visits are provided during a 60-day episode, Medicare pays the home health agency (HHA) a per-visit amount that varies by type of visit, rather than the per-episode amount. These wage-adjusted rates might be a suitable basis for a per-visit fee schedule. A per-visit payment method can provide incentives for excess utilization but, in the absence of a good case mix adjustment, it is still preferable to excluding home care from the OMFS. The appropriateness of the rates for home health aide/homemaker services covered by the CWCP would need to be evaluated because there can be considerable variation in the duration of these visits.

Ambulance Services

Following negotiated rulemaking with affected parties, CMS implemented a fee schedule for ambulance services in April 2002. Under the fee schedule, payment is based on the relative value for the service, a geographic adjustment factor (based on the RB-RVS GPCI for practice expense), and a uniform conversion factor. Fourteen HCPCS codes are used to describe the level of service, supplies, and equipment used, and mileage. In addition, ambulance suppliers may bill two CPT-4 codes for electrocardiograms. Ambulance-administered drugs are considered part of the supplies and are not paid separately. Separate mileage rates apply to air and ground transport and add-ons apply to rural trips.

CMS has established a five-year transition period using a blend of old and new payment amounts, but only the new payment system is feasible for the OMFS to consider. The fee schedule rates are to be updated annually based on the rate of increase in the CPI-U. Through FY 2006, Medicare payments under the fee schedule are to be budget-neutral to estimated payments that would have been made under the prior payment system. As a result, the update factor that is applied to the conversion factor may not be appropriate for the CWCP and consideration should be given to applying only the CPI-U.

A program memorandum was issued with the 2003 update in the fee schedule. We were unable to locate a public-use electronic file of the procedure codes and payment amounts. However, because making a public-use file available has become standard practice for other CMS fee schedules, we assume that one will become available for ambulance services on a regular basis in the future.

Summary of Findings

Over the past five years, Medicare has implemented new fee schedules for services provided by skilled nursing facilities, home health agencies, and ambulance companies. Both prospective payment systems for post-acute-care services (per-diem for SNF care and per-episode for home health care) are tailored to the particular coverage policies of the Medicare program, and further analysis is advisable to ascertain whether they also provide appropriate payment for services needed by CWCP patients. The ambulance fee schedule, while also new, is for a more narrowly defined service and should not be problematic. The fee schedules for laboratory tests and durable medical equipment, prosthetics, orthotics, and supplies are well established. As with the other services, the main issues concern the overall payment levels, whether payment-related policies should be adopted at the same time as the fee schedules, and whether there are some services covered by CWCP for which Medicare has not established payment rates.

6. Findings and Areas for Further Consideration

Across all types of medical services, this report explores issues related to adapting Medicare's fee schedules to the CWCP and providing for automatic updates in the future. This study highlights various considerations that would need to be addressed and opportunities for reducing program expenditures and administrative costs if the OMFS were to be linked to Medicare fee schedules. A number of crosscutting issues emerged from our analysis of the individual Medicare fee schedules:

- Generally, Medicare's fee schedules cover the broad range of services covered by CWCP. Some attention, however, needs to be given to individual services that are unique to CWCP or to providers that are not covered by Medicare, such as acupuncturists and family therapists.

- Linking the OMFS to the Medicare fee schedules shifts the administrative burden of ongoing refinement and updates to the Centers for Medicare Services. Medicare fee schedules are updated on a regular basis with opportunity for public comment. An independent commission is charged with reviewing and making recommendations concerning Medicare payment policies. In addition, other advisory committees provide CMS with regular input on potential refinements to the Medicare payment systems.

- Medicare fee schedules consist of more than just a set of prices; coding standards and payment policies are implicit in the prices and often differ from those currently used by the OMFS or have features that the OMFS lacks. A number of policy issues would need to be addressed at the outset. However, after the decisions are made on these issues, they can be imbedded in the OMFS and should not preclude automatic updates in the future based on Medicare fee schedule updates.

- Medicare fee schedules have evolved over time to become systems that are organized according to the *provider* who is furnishing the care and the setting where that care is delivered. When services are provided in a facility setting, separate payments are made to the physician or other practitioner and to the facility. Total payment for many ambulatory procedures vary based on the setting in which those procedures are done. In contrast, the current OMFS establishes maximum payments for *services* and, except for surgical procedures and emergency room services for which separate facility fees are allowed, the amounts do not vary based on the ambulatory setting in which the services are provided. Important decisions to be made in this area are whether to (1) continue current OMFS rules regarding separate facility fees or establish separate facility fees for all hospital outpatient services; (2) establish the same maximum facility fee payments for hospital outpatient departments and ambulatory surgical centers; or (3) adopt Medicare's payment differentials for physician services furnished in office and facility settings. How these issues are addressed will affect both the incentives for where care is delivered and total California workers' compensation medical care expenditures.

- The unit of service covered by a Medicare fee schedule payment ranges from a bundled payment for a group of services (for example, the PPS for inpatient services covers all facility services provided during an inpatient stay) to a separate payment for each individual service or diagnostic test. While the current OMFS for inpatient hospital services demonstrates that the Medicare bundled payments can be adapted for workers' compensation patients, Medicare payments for an inpatient stay (e.g., for services delivered in rehabilitation facilities) or payments for an episode of care (e.g., for home health care services) should be assessed to determine if the payments are appropriate for workers' compensation patients.

- Medicare has policies governing which items and services are included in payments for professional and facility services and which services may be billed separately. Most fee schedules include a relative value or weight that measures the resources required for a given service or group of services relative to other services. These relative weights are consistent with the service definition and may not be appropriate if the OMFS retains different policies on items and services that may be separately billed.

- For most fee schedules, Medicare applies a dollar amount conversion factor to the relative value for a given service to convert that value into a payment amount. A key question is what the appropriate conversion factor should be for services furnished to California workers' compensation patients. Although there is no "gold standard" that can be used to answer this question, a number of factors should be taken into account in any case. Those factors include whether there is adequate access to care, the current maximum allowable fees, the relationship between Medicare and private-payer fee levels in California, and the available information on the cost of providing specific services. A multiplier can be applied to the Medicare conversion factor to establish an overall payment level that is adequate to provide access to high-quality care. Setting the rate too low may create access problems, whereas setting the rate too high may encourage unnecessary utilization and result in excessive program expenditures.

- The OMFS is not adjusted for inflation on a regular basis, and most payments have been frozen for at least several years. The result is lower aggregate expenditures than the expenditures that would have resulted with regular inflation updates. While program expenditures tend to be higher with regular updates, the annual adjustments increase payment equity and predictability and should keep payments in line with the resources required to provide medical services.

- Medicare's annual update factors are set by law and include policy adjustments as well as an inflation adjustment. The policy adjustments meet Medicare programmatic needs and may not be appropriate for updates to the OMFS. Inflation adjustments other than those used by the CMS may be more suitable for the OMFS. Input price indices account for changes in the input costs of providing services and would relate payment changes to changes in the costs of providing medical services, and medical price indices account for changes in the amounts paid by consumers and/or third-party payers for medical services. The selection of an appropriate measure depends on the underlying policy goal in making an inflation adjustment.

- The potential payment changes are quite large for some service sectors and may require a transition period to allow providers time to adjust to the new payment levels. Depending on the service sector and whether the OMFS already applies, transition policies that might be considered include
    - thresholds for the maximum change that can occur in a single year
    - blended rates that over several years provide a decreasing proportion of the payment based on the OMFS and an increasing proportion based on the Medicare fee schedule
    - hold-harmless provisions that freeze the current maximum allowable fee until it is less than the inflation-adjusted Medicare fee schedule amount
    - reducing over time the OMFS multiplier that is applied to the Medicare conversion factor.
- While any of the aforementioned transition strategies involve some administrative burden, those that require maintaining procedure-specific information on amounts currently payable under the OMFS are the most burdensome. Transition policies that phase in the payment changes through adjustments in the conversion factor are the least burdensome. The annual updating burden will be minimized if the transition policies are established at the outset of linking the OMFS to the Medicare fee schedules.
- The impact on program expenditures from tying the OMFS to the Medicare fee schedules would largely depend on certain decisions regarding payment levels: the multiplier used to adjust the Medicare conversion factor, the update methodology, and transition policies. Administrative savings should accrue from regular and predictable updates, but the actual level of administrative savings may be affected by the extent to which modifications are made in the Medicare fee schedules to address particular CWCP concerns.
- The decisions regarding payment levels and fee schedule modifications also have major implications for workers' compensation patients' continued access to quality care. The lack of a single statewide database containing all or a representative sample of current California workers' compensation claims makes it difficult to evaluate the impact of various policy options. With the potentially large payment changes that are likely to occur in some sectors, ongoing monitoring to watch for unintended consequences is highly recommended if the Medicare fee schedules are adopted. If monitoring is done during the transition period, potential problems can be identified and addressed promptly, and any necessary mid-course corrections can be made before final payment levels are established.
- Adopting Medicare's patient classifications will allow the DWC to compare costs for comparable services across providers, compare costs with other programs' costs for services,

and monitor access and utilization trends for specific services. Such analyses are predicated on obtaining administrative data on an ongoing basis.

Our analysis of the policy considerations involved in linking the OMFS to the Medicare fee schedules highlighted the need for ongoing data collection on the services provided to CWCP patients. In the short run, the lack of readily available data limits the ability to model the impact of moving from the current OMFS to the Medicare fee schedules and to understand how overall OMFS payment levels compare with Medicare's payment levels and those of private payers. This information would be helpful in establishing the OMFS conversion factor and in determining transition policies for ambulatory surgery facility services, laboratory tests, and DMEPOS fee schedules. The 2002 Lewin Group study cited in this report provides necessary information on the impact of the RB-RVS relative to current OMFS payment levels, but additional information on private-payer fee levels would be beneficial.

Other areas in which further analysis would benefit the policymaking process include the following:

- Evaluating the impact of adopting the geographic adjustment factor and the impact of other policy choices in adopting the RB-RVS for physician and other practitioner services
- Modeling the financial implications of alternative fee schedules for ambulatory surgical center facility services and hospital outpatient services
- Evaluating whether the bundled payments for inpatient services furnished in rehabilitation facilities, long-term care hospitals, and skilled nursing facilities and the bundled payments for home health episodes of care are appropriate for worker's compensation patients.

In the longer term, additional research is also needed to inform decisions regarding potential refinements to the payment system. Further analyses that would benefit decision-making include:

- Assessing whether patient characteristics affect where ambulatory surgery is performed and whether outcomes differ across settings
- Determining the hardware and instrumentation costs that are included in the back and neck DRG payments for inpatient hospital services
- Reviewing the medical literature on back and spinal procedures to determine if the evidence would support practice guidelines for the procedures and the use of new technology hardware and instrumentation.

Linking the OMFS to Medicare fee schedules would expand the services covered by the OMFS and reduce the administrative burden of keeping the rates current by capitalizing on the regular updates that the Centers for Medicare and Medicaid Services perform for Medicare. The impact on both patient access to quality medical care and program expenditures will be largely determined by the overall level at which payments are set. Ongoing data collection and analysis would be needed to monitor access, cost, and quality and to address other areas of potential concern. This activity is needed to ensure that linking the OMFS to Medicare fee schedules does not have unintended consequences affecting program expenditures or CWCP patient access to medically appropriate services.

A. DRG Classification Changes Affecting the Payment Simulations in Chapter 2

Changes to Medicare diagnosis-related groups to reflect ICD-9-CM coding changes occur every October 1 as part of the annual update process for the Medicare acute care PPS (as discussed in Chapter 2). These changes are made to reduce the variation of resource use among Medicare patients assigned to a given DRG, and they frequently reflect technology diffusion and other changes in practice patterns that affect resource use.

DRG refinements are often facilitated by the ICD-9-CM coding changes, which increase differentiation among patients. In this regard, when changes are made in either the diagnosis or procedure codes, CMS's policy historically has been to initially assign the replacement codes to the same DRGs to which patients with the codes that are being modified or replaced are currently classified. When the data become available that reflect the new codes, the DRG classification logic is examined two years after the new codes are implemented to determine if changes in a DRG are warranted. More recently, some DRG changes have coincided with the ICD-9-CM coding changes in an effort to give immediate recognition to the use of new technology.

Potentially significant changes can be taken into account in the payment simulations presented in Chapter 2 (see Table 2.4) through either one of two basic ways:

- By using CWCP claims data that contain diagnosis and procedure codes, patients can be mapped into the DRGs to which they would have been assigned had the revised DRGs been in effect in FY 2000 (the year for which CWCP claims data are available).[63] This method works only for those changes that involve diagnosis and procedure codes that were used in FY 2000. It cannot be used for changes involving codes that were introduced after FY 2000 because the codes needed for the mapping are not on the bills.

- New DRGs can be recombined with the DRGs from the cases that were reassigned when the new DRGs were created. Developing an estimate of what the payments would have been in the absence of the DRG changes involves (1) applying an average of the FY 2003 relative weights of the old and new DRGs weighted by the number of Medicare cases assigned to the affected DRGs and (2) applying the revised DRG relative weight to the FY 2000 CWCP DRG assignments.

As explained in Chapter 2, patients are assigned to DRGs using the Medicare GROUPER program that contains the DRG logic for the payment year. In each year's final PPS rule, CMS produces tables showing the distribution of discharges across DRGs based on the GROUPER

[63]As stated in Chapter 2, we accounted for changes in the DRG classification system between FY 2000 and FY 2003. Where feasible, we mapped inpatient stays from old DRG assignments to new DRG assignments based on the ICD-9-CM diagnosis and procedure codes reported in the administrative data.

version currently in effect and on the version that will be implemented in the upcoming fiscal year. The distribution uses Medicare discharges for the prior fiscal year. For example, the final rule announcing the DRG changes and PPS rates for FY 2003 contains tables comparing the distribution of FY 2001 Medicare discharges based on the FY 2002 GROUPER to the same discharges based on the FY 2003 GROUPER.

The remainder of this appendix summarizes the changes in the DRG classification system that occurred between FY 2000 and FY 2003 that we considered in modeling FY 2003 CWCP payments (see Chapter 2). We studied information from tables in the Medicare final rules to understand the likely magnitude of each change on DRG assignments and to identify those changes that invalidated specific DRGs. We used CWCP 2000 claims data on the number of workers' compensation patients assigned to each DRG to identify those changes that were likely to affect the DRG assignment of at least ten workers' compensation patients. We did not take into account other changes that at most might affect only a few patients because they should not have a significant impact on the payment simulations.

For most of the changes, we mapped the FY 2000 cases into their FY 2003 DRG assignments. Where the changes could not be modeled (e.g., the codes were not in effect), we collapsed the FY 2003 DRGs and determined a weighted average relative weight.

The changes that we took into consideration when mapping cases with applicable diagnostic and procedure codes into their FY 2003 DRG assignments are as follows:

- **Spinal fusion procedures.** In FY 2002, new codes were created for refusions. Cervical fusions and refusions with and without complications were assigned to new DRGs. Also, lumbar and lumbosacral fusion, lateral traverse technique (ICD-CM procedure code 81.07), was reassigned from DRGs 497 and 498 to DRG 496 when used with an anterior technique or refusion. The impact of creating new codes for refusions cannot be modeled until claims data using the new codes become available. The reclassification of CWCP cases is shown in Table A.1.

Table A.1
FY 2002 DRG Reclassification of Spinal Fusion Cases

FY 2000/FY 2001 DRG		Cases (N)	FY 2000 Relative Weight	FY 2003 DRG		Cases (N)	FY 2003 Relative Weight
496	Combined anterior/posterior spinal fusion	543	5.6871	496	Combined anterior/posterior spinal fusion	725	5.7988
497	Spinal fusion with CC	1,077	2.8441	497	Spinal fusion except cervical with CC	840	3.3938
498	Spinal fusion without CC	3,507	1.7952	498	Spinal fusion except cervical without CC	2,048	2.4738
–	N/A	–	–	519	Cervical spinal fusion with CC	171	2.3551
–	N/A	–	–	520	Cervical spinal fusion without CC	1,336	1.5389

N = Number.

- **Cardiac surgical cases.** Major restructuring of the cardiac surgery cases has occurred since FY 2000. The results are shown in Table A.2.

Table A.2
DRG Reclassification of Cardiac Surgery Cases

		Cases (N)	FY 2000 Relative Weight	FY 2003 DRG		Cases (N)	FY 2003 Relative Weight
104	Cardiac valve procedures with cardiac catheterization	31	7.2361	104	Cardiac valve and other major cardiothoracic procedure with cardiac catheterization	4	7.9916
105	Cardiac valve procedures without cardiac catheterization	18	5.6607	105	Cardiac valve and other major cardiothoracic procedure without cardiac catheterization	9	5.8063
112[a]	Percutaneous cardiovascular procedures	71	1.9222	–	N/A	–	–
116	Other permanent cardiac pacemaker implant or PTCA with coronary artery stent	219	2.4651	116	Other permanent cardiac pacemaker implant	277	2.3078
–	N/A	–	–	514	Cardiac defibrillator implant with cardiac catheterization	27	6.3376
–	N/A	–	–	515	Cardiac defibrillator implant without cardiac catheterization	9	5.0562
–	N/A	–	–	516	Percutaneous cardiovascular procedure with AMI	57	2.7273
–	N/A	–	–	517	Percutaneous cardiovascular procedure with non-drug eluting stent without AMI	8	2.1789
–	N/A	–	–	518	Percutaneous cardiovascular procedure without coronary artery stent or AMI	64	1.7297

[a] Invalidated in FY 2002.

- New DRGs were created for patients receiving cardiac defibrillators in FY 2002 and for heart assist procedures in FY 2003.

- In FY 2002, the DRG logic for cases involving percutaneous transluminal coronary angioplasty (PTCA) was restructured to consider whether an acute myocardial infarction (AMI) was involved. The changes invalidated DRG 112 (i.e., all cases were reassigned) and resulted in a 70-percent reduction in the number of Medicare discharges assigned to DRG 116.

- In FY 2003, the DRGs were restructured again with the creation of new procedure codes and DRGs for drug-eluting stents. The new DRGs were scheduled to become effective the later of April 1, 2003, or when FDA approval is granted for the stents. In determining the relative weights, CMS estimated that 21.5 percent of all FY 2003 stent patients would receive drug-eluting stents with increased charges of $3,996. We applied these assumptions to the CWCP cases.

We took the following changes in the DRG classification system into consideration by collapsing the new DRGs and determining a weighted average relative weight:

- **Craniotomy.** In FY 2002, the two DRGs for adult craniotomy procedures were restructured to split on the presence or absence of complications and comorbidities instead of the presence or absence of trauma. Mapping patients to the revised DRGs is difficult without a GROUPER; therefore, we used a weighted average relative weight of 3.1453 for the revised DRGs. A relatively small number of CWCP discharges is assigned to these DRGs.
- **Alcohol and Drug Abuse DRGs.** In FY 2002, the alcohol and drug abuse DRGs were restructured to first split on the presence or absence of CCs. The non-CC category was then split on the presence or absence of rehabilitation. This restructuring is not an issue for modeling the current CWCP payment system because these DRGs are excluded. Because the changes cannot be modeled easily without a GROUPER, we applied a weighted average relative weight of 0.61268 to estimate the potential impact of bringing these conditions under the DRG fee schedule.

B. Payment-to-Cost Ratios and Outlier Payments for CWCP Patients

This appendix presents the results of the analyses described in Chapter 2 regarding the payment-to-cost ratios and outlier payments that would have been made for California workers' compensation patients using Medicare payment rules in effect during 2000. It expands on the information presented in Table 2.1 by presenting the information for all DRGs with ten or more workers' compensation patients in 2000.

Table B.1
Average Cost per Discharge, Payment per Discharge, Payment-to-Cost Ratios, and Outlier Payments for CWCP Patients, Using 2000 Medicare Payment Rules

DRG	DRG Description	CWCP Stays (N)	% of Total Stays in DRG	Average Cost per Case ($)	Average Payment per Case ($)	Average Payment-to-Cost Ratio	Payment-to-Cost Ratio: 25th Percentile	Payment-to-Cost Ratio: 75th Percentile	Outlier Cases (N)	Average Outlier Payment ($)	Outlier Payment as % of Total Pay
1	CRANIOTOMY AGE >17 EXCEPT FOR TRAUMA	29	0.27	27,168	29,968	1.10	0.82	2.45	9	25,080	26.0
2	CRANIOTOMY FOR TRAUMA AGE >17	61	2.85	27,159	30,559	1.13	0.80	1.84	21	28,986	32.7
4	SPINAL PROCEDURES	280	10.56	9,264	17,009	1.84	1.51	5.15	19	28,390	11.3
5	EXTRACRANIAL VASCULAR PROCEDURES	29	0.26	7,528	9,886	1.31	1.27	1.86	1	23,210	8.1
6	CARPAL TUNNEL RELEASE	34	27.87	3,306	4,666	1.41	1.15	2.16	0		
7	PERIPH & CRANIAL NERVE & OTHER NERV SYST PROC W CC	37	1.73	9,341	15,427	1.65	1.16	3.81	0		
8	PERIPH & CRANIAL NERVE & OTHER NERV SYST PROC W/O CC	146	6.82	6,419	10,202	1.59	1.44	3.14	5	42,873	14.4
9	SPINAL DISORDERS & INJURIES	34	4.27	7,558	9,176	1.21	0.82	1.97	4	12,164	15.6
14	SPECIFIC CEREBROVASCULAR DISORDERS EXCEPT TIA [transischemic attack]	54	0.11	7,901	8,103	1.03	0.84	1.76	3	9,093	6.2
15	TRANSIENT ISCHEMIC ATTACK & PRECEREBRAL OCCLUSIONS	20	0.11	2,579	4,253	1.65	1.30	2.43	0		
18	CRANIAL & PERIPHERAL NERVE DISORDERS W CC	37	0.85	6,782	5,851	0.86	0.72	2.32	1	199	0.1
19	CRANIAL & PERIPHERAL NERVE DISORDERS W/O CC	69	3.47	3,714	4,086	1.10	1.01	2.43	0		
20	NERVOUS SYSTEM INFECTION EXCEPT VIRAL MENINGITIS	18	0.60	8,493	16,817	1.98	1.22	4.38	1	186	0.1
24	SEIZURE & HEADACHE AGE >17 W CC	36	0.35	4,436	5,827	1.31	1.05	2.46	0		
25	SEIZURE & HEADACHE AGE >17 W/O CC	99	1.22	3,107	3,497	1.13	0.92	2.27	0		
27	TRAUMATIC STUPOR & COMA, COMA >1 HR	33	2.02	13,624	13,558	1.00	0.96	1.82	6	23,407	31.4
28	TRAUMATIC STUPOR & COMA, COMA <1 HR AGE >17 W CC	40	1.42	9,011	9,490	1.05	0.80	1.79	4	7,702	8.1
29	TRAUMATIC STUPOR & COMA, COMA <1 HR AGE >17 W/O CC	130	6.59	5,566	4,891	0.88	0.65	1.65	4	6,958	4.4
31	CONCUSSION AGE >17 W CC	42	2.74	5,542	5,087	0.92	0.75	1.46	0		
32	CONCUSSION AGE >17 W/O CC	155	9.55	3,473	3,245	0.93	0.73	1.55	1	5,028	1.0

DRG	DRG Description	CWCP Stays (N)	% of Total Stays in DRG	Average Cost per Case ($)	Average Payment per Case ($)	Average Payment-to-Cost Ratio	Payment-to-Cost Ratio: 25th Percentile	Payment-to-Cost Ratio: 75th Percentile	Outlier Cases (N)	Average Outlier Payment ($)	Outlier Payment as % of Total Pay
34	OTHER DISORDERS OF NERVOUS SYSTEM W CC	23	0.54	8,895	8,529	0.96	0.76	2.22	2	24,183	24.7
35	OTHER DISORDERS OF NERVOUS SYSTEM W/O CC	20	1.12	3,878	3,517	0.91	0.65	1.77	0		
37	ORBITAL PROCEDURES	28	4.48	5,628	6,657	1.18	0.89	1.69	0		
40	EXTRAOCULAR PROCEDURES EXCEPT ORBIT AGE >17	14	3.65	5,780	6,224	1.08	1.05	1.88	1	4,423	5.1
42	INTRAOCULAR PROCEDURES EXCEPT RETINA, IRIS & LENS	32	6.56	4,122	4,298	1.04	1.07	1.47	0		
47	OTHER DISORDERS OF THE EYE AGE >17 W/O CC	13	2.47	1,983	3,122	1.57	1.29	2.21	0		
63	OTHER EAR, NOSE, MOUTH & THROAT O.R. PROCEDURES	48	1.34	7,704	9,131	1.19	1.02	1.73	3	11,126	7.6
72	NASAL TRAUMA & DEFORMITY	11	2.92	3,504	4,662	1.33	0.82	3.20	0		
73	OTHER EAR, NOSE, MOUTH & THROAT DIAGNOSES AGE >17	13	0.80	4,211	4,994	1.19	0.74	2.29	0		
75	MAJOR CHEST PROCEDURES	28	0.34	20,159	21,789	1.08	0.87	1.71	7	13,763	15.8
76	OTHER RESP SYSTEM O.R. PROCEDURES W CC	20	0.36	14,770	18,932	1.28	0.92	2.50	2	21,147	11.2
78	PULMONARY EMBOLISM	44	0.71	5,711	7,751	1.36	0.97	2.11	0		
79	RESPIRATORY INFECTIONS & INFLAMMATIONS AGE >17 W CC	26	0.11	13,338	11,676	0.88	0.66	1.87	6	7,201	14.2
83	MAJOR CHEST TRAUMA W CC	44	3.36	6,152	6,134	1.00	0.82	2.08	2	2,608	1.9
84	MAJOR CHEST TRAUMA W/O CC	26	4.40	4,201	3,493	0.83	0.60	1.14	1	432	0.5
88	CHRONIC OBSTRUCTIVE PULMONARY DISEASE	49	0.10	4,981	5,421	1.09	0.82	1.84	0		
89	SIMPLE PNEUMONIA & PLEURISY AGE >17 W CC	61	0.09	6,861	6,052	0.88	0.68	1.68	1	214	0.1
90	SIMPLE PNEUMONIA & PLEURISY AGE >17 W/O CC	17	0.16	4,095	3,912	0.96	0.79	1.28	0		
94	PNEUMOTHORAX W CC	29	1.03	7,947	8,698	1.09	0.84	1.96	2	11,751	9.3
95	PNEUMOTHORAX W/O CC	42	2.30	3,603	3,466	0.96	0.70	1.82	0		
97	BRONCHITIS & ASTHMA AGE >17 W/O CC	34	0.32	2,867	3,586	1.25	0.90	2.35	0		
100	RESPIRATORY SIGNS & SYMPTOMS W/O CC	18	0.62	2,737	3,062	1.12	0.75	2.13	0		

DRG	DRG Description	CWCP Stays (N)	% of Total Stays in DRG	Average Cost per Case ($)	Average Payment per Case ($)	Average Payment-to-Cost Ratio	Payment-to-Cost Ratio: 25th Percentile	Payment-to-Cost Ratio: 75th Percentile	Outlier Cases (N)	Average Outlier Payment ($)	Outlier Payment as % of Total Pay
101	OTHER RESPIRATORY SYSTEM DIAGNOSES W CC	59	1.49	5,594	5,695	1.02	0.76	1.69	4	5,535	6.6
102	OTHER RESPIRATORY SYSTEM DIAGNOSES W/O CC	69	2.76	3,925	3,736	0.95	0.82	1.41	0		
104	CARDIAC VALVE AND OTHER MAJOR CARDIOTHORACIC PROC W CARDIAC CATH	31	0.52	27,114	42,717	1.58	1.38	2.08	2	5,725	0.9
105	CARDIAC VALVE AND OTHER MAJOR CARDIOTHORACIC PROC W/ O CARDIAC CATH	18	0.30	25,775	35,965	1.40	1.31	1.69	3	17,479	8.1
107	CORONARY BYPASS W CARDIAC CATH.	66	0.41	27,048	36,525	1.35	1.10	1.63	14	31,436	18.3
109	CORONARY BYPASS W/O CARDIAC CATH OR PTCA	50	0.51	20,616	23,607	1.15	0.89	1.52	8	10,410	7.1
110	MAJOR CARDIOVASCULAR PROCEDURES W CC	21	0.28	22,137	30,765	1.39	0.95	3.36	3	45,971	21.3
112	PERCUTANEOUS CARDIOVASCULAR PROCEDURES	70	0.63	8,887	11,314	1.27	1.03	2.26	1	8,715	1.1
113	AMPUTATION FOR CIRC SYSTEM DISORDERS EXCEPT UPPER LIMB & TOE	12	0.24	14,488	19,050	1.31	0.92	3.80	1	18,262	8.0
116	OTH PERM CARDIAC PACEMAKER IMPLANT OR PTCA W CORONARY ART STENT	277	0.53	10,672	13,672	1.28	1.09	1.72	12	4,100	1.3
120	OTHER CIRCULATORY SYSTEM O.R. PROCEDURES	12	0.23	10,762	11,273	1.05	0.74	1.69	1	961	0.7
121	CIRCULATORY DISORDERS W AMI & MAJOR COMP DISCH ALIVE	18	0.08	6,482	7,297	1.13	0.91	1.62	5	1,512	5.8
122	CIRCULATORY DISORDERS W AMI W/O MAJOR COMP DISCH	48	0.30	5,867	6,747	1.15	0.81	1.84	8	6,542	16.2
124	CIRCULATORY DISORDERS EXCEPT AMI, W CARD CATH & COMPLEX DIAG	67	0.37	5,785	8,022	1.39	1.10	1.89	3	4,280	2.4
125	CIRCULATORY DISORDERS EXCEPT AMI, W CARD CATH W/ O COMPLEX DIAG	74	0.52	4,884	5,946	1.22	1.04	1.60	0		
127	HEART FAILURE & SHOCK	82	0.10	4,731	5,654	1.20	0.99	2.40	1	15,555	3.4
128	DEEP VEIN THROMBOPHLEBITIS	17	1.20	3,005	4,102	1.36	0.95	2.00	0		
130	PERIPHERAL VASCULAR DISORDERS W CC	67	0.52	5,739	6,812	1.19	0.98	2.15	2	49,023	21.5
131	PERIPHERAL VASCULAR DISORDERS W/O CC	83	1.67	3,871	3,650	0.94	0.72	1.72	2	7,441	4.9
132	ATHEROSCLEROSIS W CC	68	0.33	2,873	3,527	1.23	0.94	1.86	1	1,894	0.8

DRG	DRG Description	CWCP Stays (N)	% of Total Stays in DRG	Average Cost per Case ($)	Average Payment per Case ($)	Average Payment-to-Cost Ratio	Payment-to-Cost Ratio: 25th Percentile	Payment-to-Cost Ratio: 75th Percentile	Outlier Cases (N)	Average Outlier Payment ($)	Outlier Payment as % of Total Pay
133	ATHEROSCLEROSIS W/O CC	11	0.47	2,577	2,941	1.14	0.74	2.35	0		
134	HYPERTENSION	10	0.18	2,625	3,282	1.25	1.08	1.90	0		
138	CARDIAC ARRHYTHMIA & CONDUCTION DISORDERS W CC	49	0.20	4,463	5,455	1.22	1.31	3.11	4	11,619	17.4
139	CARDIAC ARRHYTHMIA & CONDUCTION DISORDERS W/O CC	57	0.37	2,142	2,765	1.29	1.02	2.17	0		
140	ANGINA PECTORIS	34	0.27	2,709	2,993	1.10	0.88	1.82	2	598	1.2
141	SYNCOPE & COLLAPSE W CC	19	0.18	2,555	4,193	1.64	1.32	2.27	0		
142	SYNCOPE & COLLAPSE W/O CC	45	0.59	2,703	3,223	1.19	0.87	1.64	0		
143	CHEST PAIN	228	0.39	2,356	3,147	1.34	1.08	2.01	0		
144	OTHER CIRCULATORY SYSTEM DX W CC	34	0.23	8,172	8,741	1.07	0.82	2.49	1	72,442	24.4
145	OTHER CIRCULATORY SYSTEM DX W/O CC	15	0.68	2,243	3,782	1.69	1.42	2.37	0		
148	MAJOR SMALL & LARGE BOWEL PROC W CC	38	0.18	18,454	27,552	1.49	0.93	2.17	6	45,183	25.9
149	MAJOR SMALL & LARGE BOWEL PROC W/O CC	10	0.17	9,919	10,117	1.02	0.92	1.41	0		
159	HERNIA PROCEDURES EXCEPT INGUINAL & FEMORAL AGE >17 W CC	36	1.37	6,092	8,198	1.35	1.14	2.44	1	16,928	5.7
160	HERNIA PROCEDURES EXCEPT INGUINAL & FEMORAL AGE >17 W/O CC	82	2.13	4,023	4,560	1.13	0.94	1.56	0		
162	INGUINAL & FEMORAL HERNIA PROC AGE >17 W/O CC	69	4.43	3,355	3,752	1.12	0.95	1.59	0		
174	G.I. HEMORRHAGE W CC	23	0.07	3,621	5,319	1.47	1.17	2.32	0		
180	G.I. OBSTRUCTION W CC	16	0.13	3,078	5,063	1.64	1.07	2.41	0		
181	G.I. OBSTRUCTION W/O CC	16	0.23	3,159	2,948	0.93	0.69	1.40	0		
182	ESOPHAGITIS, GASTROENT & MISC DIGEST DISORDERS AGE >17 W CC	57	0.16	2,934	4,388	1.50	0.99	2.75	0		
183	ESOPHAGITIS, GASTROENT & MISC DIGEST DISORDERS AGE >17 W/O CC	77	0.33	2,362	3,538	1.50	1.06	2.82	0		
185	DENTAL & ORAL DIS EXCEPT EXTRACTIONS & RESTORATIONS, AGE >17	25	1.12	5,624	6,147	1.09	0.84	1.99	1	6,439	4.2
188	OTHER DIGESTIVE SYSTEM DX [diagnosis] AGE >17 W CC	30	0.22	3,713	6,356	1.71	1.23	4.90	0		
189	OTHER DIGESTIVE SYSTEM DX AGE >17 W/O CC	20	0.48	3,148	3,602	1.14	0.91	2.76	0		

DRG	DRG Description	CWCP Stays (N)	% of Total Stays in DRG	Average Cost per Case ($)	Average Payment per Case ($)	Average Payment-to-Cost Ratio	Payment-to-Cost Ratio: 25th Percentile	Payment-to-Cost Ratio: 75th Percentile	Outlier Cases (N)	Average Outlier Payment ($)	Outlier Payment as % of Total Pay
204	DISORDERS OF PANCREAS EXCEPT MALIGNANCY	14	0.08	9,200	9,353	1.02	0.80	1.79	2	21,670	33.1
205	DISORDERS OF LIVER EXCEPT MALIG, CIRR, ALC HEPA W CC	14	0.19	5,224	7,668	1.47	0.84	2.84	0		
209	MAJOR JOINT & LIMB REATTACHMENT PROCEDURES OF LOWER EXTREMITY	1280	2.53	11,206	12,314	1.10	0.95	1.36	45	7,876	2.2
210	HIP & FEMUR PROCEDURES EXCEPT MAJOR JOINT AGE >17 W CC	111	0.81	12,999	12,607	0.97	0.78	1.36	16	10,839	12.4
211	HIP & FEMUR PROCEDURES EXCEPT MAJOR JOINT AGE >17 W/O CC	215	3.49	8,326	8,079	0.97	0.78	1.36	10	6,838	3.9
213	AMPUTATION FOR MUSCULOSDELETAL SYSTEM & CONN TISSUE DISORDERS	24	1.87	8,197	12,812	1.56	1.26	2.98	2	4,790	3.1
216	BIOPSIES OF MUSCULOSDELETAL SYSTEM & CONNECTIVE TISSUE	19	1.67	10,201	12,662	1.24	0.88	2.40	2	620	0.5
217	WND DEBRID & SKN GRFT EXCEPT HAND, FOR MUSCSDELET & CONN TISS DIS	370	7.39	14,319	21,683	1.51	1.14	3.93	53	26,929	17.8
218	LOWER EXTREM & HUMER PROC EXCEPT HIP, FOOT, FEMUR AGE >17 W CC	194	4.06	9,453	10,316	1.09	0.81	1.75	16	14,837	11.9
219	LOWER EXTREM & HUMER PROC EXCEPT HIP, FOOT, FEMUR AGE >17 W/O CC	1065	8.64	6,110	6,270	1.03	0.84	1.57	28	8,274	3.5
223	MAJOR SHOULDER/ELBOW PROC, OR OTHER UPPER EXTREMITY PROC W CC	556	14.90	4,083	5,395	1.32	1.05	2.04	3	2,587	0.3
224	SHOULDER, ELBOW OR FOREARM PROC, EXC MAJOR JOINT PROC, W/O CC	700	10.74	4,368	4,675	1.07	0.89	1.60	6	7,881	1.4
225	FOOT PROCEDURES	233	9.10	6,072	7,418	1.22	1.07	1.94	7	34,758	14.1
226	SOFT TISSUE PROCEDURES W CC	57	3.90	5,841	8,455	1.45	1.24	2.60	1	94	
227	SOFT TISSUE PROCEDURES W/O CC	344	10.92	4,497	5,035	1.12	0.95	1.67	4	26,656	6.2
228	MAJOR THUMB OR JOINT PROC, OR OTH HAND OR WRIST PROC W CC	92	10.63	5,125	6,448	1.26	1.02	2.23	2	8,967	3.0
229	HAND OR WRIST PROC, EXCEPT MAJOR JOINT PROC, W/O CC	385	18.79	4,622	5,407	1.17	0.99	1.84	7	47,307	15.9
230	LOCAL EXCISION & REMOVAL OF INT FIX DEVICES OF HIP & FEMUR	38	4.96	4,418	7,118	1.61	1.26	2.89	0		
231	LOCAL EXCISION & REMOVAL OF INT FIX DEVICES EXCEPT HIP & FEMUR	767	15.47	5,268	8,245	1.57	1.34	2.32	13	23,964	4.9

DRG	DRG Description	CWCP Stays (N)	% of Total Stays in DRG	Average Cost per Case ($)	Average Payment per Case ($)	Average Payment-to-Cost Ratio	Payment-to-Cost Ratio: 25th Percentile	Payment-to-Cost Ratio: 75th Percentile	Outlier Cases (N)	Average Outlier Payment ($)	Outlier Payment as % of Total Pay
232	ARTHROSCOPY	67	17.87	4,472	6,757	1.51	1.29	2.04	0		
233	OTHER MUSCULOSKELET SYS & CONN TISS O.R. PROC W CC	44	3.49	16,091	14,902	0.93	0.69	1.79	8	11,649	14.2
234	OTHER MUSCULOSKELET SYS & CONN TISS O.R. PROC W/O CC	124	7.49	7,639	8,121	1.06	0.80	2.10	6	14,066	8.4
235	FRACTURES OF FEMUR	13	0.85	4,778	4,588	0.96	0.81	1.43	0		
236	FRACTURES OF HIP & PELVIS	124	1.38	4,295	4,538	1.06	0.82	2.07	5	5,696	5.1
238	OSTEOMYELITIS	36	1.60	5,324	7,540	1.42	1.10	3.04	1	8,604	3.2
242	SEPTIC ARTHRITIS	20	2.43	5,406	6,554	1.21	1.02	2.74	1	13,362	10.2
243	MEDICAL BACK PROBLEMS	1126	6.19	3,298	4,303	1.30	1.03	2.83	10	8,214	1.7
244	BONE DISEASES & SPECIFIC ARTHROPATHIES W CC	24	0.90	4,099	4,847	1.18	1.00	1.78	1	13,933	12.0
245	BONE DISEASES & SPECIFIC ARTHROPATHIES W/O CC	91	3.06	2,320	2,739	1.18	0.93	2.02	0		
247	SIGNS & SYMPTOMS OF MUSCULOSKELETAL SYSTEM & CONN TISSUE	106	3.01	3,073	3,539	1.15	1.00	3.04	3	1,448	1.2
248	TENDONITIS, MYOSITIS & BURSITIS	62	2.43	2,526	4,710	1.86	1.42	3.54	1	3,040	1.0
249	AFTERCARE, MUSCULOSKELETAL SYSTEM & CONNECTIVE TISSUE	136	2.20	3,311	4,005	1.21	1.01	2.68	4	10,711	7.9
250	FX, SPRN, STRN & DISL OF FOREARM, HAND, FOOT AGE >17 W CC	24	3.14	4,217	4,453	1.06	0.74	2.12	0		
251	FX, SPRN, STRN & DISL OF FOREARM, HAND, FOOT AGE >17 W/O CC	101	7.76	3,123	3,186	1.02	0.87	2.51	0		
253	FX, SPRN, STRN & DISL OF UPARM, LOWLEG EX FOOT AGE >17 W CC	57	1.53	5,226	5,270	1.01	0.79	1.78	2	15,326	10.2
254	FX, SPRN, STRN & DISL OF UPARM, LOWLEG EX FOOT AGE >17 W/O CC	181	5.10	2,650	2,719	1.03	0.77	2.24	1	37	
256	OTHER MUSCULOSKELETAL SYSTEM & CONNECTIVE TISSUE DIAGNOSES	56	2.80	4,522	6,072	1.34	1.18	3.28	1	64,849	19.1
263	SKIN GRAFT &/OR DEBRID FOR SKN ULCER OR CELLULITIS W CC	40	1.12	12,975	15,312	1.18	0.99	2.48	4	25,589	16.7
264	SKIN GRAFT &/OR DEBRID FOR SKN ULCER OR CELLULITIS W/ O CC	38	3.81	4,633	6,706	1.45	1.17	2.36	0		
265	SKIN GRAFT &/OR DEBRID EXCEPT FOR SKIN ULCER OR CELLULITIS W CC	13	1.30	14,700	18,346	1.25	1.01	1.93	4	25,404	42.6

DRG	DRG Description	CWCP Stays (N)	% of Total Stays in DRG	Average Cost per Case ($)	Average Payment per Case ($)	Average Payment-to-Cost Ratio	Payment-to-Cost Ratio: 25th Percentile	Payment-to-Cost Ratio: 75th Percentile	Outlier Cases (N)	Average Outlier Payment ($)	Outlier Payment as % of Total Pay
266	SKIN GRAFT &/OR DEBRID EXCEPT FOR SKIN ULCER OR CELLULITIS W/O CC	81	5.79	6,199	6,205	1.00	0.82	2.00	3	13,608	8.1
268	SKIN, SUBCUTANEOUS TISSUE & BREAST PLASTIC PROCEDURES	18	1.38	4,086	8,238	2.02	1.81	2.45	0		
269	OTHER SKIN, SUBCUT TISS & BREAST PROC W CC	11	0.54	12,329	10,099	0.82	0.59	1.15	1	1,372	1.2
270	OTHER SKIN, SUBCUT TISS & BREAST PROC W/O CC	58	3.27	4,714	4,798	1.02	0.89	1.82	1	7,667	2.8
271	SKIN ULCERS	13	0.34	6,115	6,497	1.06	0.83	1.85	0		
277	CELLULITIS AGE >17 W CC	135	0.72	3,893	4,950	1.27	0.99	2.61	1	10,472	1.6
278	CELLULITIS AGE >17 W/O CC	310	3.01	2,649	3,386	1.28	0.95	2.29	2	755	0.1
280	TRAUMA TO THE SKIN, SUBCUT TISS & BREAST AGE >17 W C	54	1.26	3,331	4,415	1.33	0.95	2.29	0		
281	TRAUMA TO THE SKIN, SUBCUT TISS & BREAST AGE >17 W/O CC	208	4.70	3,066	3,073	1.00	0.74	1.94	0		
285	AMPUTAT OF LOWER LIMB FOR ENDOCRINE, NUTRIT, & METABOL DISORDERS	10	0.84	29,855	30,872	1.03	0.94	1.87	3	60,544	58.8
287	SKIN GRAFTS & WOUND DEBRID FOR ENDOC, NUTRIT & METAB DISORDERS	10	1.36	12,029	12,443	1.03	0.79	2.41	1	13,866	11.1
288	O.R. PROCEDURES FOR OBESITY	13	0.18	12,442	14,894	1.20	0.90	1.63	2	12,057	12.5
294	DIABETES AGE >35	19	0.10	4,919	4,668	0.95	1.01	1.67	0		
296	NUTRITIONAL & MISC METABOLIC DISORDERS AGE >17 W CC	31	0.10	5,217	5,788	1.11	0.87	2.27	1	34,988	19.5
297	NUTRITIONAL & MISC METABOLIC DISORDERS AGE >17 W/O CC	23	0.28	2,553	2,991	1.17	0.89	2.57	0		
313	URETHRAL PROCEDURES, AGE >17 W/O CC	11	3.69	4,962	5,102	1.03	0.86	1.33	0		
316	RENAL FAILURE	11	0.06	6,967	7,009	1.01	0.86	2.08	1	1,334	1.7
320	KIDNEY & URINARY TRACT INFECTIONS AGE >17 W CC	32	0.12	4,951	5,352	1.08	0.83	2.29	1	5,717	3.3
321	KIDNEY & URINARY TRACT INFECTIONS AGE >17 W/O CC	14	0.17	3,458	3,102	0.90	0.68	1.71	0		
331	OTHER KIDNEY & URINARY TRACT DIAGNOSES AGE >17 W CC	17	0.20	5,112	5,892	1.15	0.70	3.37	0		
332	OTHER KIDNEY & URINARY TRACT DIAGNOSES AGE >17 W/ O CC	10	0.64	3,253	4,190	1.29	0.95	2.09	0		

DRG	DRG Description	CWCP Stays (N)	% of Total Stays in DRG	Average Cost per Case ($)	Average Payment per Case ($)	Average Payment-to-Cost Ratio	Payment-to-Cost Ratio: 25th Percentile	Payment-to-Cost Ratio: 75th Percentile	Outlier Cases (N)	Average Outlier Payment ($)	Outlier Payment as % of Total Pay
339	TESTES PROCEDURES, NON- MALIGNANCY AGE >17	11	2.55	3,430	5,783	1.69	1.27	3.14	0		
350	INFLAMMATION OF THE MALE REPRODUCTIVE SYSTEM	11	0.73	2,474	4,104	1.66	1.28	3.66	0		
359	UTERINE & ADNEXA PROC FOR NON-MALIGNANCY W/O CC	19	0.04	5,001	4,612	0.92	0.78	1.08	0		
373	VAGINAL DELIVERY W/O COMPLICATING DIAGNOSES	19	0.01	1,954	2,200	1.13	0.96	1.77	0		
391	NORMAL NEWBORN	24	0.01	568	749	1.32	1.19	2.10	0		
395	RED BLOOD CELL DISORDERS AGE >17	16	0.10	4,198	4,752	1.13	1.89	3.12	0		
398	RETICULOENDOTHELIAL & IMMUNITY DISORDERS W CC	10	0.22	6,065	8,180	1.35	0.70	2.74	0		
415	O.R. PROCEDURE FOR INFECTIOUS & PARASITIC DISEASES	258	3.54	10,526	22,460	2.13	1.85	4.77	14	26,841	6.5
416	SEPTICEMIA AGE >17	40	0.15	8,823	11,052	1.25	0.97	2.76	4	26,003	23.5
418	POSTOPERATIVE & POST- TRAUMATIC INFECTIONS	185	2.72	4,208	5,956	1.42	1.10	2.95	1	9,895	0.9
423	OTHER INFECTIOUS & PARASITIC DISEASES DIAGNOSES	10	0.48	5,750	8,236	1.43	1.32	2.48	0		
425	ACUTE ADJUST REACT & DISTURBANCES OF PSYCHOSOCIAL DYSFUNCTION 13	15	0.47	3,728	3,872	1.04	0.74	1.43	0		
426	DEPRESSIVE NEUROSES.	14	0.18	1,831	3,449	1.88	1.47	5.19	0		
427	NEUROSES EXCEPT DEPRESSIVE.	12	0.51	2,277	3,923	1.72	1.21	8.27	0		
429	ORGANIC DISTURBANCES & MENTAL RETARDATION	14	0.28	4,552	5,082	1.12	0.82	2.06	0		
430	PSYCHOSES	170	0.19	6,124	6,298	1.03	0.84	3.65	14	20,102	26.3
434	ALC/DRUG ABUSE OR DEPEND, DETOX OR OTH SYMPT TREAT W CC.	16	0.19	5,345	4,349	0.81	0.60	1.46	0		
435	ALC/DRUG ABUSE OR DEPEND, DETOX OR OTH SYMPT TREAT W/ O CC	39	0.36	2,816	2,432	0.86	0.68	2.35	0		
439	SKIN GRAFTS FOR INJURIES	39	7.94	14,874	19,093	1.28	1.06	3.64	6	52,929	42.6
440	WOUND DEBRIDEMENTS FOR INJURIES	207	12.17	11,444	16,026	1.40	1.10	3.76	33	22,876	22.8
441	HAND PROCEDURES FOR INJURIES	302	34.53	6,529	6,888	1.05	0.76	2.31	22	10,783	11.4
442	OTHER O.R. PROC FOR INJURIES W CC	49	1.38	13,481	18,466	1.37	1.19	3.23	8	24,140	21.3
443	OTHER O.R. PROC FOR INJURIES W/O CC	149	6.45	5,437	6,486	1.19	0.95	2.09	4	20,572	8.5

DRG	DRG Description	CWCP Stays (N)	% of Total Stays in DRG	Average Cost per Case ($)	Average Payment per Case ($)	Average Payment-to-Cost Ratio	Payment-to-Cost Ratio: 25th Percentile	Payment-to-Cost Ratio: 75th Percentile	Outlier Cases (N)	Average Outlier Payment ($)	Outlier Payment as % of Total Pay
444	TRAUMATIC INJURY AGE >17 W CC	52	3.04	4,723	4,564	0.97	0.66	1.86	1	3,303	1.4
445	TRAUMATIC INJURY AGE >17 W/ O CC	206	9.98	3,022	3,296	1.09	0.77	2.30	0		
447	ALLERGIC REACTIONS AGE >17	18	1.27	2,133	3,139	1.47	1.15	3.52	1	1,756	3.1
449	POISONING & TOXIC EFFECTS OF DRUGS AGE >17 W CC	42	0.38	3,771	4,417	1.17	1.00	2.69	1	1,199	0.6
450	POISONING & TOXIC EFFECTS OF DRUGS AGE >17 W/O CC	110	2.16	2,431	2,570	1.06	0.81	2.37	0		
452	COMPLICATIONS OF TREATMENT W CC	28	0.56	4,410	5,898	1.34	0.95	2.29	1	210	0.1
453	COMPLICATIONS OF TREATMENT W/O CC	48	2.27	2,703	2,983	1.10	0.92	2.21	0		
454	OTHER INJURY, POISONING & TOXIC EFFECT DIAG W CC.	38	2.40	3,756	5,533	1.47	1.23	2.94	0		
455	OTHER INJURY, POISONING & TOXIC EFFECT DIAG W/O CC	99	6.08	2,810	3,160	1.12	0.88	2.29	0		
461	O.R. PROC W DIAGNOSES OF OTHER CONTACT W HEALTH SERVICES	76	2.60	11,526	12,949	1.12	1.01	1.86	10	43,220	43.9
462	REHABILITATION	768	1.85	10,731	11,189	1.04	0.78	2.55	93	25,149	27.2
466	AFTERCARE W/O HISTORY OF MALIGNANCY AS SECONDARY DIAGNOSIS	92	0.90	4,937	4,547	0.92	0.74	2.39	7	4,691	7.8
467	OTHER FACTORS INFLUENCING HEALTH STATUS	26	0.59	2,267	2,877	1.27	0.81	4.35	0		
468	EXTENSIVE O.R. PROCEDURE UNRELATED TO PRINCIPAL DIAGNOSIS	86	0.88	11,322	24,080	2.13	1.76	5.82	6	35,846	10.4
471	BILATERAL OR MULTIPLE MAJOR JOINT PROCS OF LOWER EXTREMITY	18	1.57	17,459	19,940	1.14	0.96	1.43	5	6,844	9.5
475	RESPIRATORY SYSTEM DIAGNOSIS WITH VENTILATOR SUPPORT	36	0.17	30,997	34,508	1.11	0.85	1.90	11	38,416	34.0
477	NON-EXTENSIVE O.R. PROCEDURE UNRELATED TO PRINCIPAL DIAGNOSIS.	57	1.41	5,407	10,453	1.93	1.53	3.23	1	2,631	0.4
478	OTHER VASCULAR PROCEDURES W CC	34	0.24	12,878	18,173	1.41	1.07	2.20	4	35,314	22.9
479	OTHER VASCULAR PROCEDURES W/ O CC	22	0.59	8,549	9,527	1.11	0.96	1.88	1	12,209	5.8
483	TRACHEOSTOMY EXCEPT FOR FACE, MOUTH & NECD DIAGNOSES	62	0.74	130,388	161,517	1.24	1.01	1.78	40	86,444	34.5
484	CRANIOTOMY FOR MULTIPLE SIGNIFICANT TRAUMA	14	4.55	53,462	68,249	1.28	1.12	1.90	8	58,805	49.2

DRG	DRG Description	CWCP Stays (N)	% of Total Stays in DRG	Average Cost per Case ($)	Average Payment per Case ($)	Average Payment-to-Cost Ratio	Payment-to-Cost Ratio: 25th Percentile	Payment-to-Cost Ratio: 75th Percentile	Outlier Cases (N)	Average Outlier Payment ($)	Outlier Payment as % of Total Pay
485	LIMB REATTACHMENT, HIP AND FEMUR PROC FOR MULTIPLE SIGNIFICANT TR	41	4.13	34,102	34,544	1.01	0.78	1.40	20	30,021	42.4
486	OTHER O.R. PROCEDURES FOR MULTIPLE SIGNIFICANT TRAUMA	106	3.74	37,488	47,552	1.27	0.94	2.14	34	45,077	30.4
487	OTHER MULTIPLE SIGNIFICANT TRAUMA	79	3.44	12,771	14,480	1.13	0.81	2.46	14	11,840	14.5
491	MAJOR JOINT & LIMB REATTACHMENT PROCEDURES OF UPPER EXTREMITY	104	5.75	8,836	10,416	1.18	0.95	1.51	4	15,258	5.6
496	COMBINED ANTERIOR/POSTERIOR SPINAL FUSION	543	35.31	20,077	33,682	1.68	1.45	2.29	47	12,233	3.1
497	SPINAL FUSION W CC	1071	18.09	16,067	17,968	1.12	0.87	1.65	130	11,421	7.7
498	SPINAL FUSION W/O CC	3490	26.07	10,803	11,126	1.03	0.82	1.54	289	7,619	5.7
499	BACK & NECK PROCS EXCEPT SPINAL FUSION W CC	443	8.16	7,240	8,658	1.20	1.02	1.84	17	7,048	3.1
500	BACK & NECK PROCS EXCEPT SPINAL FUSION W/O CC	3229	17.49	5,224	5,638	1.08	0.90	1.53	27	4,215	0.6
501	KNEE PROC W PDX OF INFECTION W CC	14	3.89	9,669	15,121	1.56	1.41	2.51	0		
502	KNEE PROC W PDX OF INFECTION W/O CC	18	8.60	8,503	9,102	1.07	0.92	1.74	2	2,343	2.9
503	KNEE PROCEDURES W/O PDX [principal diagnosis] OF INFECTION	657	13.36	5,884	7,065	1.20	0.96	1.83	7	14,228	2.1
504	EXTENSIVE 3RD DEGREE BURNS W SKIN GRAFT	17	11.72	80,375	115,473	1.44	1.10	2.16	7	52,107	18.6
506	FULL THICKNESS BURN W SKIN GRAFT OR INHAL INJ W CC OR SIG TRAUMA	51	12.17	28,959	35,133	1.21	0.94	1.94	11	25,983	16.0
507	FULL THICKNESS BURN W SKIN GRFT OR INHAL INJ W/O CC OR SIG TRAUMA	111	20.15	13,395	14,372	1.07	0.71	1.91	17	12,795	13.6
508	FULL THICKNESS BURN W/O SKIN GRFT OR INHAL INJ W CC OR SIG TRAUMA	15	8.15	10,780	14,516	1.35	0.69	2.49	2	27,399	25.2
509	FULL THICKNESS BURN W/O SKIN GRFT OR INH INJ W/O CC OR SIG TRAUMA	25	13.23	4,267	5,978	1.40	1.07	4.68	1	161	0.1
510	NON-EXTENSIVE BURNS W CC OR SIGNIFICANT TRAUMA	25	4.46	13,694	14,775	1.08	0.90	5.25	5	21,725	29.4
511	NON-EXTENSIVE BURNS W/O CC	152	12.07	5,797	7,158	1.23	1.11	3.51	14	12,254	15.8

SOURCE: Centers for Medicare and Medicaid Services, n.d.

NOTES: Blank cells in this table are not applicable to the category.

DRG titles listed here were in effect during FY 2000, or on the date the DRG was created, if later.

DRGs that were retitled during FY 2001–2003 are as follows.

DRGs 1 and 2 retitled effective FY 2003 to "Craniotomy > Age 17 with and without CC."

DRG 14 retitled effective FY 2003 to "Intracranial Hemorrhage and Stroke with Infarction"

DRG 15 retitled effective FY 2003 to "Nonspecific Cerebrovascular Accident and Precerebral Occlusion without Infarction."

DRGs 497 and 498 retitled effective FY 2002 as "Spinal Fusion Except Cervical with and without CC."

C. Medicare 2003 National Physician Fee Schedule Relative Value Units

The table in this appendix provides information on the relative values assigned to each component of the Medicare fee schedule for high-volume workers' compensation patients. It provides procedure-specific information to supplement the discussions in Chapter 3 on the physician fee schedule related to issues such as site-of-service differentials, global billing periods, and multiple procedure discounting. The list of high-volume procedures was identified by WCRI (Eccleston et al., 2002).

Table C.1
Medicare 2003 National Physician Fee Schedule Relative Value Units, Global Billing Period, and Multiple Procedure Discount Policies for High-Volume Workers' Compensation Procedures

HCPCS CODE	MODI-FIER CODE	DESCRIPTION	WORK RVU	NON-FACILITY PRAC-TICE EXPENSE RVU	FACILITY PRAC-TICE EXPENSE RVU	MAL-PRAC-TICE RVU	NON-FACILITY TOTAL	FACILITY TOTAL	GLOBAL DAYS[a]	MULTI. PROC.[b]
12001		Repair superficial wound(s)	1.7	2.16	0.44	0.13	3.99	2.27	10	2
12002		Repair superficial wound(s)	1.86	2.23	0.92	0.15	4.24	2.93	10	2
13102		Repair wound/lesion add-on	1.24	0.76	0.58	0.1	2.1	1.92	ZZZ	0
13132		Repair of wound or lesion	5.95	4.72	3.25	0.32	10.99	9.52	10	2
14040		Skin tissue rearrangement	7.87	8.77	7.05	0.55	17.19	15.47	90	2
15100		Skin split graft	9.05	11.7	8.09	0.94	21.69	18.08	90	2
15101		Skin split graft add-on	1.72	3.27	1.48	0.18	5.17	3.38	ZZZ	0
15240		Skin full graft	9.04	9.25	7.01	0.8	19.09	16.85	90	2
20550		Injured tendon sheath/ligament	0.75	0.76	0.24	0.06	1.57	1.05	0	2
20605		Drain/inject, joint/bursa	0.68	0.78	0.37	0.06	1.52	1.11	0	2
20610		Drain/inject, joint/bursa	0.79	0.97	0.42	0.08	1.84	1.29	0	2
20680		Removal of support implant	3.35	5.37	5.37	0.46	9.18	9.18	90	2
20937		Spinal bone autograft	2.79	1.49	1.49	0.43	4.71	4.71	ZZZ	0
22554		Neck spine fusion	18.62	12.63	12.63	3.51	34.76	34.76	90	2
22558		Lumbar spine fusion	22.28	13.4	13.4	3.18	38.86	38.86	90	2
22585		Additional spinal fusion	5.53	2.87	2.87	0.98	9.38	9.38	ZZZ	0
22612		Lumbar spine fusion	21	14.36	14.36	3.28	38.64	38.64	90	2
22614		Spine fusion, extra segment	6.44	3.44	3.44	1.04	10.92	10.92	ZZZ	0
22630		Lumbar spine fusion	20.84	14.01	14.01	3.79	38.64	38.64	90	2
22840		Insert spine fixation device	12.54	6.67	6.67	2.03	21.24	21.24	ZZZ	0
22842		Insert spine fixation device	12.58	6.69	6.69	2.04	21.31	21.31	ZZZ	0
22845		Insert spine fixation device	11.96	6.24	6.24	2.22	20.42	20.42	ZZZ	0
22851		Apply spine prosthetic device	6.71	3.45	3.45	1.11	11.27	11.27	ZZZ	0
23120		Partial removal, collar bone	7.11	9.97	9.97	0.99	18.07	18.07	90	2
23130		Remove shoulder bone, partial	7.55	10.2	10.2	1.06	18.81	18.81	90	2
23410		Repair rotator cuff, acute	12.45	12.81	12.81	1.72	26.98	26.98	90	2
23412		Repair rotator cuff, chronic	13.31	13.32	13.32	1.86	28.49	28.49	90	2
23420		Repair of shoulder	13.3	14.31	14.31	1.86	29.47	29.47	90	2
23455		Repair shoulder capsule	14.37	13.88	13.88	2.01	30.26	30.26	90	2
23466		Repair shoulder capsule	14.22	13.84	13.84	2	30.06	30.06	90	2
24356		Revision of tennis elbow	6.68	7.33	7.33	0.9	14.91	14.91	90	2
25000		Incision of tendon sheath	3.38	7.59	7.59	0.45	11.42	11.42	90	2
25111		Remove wrist tendon lesion	3.39	6.67	6.67	0.42	10.48	10.48	90	2
26055		Incise finger tendon sheath	2.69	15.46	3.59	0.36	18.51	6.64	90	2
26356		Repair finger/hand tendon	8.07	21.49	21.49	0.99	30.55	30.55	90	2
26418		Repair finger tendon	4.25	16.13	16.13	0.5	20.88	20.88	90	2
26735		Treat finger fracture, each	5.98	8.91	8.91	0.77	15.66	15.66	90	2
26765		Treat finger fracture, each	4.17	7.97	7.97	0.51	12.65	12.65	90	2
26951		Amputation of finger/ thumb	4.59	13.06	13.06	0.56	18.21	18.21	90	2
26952		Amputation of finger/ thumb	6.31	14.25	14.25	0.74	21.3	21.3	90	2
27425		Lat retinacular release open	5.22	7.58	7.58	0.73	13.53	13.53	90	2
27447		Total knee arthroplasty	21.48	14.82	14.82	3	39.3	39.3	90	2
27814		Treatment of ankle fracture	10.68	11.19	11.19	1.5	23.37	23.37	90	2
29822		Shoulder arthroscopy/	7.43	6.77	6.77	1.04	15.24	15.24	90	3

HCPCS CODE	MODI- FIER CODE	DESCRIPTION	WORK RVU	NON-FACILITY PRAC-TICE EXPENSE RVU	FACILITY PRAC-TICE EXPENSE RVU	MAL-PRAC-TICE RVU	NON-FACILITY TOTAL	FACILITY TOTAL	GLOBAL DAYS[a]	MULTI. PROC.[b]
		surgery								
29823		Shoulder arthroscopy/ surgery	8.17	7.32	7.32	1.15	16.64	16.64	90	3
29826		Shoulder arthroscopy/ surgery	8.99	7.63	7.63	1.26	17.88	17.88	90	3
29846		Wrist arthroscopy/surgery	6.75	6.19	6.19	0.89	13.83	13.83	90	3
29848		Wrist endoscopy/surgery	5.44	5.69	5.69	0.72	11.85	11.85	90	2
29870		Knee arthroscopy, dx	5.07	5	5	0.67	10.74	10.74	90	2
29875		Knee arthroscopy/surgery	6.31	5.98	5.98	0.88	13.17	13.17	90	3
29876		Knee arthroscopy/surgery	7.92	7.12	7.12	1.11	16.15	16.15	90	3
29877		Knee arthroscopy/surgery	7.35	6.81	6.81	1.03	15.19	15.19	90	3
29879		Knee arthroscopy/surgery	8.04	7.21	7.21	1.13	16.38	16.38	90	3
29880		Knee arthroscopy/surgery	8.5	7.46	7.46	1.19	17.15	17.15	90	3
29881		Knee arthroscopy/surgery	7.76	7.04	7.04	1.09	15.89	15.89	90	3
29882		Knee arthroscopy/surgery	8.65	7.34	7.34	1.09	17.08	17.08	90	3
29888		Knee arthroscopy/surgery	13.9	10.42	10.42	1.95	26.27	26.27	90	2
35207		Repair blood vessel lesion	10.15	9.76	9.76	1.15	21.06	21.06	90	2
49505		Prp i/hern init reduc>5 yr	7.6	4.48	4.01	0.65	12.73	12.26	90	2
49585		Rpr umbil hern, reduc > 5 yr	6.23	4.04	4.04	0.53	10.8	10.8	90	2
49650		Laparo hernia repair initial	6.27	3.23	3.23	0.64	10.14	10.14	90	2
62284		Injection for myelogram	1.54	5.07	0.61	0.1	6.71	2.25	0	0
62290		Inject for spine disk x-ray	3	8.54	1.29	0.2	11.74	4.49	0	2
62310		Inject spine c/t	1.91	4.91	0.51	0.11	6.93	2.53	0	2
62311		Inject spine l/s (cd)	1.54	5.02	0.45	0.09	6.65	2.08	0	2
63012		Removal of spinal lamina	15.4	10.45	10.45	2.71	28.56	28.56	90	2
63020		Neck spine disk surgery	14.81	10.08	10.08	2.89	27.78	27.78	90	2
63030		Low back disk surgery	12	8.75	8.75	2.21	22.96	22.96	90	2
63035		Spinal disk surgery add-on	3.15	1.63	1.63	0.57	5.35	5.35	ZZZ	0
63042		Laminotomy, single lumbar	17.47	11.71	11.71	3.11	32.29	32.29	90	2
63047		Removal of spinal lamina	14.61	10.23	10.23	2.61	27.45	27.45	90	2
63048		Remove spinal lamina add-on	3.26	1.71	1.71	0.58	5.55	5.55	ZZZ	0
63075		Neck spine disk surgery	19.41	12.53	12.53	3.73	35.67	35.67	90	2
63076		Neck spine disk surgery	4.05	2.11	2.11	0.78	6.94	6.94	ZZZ	0
63081		Removal of vertebral body	23.73	14.8	14.8	4.46	42.99	42.99	90	2
63090		Removal of vertebral body	28.16	16.4	16.4	4.27	48.83	48.83	90	2
63650		Implant neuroelectrodes	6.74	2.96	2.96	0.48	10.18	10.18	90	2
64450		N block, other peripheral	1.27	1.3	0.42	0.08	2.65	1.77	0	2
64475		Inj paravertebral l/s	1.41	4.65	0.48	0.09	6.15	1.98	0	2
64476		Inj paravertebral l/s add-on	0.98	1.86	0.25	0.06	2.9	1.29	ZZZ	0
64479		Inj foramen epidural c/t	2.2	7.32	0.73	0.14	9.66	3.07	0	2
64480		Inj foramen epidural add-on	1.54	2.36	0.48	0.09	3.99	2.11	ZZZ	0
64510		N block, stellate ganglion	1.22	3.19	0.38	0.07	4.48	1.67	0	2
64520		N block, lumbar/thoracic	1.35	4.54	0.42	0.08	5.97	1.85	0	2
64622		Destr paravertebrl nerve l/s	3	8.53	1.17	0.17	11.7	4.34	10	2
64708		Revise arm/leg nerve	6.12	5.12	5.12	0.82	12.06	12.06	90	2
64718		Revise ulnar nerve at elbow	5.99	5.3	5.3	0.87	12.16	12.16	90	2
64721		Carpal tunnel surgery	4.29	5.97	5.64	0.59	10.85	10.52	90	2
64722		Relieve pressure on nerve(s)	4.7	3.33	3.33	0.32	8.35	8.35	90	2
64831		Repair of digit nerve	9.44	7.24	7.24	1.14	17.82	17.82	90	2
65222		Remove foreign body from eye	0.93	0.78	0.28	0.04	1.75	1.25	0	2

HCPCS CODE	MODI-FIER CODE	DESCRIPTION	WORK RVU	NON-FACILITY PRAC-TICE EXPENSE RVU	FACILITY PRAC-TICE EXPENSE RVU	MAL-PRAC-TICE RVU	NON-FACILITY TOTAL	FACILITY TOTAL	GLOBAL DAYS[a]	MULTI. PROC.[b]
70450		Ct head/brain w/o dye	0.85	4.99	4.99	0.25	6.09	6.09	N/A	0
70450	TC	Ct head/brain w/o dye	0	4.7	4.7	0.21	4.91	4.91	N/A	0
70450	26	Ct head/brain w/o dye	0.85	0.29	0.29	0.04	1.18	1.18	N/A	0
70551		MRI brain w/o dye	1.48	11.67	11.67	0.56	13.71	13.71	N/A	0
70551	TC	MRI brain w/o dye	0	11.16	11.16	0.49	11.65	11.65	N/A	0
70551	26	MRI brain w/o dye	1.48	0.51	0.51	0.07	2.06	2.06	N/A	0
71020		Chest X-ray	0.22	0.69	0.69	0.04	0.95	0.95	N/A	0
71020	TC	Chest X-ray	0	0.62	0.62	0.03	0.65	0.65	N/A	0
71020	26	Chest X-ray	0.22	0.07	0.07	0.01	0.3	0.3	N/A	0
72040		X-ray exam of neck spine	0.22	0.67	0.67	0.04	0.93	0.93	N/A	0
72040	TC	X-ray exam of neck spine	0	0.6	0.6	0.03	0.63	0.63	N/A	0
72040	26	X-ray exam of neck spine	0.22	0.07	0.07	0.01	0.3	0.3	N/A	0
72050		X-ray exam of neck spine	0.31	1	1	0.07	1.38	1.38	N/A	0
72050	TC	X-ray exam of neck spine	0	0.89	0.89	0.05	0.94	0.94	N/A	0
72050	26	X-ray exam of neck spine	0.31	0.11	0.11	0.02	0.44	0.44	N/A	0
72052		X-ray exam of neck spine	0.36	1.24	1.24	0.07	1.67	1.67	N/A	0
72052	TC	X-ray exam of neck spine	0	1.12	1.12	0.05	1.17	1.17	N/A	0
72052	26	X-ray exam of neck spine	0.36	0.12	0.12	0.02	0.5	0.5	N/A	0
72070		X-ray exam of thoracic spine	0.22	0.72	0.72	0.04	0.98	0.98	N/A	0
72070	TC	X-ray exam of thoracic spine	0	0.65	0.65	0.03	0.68	0.68	N/A	0
72070	26	X-ray exam of thoracic spine	0.22	0.07	0.07	0.01	0.3	0.3	N/A	0
72100		X-ray exam of lower spine	0.22	0.75	0.75	0.05	1.02	1.02	N/A	0
72100	TC	X-ray exam of lower spine	0	0.67	0.67	0.03	0.7	0.7	N/A	0
72100	26	X-ray exam of lower spine	0.22	0.08	0.08	0.02	0.32	0.32	N/A	0
72110		X-ray exam of lower spine	0.31	1.02	1.02	0.07	1.4	1.4	N/A	0
72110	TC	X-ray exam of lower spine	0	0.91	0.91	0.05	0.96	0.96	N/A	0
72110	26	X-ray exam of lower spine	0.31	0.11	0.11	0.02	0.44	0.44	N/A	0
72125		Ct neck spine w/o dye	1.16	6.27	6.27	0.31	7.74	7.74	N/A	0
72125	TC	Ct neck spine w/o dye	0	5.88	5.88	0.26	6.14	6.14	N/A	0
72125	26	Ct neck spine w/o dye	1.16	0.39	0.39	0.05	1.6	1.6	N/A	0
72131		Ct lumbar spine w/o dye	1.16	6.28	6.28	0.31	7.75	7.75	N/A	0
72131	TC	Ct lumbar spine w/o dye	0	5.88	5.88	0.26	6.14	6.14	N/A	0
72131	26	Ct lumbar spine w/o dye	1.16	0.4	0.4	0.05	1.61	1.61	N/A	0
72132		Ct lumbar spine w/dye	1.22	7.45	7.45	0.37	9.04	9.04	N/A	0
72132	TC	Ct lumbar spine w/dye	0	7.04	7.04	0.31	7.35	7.35	N/A	0
72132	26	Ct lumbar spine w/dye	1.22	0.41	0.41	0.06	1.69	1.69	N/A	0
72141		MRI neck spine w/o dye	1.6	11.71	11.71	0.56	13.87	13.87	N/A	0
72141	TC	MRI neck spine w/o dye	0	11.16	11.16	0.49	11.65	11.65	N/A	0
72141	26	MRI neck spine w/o dye	1.6	0.55	0.55	0.07	2.22	2.22	N/A	0
72146		MRI chest spine w/o dye	1.6	12.94	12.94	0.6	15.14	15.14	N/A	0
72146	TC	MRI chest spine w/o dye	0	12.39	12.39	0.53	12.92	12.92	N/A	0
72146	26	MRI chest spine w/o dye	1.6	0.55	0.55	0.07	2.22	2.22	N/A	0
72148		MRI lumbar spine w/o dye	1.48	12.9	12.9	0.6	14.98	14.98	N/A	0
72148	TC	MRI lumbar spine w/o dye	0	12.39	12.39	0.53	12.92	12.92	N/A	0
72148	26	MRI lumbar spine w/o dye	1.48	0.51	0.51	0.07	2.06	2.06	N/A	0
72158		MRI lumbar spine w/o & w/dye	2.36	25.59	25.59	1.2	29.15	29.15	N/A	0
72158	TC	MRI lumbar spine w/o & w/dye	0	24.78	24.78	1.09	25.87	25.87	N/A	0
72158	26	MRI lumbar spine w/o & w/dye	2.36	0.81	0.81	0.11	3.28	3.28	N/A	0
72265		Contrast X-ray, lower spine	0.83	4.31	4.31	0.22	5.36	5.36	N/A	0
72265	TC	Contrast X-ray, lower spine	0	4.05	4.05	0.18	4.23	4.23	N/A	0

HCPCS CODE	MODI- FIER CODE	DESCRIPTION	WORK RVU	NON-FACILITY PRAC-TICE EXPENSE RVU	FACILITY PRAC-TICE EXPENSE RVU	MAL-PRAC-TICE RVU	NON-FACILITY TOTAL	FACILITY TOTAL	GLOBAL DAYS[a]	MULTI. PROC.[b]
72265	26	Contrast X-ray, lower spine	0.83	0.26	0.26	0.04	1.13	1.13	N/A	0
73030		X-ray exam of shoulder	0.18	0.63	0.63	0.04	0.85	0.85	N/A	0
73030	TC	X-ray exam of shoulder	0	0.57	0.57	0.03	0.6	0.6	N/A	0
73030	26	X-ray exam of shoulder	0.18	0.06	0.06	0.01	0.25	0.25	N/A	0
73110		X-ray exam of wrist	0.17	0.59	0.59	0.03	0.79	0.79	N/A	0
73110	TC	X-ray exam of wrist	0	0.53	0.53	0.02	0.55	0.55	N/A	0
73110	26	X-ray exam of wrist	0.17	0.06	0.06	0.01	0.24	0.24	N/A	0
73130		X-ray exam of hand	0.17	0.59	0.59	0.03	0.79	0.79	N/A	0
73130	TC	X-ray exam of hand	0	0.53	0.53	0.02	0.55	0.55	N/A	0
73130	26	X-ray exam of hand	0.17	0.06	0.06	0.01	0.24	0.24	N/A	0
73140		X-ray exam of finger(s)	0.13	0.46	0.46	0.03	0.62	0.62	N/A	0
73140	TC	X-ray exam of finger(s)	0	0.42	0.42	0.02	0.44	0.44	N/A	0
73140	26	X-ray exam of finger(s)	0.13	0.04	0.04	0.01	0.18	0.18	N/A	0
73220		MRI upper extremity w/o & w/dye	2.15	25.52	25.52	0.78	28.45	28.45	N/A	0
73220	TC	MRI upper extremity w/o&w/dye	0	24.78	24.78	0.7	25.48	25.48	N/A	0
73220	26	MRI uppr extremity w/o&w/dye	2.15	0.74	0.74	0.08	2.97	2.97	N/A	0
73221		MRI joint upper extremity w/o dye	1.35	11.62	11.62	0.36	13.33	13.33	N/A	0
73221	TC	MRI joint upr extremity w/o dye	0	11.16	11.16	0.32	11.48	11.48	N/A	0
73221	26	MRI joint upper extremity w/o dye	1.35	0.46	0.46	0.04	1.85	1.85	N/A	0
73560		X-ray exam of knee, 1 or 2	0.17	0.58	0.58	0.04	0.79	0.79	N/A	0
73560	TC	X-ray exam of knee, 1 or 2	0	0.52	0.52	0.02	0.54	0.54	N/A	0
73560	26	X-ray exam of knee, 1 or 2	0.17	0.06	0.06	0.02	0.25	0.25	N/A	0
73562		X-ray exam of knee, 3	0.18	0.63	0.63	0.05	0.86	0.86	N/A	0
73562	TC	X-ray exam of knee, 3	0	0.57	0.57	0.03	0.6	0.6	N/A	0
73562	26	X-ray exam of knee, 3	0.18	0.06	0.06	0.02	0.26	0.26	N/A	0
73564		X-ray exam, knee, 4 or more	0.22	0.7	0.7	0.05	0.97	0.97	N/A	0
73564	TC	X-ray exam, knee, 4 or more	0	0.62	0.62	0.03	0.65	0.65	N/A	0
73564	26	X-ray exam, knee, 4 or more	0.22	0.08	0.08	0.02	0.32	0.32	N/A	0
73610		X-ray exam of ankle	0.17	0.59	0.59	0.03	0.79	0.79	N/A	0
73610	TC	X-ray exam of ankle	0	0.53	0.53	0.02	0.55	0.55	N/A	0
73610	26	X-ray exam of ankle	0.17	0.06	0.06	0.01	0.24	0.24	N/A	0
73630		X-ray exam of foot	0.17	0.59	0.59	0.03	0.79	0.79	N/A	0
73630	TC	X-ray exam of foot	0	0.53	0.53	0.02	0.55	0.55	N/A	0
73630	26	X-ray exam of foot	0.17	0.06	0.06	0.01	0.24	0.24	N/A	0
73720		MRI lowr extremity w/o & w/dye	2.15	25.51	25.51	0.78	28.44	28.44	N/A	0
73720	TC	MRI lower extremity w/o & w/dye	0	24.78	24.78	0.7	25.48	25.48	N/A	0
73720	26	MRI lower extremity w/o & w/dye	2.15	0.73	0.73	0.08	2.96	2.96	N/A	0
73721		MRI jnt of lowr extremity w/o dye	1.35	11.62	11.62	0.36	13.33	13.33	N/A	0
73721	TC	MRI jnt of lower extremity w/o dye	0	11.16	11.16	0.32	11.48	11.48	N/A	0
73721	26	MRI jnt of lower extremity w/o dye	1.35	0.46	0.46	0.04	1.85	1.85	N/A	0
90780		IV infusion therapy, 1 hour	0	1.1	1.1	0.06	1.16	1.16	N/A	0
90782		Injection, sc/im	0	0.11	0.11	0.01	0.12	0.12	N/A	0
90801		Psy dx interview	2.8	1.19	0.96	0.06	4.05	3.82	N/A	0
90806		Psytx, off, 45-50 min	1.86	0.72	0.62	0.04	2.62	2.52	N/A	0
90807		Psytx, off, 45-50 min w/e&m	2.02	0.72	0.65	0.05	2.79	2.72	N/A	0
90808		Psytx, office, 75-80 min	2.79	1.05	0.93	0.07	3.91	3.79	N/A	0
90853		Group psychotherapy	0.59	0.26	0.24	0.01	0.86	0.84	N/A	0
90862		Medication management	0.95	0.41	0.33	0.02	1.38	1.3	N/A	0
90901		Biofeedback train, any meth	0.41	0.86	0.19	0.02	1.29	0.62	0	0
92002		Eye exam, new patient	0.88	0.94	0.35	0.02	1.84	1.25	N/A	0

HCPCS CODE	MODIFIER CODE	DESCRIPTION	WORK RVU	NON-FACILITY PRACTICE EXPENSE RVU	FACILITY PRACTICE EXPENSE RVU	MALPRACTICE RVU	NON-FACILITY TOTAL	FACILITY TOTAL	GLOBAL DAYS[a]	MULTI. PROC.[b]
92004		Eye exam, new patient	1.67	1.66	0.7	0.03	3.36	2.4	N/A	0
92012		Eye exam established pat	0.67	0.99	0.3	0.01	1.67	0.98	N/A	0
93000		Electrocardiogram, complete	0.17	0.51	0.51	0.03	0.71	0.71	N/A	0
93005		Electrocardiogram, tracing	0	0.45	0.45	0.02	0.47	0.47	N/A	0
93010		Electrocardiogram report	0.17	0.06	0.06	0.01	0.24	0.24	N/A	0
95831		Limb muscle testing, manual	0.28	0.53	0.13	0.01	0.82	0.42	N/A	0
95851		Range of motion measurements	0.16	0.57	0.08	0.01	0.74	0.25	N/A	0
95860		Muscle test, one limb	0.96	1.62	1.62	0.05	2.63	2.63	N/A	0
95860	TC	Muscle test, one limb	0	1.19	1.19	0.02	1.21	1.21	N/A	0
95860	26	Muscle test, one limb	0.96	0.43	0.43	0.03	1.42	1.42	N/A	0
95861		Muscle test, 2 limbs	1.54	1.44	1.44	0.1	3.08	3.08	N/A	0
95861	TC	Muscle test, 2 limbs	0	0.74	0.74	0.05	0.79	0.79	N/A	0
95861	26	Muscle test, 2 limbs	1.54	0.7	0.7	0.05	2.29	2.29	N/A	0
95900		Motor nerve conduction test	0.42	1.12	1.12	0.03	1.57	1.57	N/A	0
95900	TC	Motor nerve conduction test	0	0.93	0.93	0.02	0.95	0.95	N/A	0
95900	26	Motor nerve conduction test	0.42	0.19	0.19	0.01	0.62	0.62	N/A	0
95903		Motor nerve conduction test	0.6	1.07	1.07	0.04	1.71	1.71	N/A	0
95903	TC	Motor nerve conduction test	0	0.8	0.8	0.02	0.82	0.82	N/A	0
95903	26	Motor nerve conduction test	0.6	0.27	0.27	0.02	0.89	0.89	N/A	0
95904		Sense nerve conduction test	0.34	0.95	0.95	0.03	1.32	1.32	N/A	0
95904	TC	Sense nerve conduction test	0	0.8	0.8	0.02	0.82	0.82	N/A	0
95904	26	Sense nerve conduction test	0.34	0.15	0.15	0.01	0.5	0.5	N/A	0
95920		Intraop nerve test add-on	2.11	2.26	2.26	0.2	4.57	4.57	ZZZ	0
95920	TC	Intraop nerve test add-on	0	1.3	1.3	0.06	1.36	1.36	ZZZ	0
95920	26	Intraop nerve test add-on	2.11	0.96	0.96	0.14	3.21	3.21	ZZZ	0
95925		Somatosensory testing	0.54	1.14	1.14	0.07	1.75	1.75	N/A	0
95925	TC	Somatosensory testing	0	0.91	0.91	0.05	0.96	0.96	N/A	0
95925	26	Somatosensory testing	0.54	0.23	0.23	0.02	0.79	0.79	N/A	0
95934		H-reflex test	0.51	0.44	0.44	0.04	0.99	0.99	N/A	0
95934	TC	H-reflex test	0	0.21	0.21	0.02	0.23	0.23	N/A	0
95934	26	H-reflex test	0.51	0.23	0.23	0.02	0.76	0.76	N/A	0
96100		Psychological testing	0	1.75	1.75	0.15	1.9	1.9	N/A	0
96117		Neuropsych test battery	0	1.75	1.75	0.15	1.9	1.9	N/A	0
97010		Hot or cold packs therapy	0.06	0.05	0.05	0.01	0.12	0.12	N/A	9
97014		Electric stimulation therapy	0.18	0.19	0.19	0.01	0.38	0.38	N/A	9
97035		Ultrasound therapy	0.21	0.11	0.11	0.01	0.33	0.33	N/A	0
97110		Therapeutic exercises	0.45	0.28	0.28	0.03	0.76	0.76	N/A	0
97124		Massage therapy	0.35	0.24	0.24	0.01	0.6	0.6	N/A	0
97140		Manual therapy	0.43	0.27	0.27	0.02	0.72	0.72	N/A	0
97530		Therapeutic activities	0.44	0.31	0.31	0.02	0.77	0.77	N/A	0
97750		Physical performance test	0.45	0.31	0.31	0.02	0.78	0.78	N/A	0
98940		Chiropractic manipulation	0.45	0.24	0.13	0.01	0.7	0.59	0	0
99183		Hyperbaric oxygen therapy	2.34	0.75	0.75	0.12	3.21	3.21	N/A	0
99203		Office/outpatient visit, new	1.34	1.1	0.49	0.08	2.52	1.91	N/A	0
99204		Office/outpatient visit, new	2	1.49	0.72	0.1	3.59	2.82	N/A	0
99205		Office/outpatient visit, new	2.67	1.79	0.95	0.12	4.58	3.74	N/A	0
99212		Office/outpatient visit, est	0.45	0.52	0.16	0.02	0.99	0.63	N/A	0
99213		Office/outpatient visit, est	0.67	0.69	0.24	0.03	1.39	0.94	N/A	0
99214		Office/outpatient visit, est	1.1	1.03	0.4	0.04	2.17	1.54	N/A	0
99215		Office/outpatient visit, est	1.77	1.34	0.64	0.07	3.18	2.48	N/A	0

HCPCS CODE	MODIFIER CODE	DESCRIPTION	WORK RVU	NON-FACILITY PRACTICE EXPENSE RVU	FACILITY PRACTICE EXPENSE RVU	MALPRACTICE RVU	NON-FACILITY TOTAL	FACILITY TOTAL	GLOBAL DAYS[a]	MULTI. PROC.[b]
99244		Office consultation	2.58	1.8	0.94	0.13	4.51	3.65	N/A	0
99245		Office consultation	3.43	2.26	1.24	0.16	5.85	4.83	N/A	0
99283		Emergency dept visit	1.24	0.32	0.32	0.08	1.64	1.64	N/A	0

NOTES: REVISED 2/28/2003.

Modifier:

TC = Technical component only.

26 = Professional component only.

[a]Number of days in global billing period for surgical procedures.

ZZZ = Code is part of another service and falls within the global period for that service

N/A = Not applicable.

[b]Multiple procedure discounting policy:

0 = Does not apply.

2 = Standard payment adjustment rules apply.

3 = Special rules for multiple endoscopic procedures apply if procedure is billed with another endoscopy in the same family.

D. Schedule of Payments for High-Volume Workers' Compensation Ambulatory Procedures

The table in this appendix compares Medicare 2003 facility payments for high-volume workers' compensation ambulatory procedures across different settings. It supplements the discussion in Chapter 4 on site-of-service differentials. For physician services, the incremental facility payment is the difference between the payment for a given procedure when it is furnished in a non-facility setting, e.g., a physician's office, and when it is furnished in a facility setting. All payment amounts are based on the Medicare 2003 national payment rate adjusted by an estimated average geographic adjustment factor for California providers. The high-volume procedures were identified by WCRI (Eccleston et al., 2002).

Table D.1
Schedule of Payments for High-Volume Workers' Compensation Ambulatory Procedures

HCPCS	DESCRIPTION	Facility PE RVU	Non-Facility PE RVU	Incre-mental Facility Payment ($)	Outpatient PPS Status Codes, Classification Groups, Relative Weights, and Payment Rates: Status Code[a]	APC	Relative Weight	Payment Rate ($)	ASC Payment Groups and Payment Rates: Group	Payment Rate ($)
12001	Repair superficial wound(s)	0.44	2.16	67	T	0024	1.8507	96.52		
12002	Repair superficial wound(s)	0.92	2.23	51	T	0024	1.8507	96.52		
13102	Repair wound/lesion add-on	0.58	0.76	7	T	0024	1.8507	96.52		
13132	Repair of wound or lesion	3.25	4.72	57	T	0024	1.8507	96.52	3	547
14040	Skin tissue rearrangement	7.05	8.77	67	T	0027	15.2225	793.87	2	478
15100	Skin split graft	8.09	11.7	141	T	0027	15.2225	793.87	2	478
15101	Skin split graft add-on	1.48	3.27	70	T	0027	15.2225	793.87	3	547
15240	Skin full graft	7.01	9.25	87	T	0027	15.2225	793.87	3	547
20550	Inj tendon sheath/ ligament	0.24	0.76	20	T	0204	2.0251	105.61		
20605	Drain/inject, joint/ bursa	0.37	0.78	16	T	0204	2.0251	105.61		
20610	Drain/inject, joint/ bursa	0.42	0.97	21	T	0204	2.0251	105.61		
20680	Removal of support implant	5.37	5.37	0	T	0022	17.393	907.06	3	547
20937	Spinal bone autograft	1.49	1.49	0	C	0	0	0		
22554	Neck spine fusion	12.63	12.63	0	C	0	0	0		
22558	Lumbar spine fusion	13.4	13.4	0	C	0	0	0		
22585	Additional spinal fusion	2.87	2.87	0	C	0	0	0		
22612	Lumbar spine fusion	14.36	14.36	0	T	0208	38.4487	2005.14		
22614	Spine fusion, extra segment	3.44	3.44	0	T	0208	38.4487	2005.14		
22630	Lumbar spine fusion	14.01	14.01	0	C	0	0	0		
22840	Insert spine fixation device	6.67	6.67	0	C	0	0	0		
22842	Insert spine fixation device	6.69	6.69	0	C	0	0	0		
22845	Insert spine fixation device	6.24	6.24	0	C	0	0	0		
22851	Apply spine prosthetic device	3.45	3.45	0	C	0	0	0		
23120	Partial removal, collar bone	9.97	9.97	0	T	0051	32.9062	1716.09	5	769
23130	Remove shoulder bone, part [partial?]	10.2	10.2	0	T	0051	32.9062	1716.09	5	769
23410	Repair rotator cuff, acute	12.81	12.81	0	T	0052	40.7646	2125.91	5	769
23412	Repair rotator cuff, chronic	13.32	13.32	0	T	0052	40.7646	2125.91	7	1067
23420	Repair of shoulder	14.31	14.31	0	T	0052	40.7646	2125.91	7	1067
23455	Repair shoulder capsule	13.88	13.88	0	T	0052	40.7646	2125.91	7	1067
23466	Repair shoulder capsule	13.84	13.84	0	T	0052	40.7646	2125.91	7	1067
24356	Revision of tennis elbow	7.33	7.33	0	T	0050	23.3037	1215.31	3	547
25000	Incision of tendon sheath	7.59	7.59	0	T	0049	18.6042	970.23	3	547
25111	Remove wrist tendon lesion	6.67	6.67	0	T	0053	14.176	739.29	3	547
26055	Incise finger tendon sheath	3.59	15.46	463	T	0053	14.176	739.29	2	478
26356	Repair finger/hand tendon	21.49	21.49	0	T	0054	22.7223	1184.99	4	676
26418	Repair finger tendon	16.13	16.13	0	T	0053	14.176	739.29	4	676
26735	Treat finger fracture, each	8.91	8.91	0	T	0046	29.292	1527.61	4	676
26765	Treat finger fracture, each	7.97	7.97	0	T	0046	29.292	1527.61	4	676
26951	Amputation of finger/ thumb	13.06	13.06	0	T	0053	14.176	739.29	2	478
26952	Amputation of finger/ thumb	14.25	14.25	0	T	0053	14.176	739.29	4	676
27425	Lat retinacular release open	7.58	7.58	0	T	0050	23.3037	1215.31	7	1067
27447	Total knee arthroplasty	14.82	14.82	0	C	0	0	0		
27814	Treatment of ankle fracture	11.19	11.19	0	T	0046	29.2920	1527.61	3	547
29822	Shoulder arthroscopy/ surgery	6.77	6.77	0	T	0041	26.1234	1362.36	3	547

					Outpatient PPS Status Codes, Classification Groups, Relative Weights, and Payment Rates				ASC Payment Groups and Payment Rates	
HCPCS	DESCRIPTION	Facility PE RVU	Non-Facility PE RVU	Incremental Facility Payment ($)	Status Code[a]	APC	Relative Weight	Payment Rate ($)	Group	Payment Rate ($)
29823	Shoulder arthroscopy/ surgery	7.32	7.32	0	T	0041	26.1234	1362.36	3	547
29826	Shoulder arthroscopy/ surgery	7.63	7.63	0	T	0042	40.968	2136.52	3	547
29846	Wrist arthroscopy/ surgery	6.19	6.19	0	T	0041	26.1234	1362.36	3	547
29848	Wrist endoscopy/ surgery	5.69	5.69	0	T	0041	26.1234	1362.36	9	1436
29870	Knee arthroscopy, dx	5	5	0	T	0041	26.1234	1362.36	3	547
29875	Knee arthroscopy/ surgery	5.98	5.98	0	T	0041	26.1234	1362.36	4	676
29876	Knee arthroscopy/ surgery	7.12	7.12	0	T	0041	26.1234	1362.36	4	676
29877	Knee arthroscopy/ surgery	6.81	6.81	0	T	0041	26.1234	1362.36	4	676
29879	Knee arthroscopy/ surgery	7.21	7.21	0	T	0041	26.1234	1362.36	3	547
29880	Knee arthroscopy/ surgery	7.46	7.46	0	T	0041	26.1234	1362.36	4	676
29881	Knee arthroscopy/ surgery	7.04	7.04	0	T	0041	26.1234	1362.36	4	676
29882	Knee arthroscopy/ surgery	7.34	7.34	0	T	0041	26.1234	1362.36	3	547
29888	Knee arthroscopy/ surgery	10.42	10.42	0	T	0042	40.968	2136.52	3	547
35207	Repair blood vessel lesion	9.76	9.76	0	T	0088	32.5768	1698.91	4	676
49505	Prp i/hern init reduc>5 yr	4.01	4.48	18	T	0154	25.7262	1341.65	4	676
49585	Rpr umbil hern, reduc > 5 yr	4.04	4.04	0	T	0154	25.7262	1341.65	4	676
49650	Laparo hernia repair initial	3.23	3.23	0	T	0131	40.2026	2096.61	4	676
62284	Injection for myelogram	0.61	5.07	174	N	0	0	0		
62290	Inject for spine disk x-ray	1.29	8.54	283	N	0	0	0		
62310	Inject spine c/t	0.51	4.91	172	T	0206	4.7867	249.63	1	357
62311	Inject spine l/s (cd)	0.45	5.02	178	T	0206	4.7867	249.63	1	357
63012	Removal of spinal lamina	10.45	10.45	0	T	0208	38.4487	2005.14		
63020	Neck spine disk surgery	10.08	10.08	0	T	0208	38.4487	2005.14		
63030	Low back disk surgery	8.75	8.75	0	T	0208	38.4487	2005.14		
63035	Spinal disk surgery add-on	1.63	1.63	0	T	0208	38.4487	2005.14		
63042	Laminotomy, single lumbar	11.71	11.71	0	T	0208	38.4487	2005.14		
63047	Removal of spinal lamina	10.23	10.23	0	T	0208	38.4487	2005.14		
63048	Remove spinal lamina add-on	1.71	1.71	0	T	0208	38.4487	2005.14		
63075	Neck spine disk surgery	12.53	12.53	0	C	0	0	0		
63076	Neck spine disk surgery	2.11	2.11	0	C	0	0	0		
63081	Removal of vertebral body	14.8	14.8	0	C	0	0	0		
63090	Removal of vertebral body	16.4	16.4	0	C	0	0	0		
63650	Implant neuroelectrodes	2.96	2.96	0	S	0225	139.3379	7266.61	2	478
64450	N block, other peripheral	0.42	1.3	34	T	0204	2.0251	105.61		
64475	Inj paravertebral l/s	0.48	4.65	163	T	0207	5.7654	300.67	1	357
64476	Inj paravertebral l/s add-on	0.25	1.86	63	T	0207	5.7654	300.67	1	357
64479	Inj foramen epidural c/t	0.73	7.32	257	T	0207	5.7654	300.67	1	357
64480	Inj foramen epidural add-on	0.48	2.36	73	T	0207	5.7654	300.67	1	357
64510	N block, stellate ganglion	0.38	3.19	110	T	0207	5.7654	300.67	1	357
64520	N block, lumbar/thoracic	0.42	4.54	161	T	0207	5.7654	300.67	1	357
64622	Destr paravertebrl nerve l/s	1.17	8.53	287	T	0203	11.7924	614.99	1	357
64708	Revise arm/leg nerve	5.12	5.12	0	T	0220	15.8136	824.7	2	478

					Outpatient PPS Status Codes, Classification Groups, Relative Weights, and Payment Rates				ASC Payment Groups and Payment Rates	
HCPCS	DESCRIPTION	Facility PE RVU	Non-Facility PE RVU	Incre-mental Facility Payment ($)	Status Code[a]	APC	Relative Weight	Payment Rate ($)	Group	Payment Rate ($)
64718	Revise ulnar nerve at elbow	5.3	5.3	0	T	0220	15.8136	824.7	2	478
64721	Carpal tunnel surgery	5.64	5.97	13	T	0220	15.8136	824.7	2	478
64722	Relieve pressure on nerve(s)	3.33	3.33	0	T	0220	15.8136	824.7	1	357
64831	Repair of digit nerve	7.24	7.24	0	T	0221	21.5208	1122.33	4	676
65222	Remove foreign body from eye	0.28	0.78	19	S	0231	2.1705	113.19		
70450	Ct head/brain w/o dye	4.99	4.99	0	S	0332	3.4398	179.39		
70450	Ct head/brain w/o dye	4.7	4.7	0	S	0332	3.4398	179.39		
70450	Ct head/brain w/o dye	0.29	0.29	0	S	0332	3.4398	179.39		
70551	MRI brain w/o dye	11.67	11.67	0	S	0336	6.5987	344.13		
70551	MRI brain w/o dye	11.16	11.16	0	S	0336	6.5987	344.13		
70551	MRI brain w/o dye	0.51	0.51	0	S	0336	6.5987	344.13		
71020	Chest x-ray	0.69	0.69	0	X	0260	0.7655	39.92		
71020	Chest x-ray	0.62	0.62	0	X	0260	0.7655	39.92		
71020	Chest x-ray	0.07	0.07	0	X	0260	0.7655	39.92		
72040	X-ray exam of neck spine	0.67	0.67	0	X	0260	0.7655	39.92		
72040	X-ray exam of neck spine	0.6	0.6	0	X	0260	0.7655	39.92		
72040	X-ray exam of neck spine	0.07	0.07	0	X	0260	0.7655	39.92		
72050	X-ray exam of neck spine	1	1	0	X	0261	1.2887	67.21		
72050	X-ray exam of neck spine	0.89	0.89	0	X	0261	1.2887	67.21		
72050	X-ray exam of neck spine	0.11	0.11	0	X	0261	1.2887	67.21		
72052	X-ray exam of neck spine	1.24	1.24	0	X	0261	1.2887	67.21		
72052	X-ray exam of neck spine	1.12	1.12	0	X	0261	1.2887	67.21		
72052	X-ray exam of neck spine	0.12	0.12	0	X	0261	1.2887	67.21		
72070	X-ray exam of thoracic spine	0.72	0.72	0	X	0260	0.7655	39.92		
72070	X-ray exam of thoracic spine	0.65	0.65	0	X	0260	0.7655	39.92		
72070	X-ray exam of thoracic spine	0.07	0.07	0	X	0260	0.7655	39.92		
72100	X-ray exam of lower spine	0.75	0.75	0	X	0260	0.7655	39.92		
72100	X-ray exam of lower spine	0.67	0.67	0	X	0260	0.7655	39.92		
72100	X-ray exam of lower spine	0.08	0.08	0	X	0260	0.7655	39.92		
72110	X-ray exam of lower spine	1.02	1.02	0	X	0261	1.2887	67.21		
72110	X-ray exam of lower spine	0.91	0.91	0	X	0261	1.2887	67.21		
72110	X-ray exam of lower spine	0.11	0.11	0	X	0261	1.2887	67.21		
72125	Ct neck spine w/o dye	6.27	6.27	0	S	0332	3.4398	179.39		
72125	Ct neck spine w/o dye	5.88	5.88	0	S	0332	3.4398	179.39		
72125	Ct neck spine w/o dye	0.39	0.39	0	S	0332	3.4398	179.39		
72131	Ct lumbar spine w/o dye	6.28	6.28	0	S	0332	3.4398	179.39		
72131	Ct lumbar spine w/o dye	5.88	5.88	0	S	0332	3.4398	179.39		
72131	Ct lumbar spine w/o dye	0.4	0.4	0	S	0332	3.4398	179.39		
72132	Ct lumbar spine w/dye	7.45	7.45	0	S	0283	4.5057	234.98		
72132	Ct lumbar spine w/dye	7.04	7.04	0	S	0283	4.5057	234.98		
72132	Ct lumbar spine w/dye	0.41	0.41	0	S	0283	4.5057	234.98		
72141	MRI neck spine w/o dye	11.71	11.71	0	S	0336	6.5987	344.13		
72141	MRI neck spine w/o dye	11.16	11.16	0	S	0336	6.5987	344.13		
72141	MRI neck spine w/o dye	0.55	0.55	0	S	0336	6.5987	344.13		
72146	MRI chest spine w/o dye	12.94	12.94	0	S	0336	6.5987	344.13		
72146	MRI chest spine w/o dye	12.39	12.39	0	S	0336	6.5987	344.13		
72146	MRI chest spine w/o dye	0.55	0.55	0	S	0336	6.5987	344.13		
72148	MRI lumbar spine w/o dye	12.9	12.9	0	S	0336	6.5987	344.13		
72148	MRI lumbar spine w/o dye	12.39	12.39	0	S	0336	6.5987	344.13		
72148	MRI lumbar spine w/o dye	0.51	0.51	0	S	0336	6.5987	344.13		
72158	MRI lumbar spine w/o & w/dye	25.59	25.59	0	S	0337	9.244	482.08		
72158	MRI lumbar spine w/o & w/dye	24.78	24.78	0	S	0337	9.244	482.08		
72158	MRI lumbar spine w/o&w/dye	0.81	0.81	0	S	0337	9.244	482.08		
72265	Contrast x-ray, lower spine	4.31	4.31	0	S	0274	3.8759	202.13		
72265	Contrast x-ray, lower spine	4.05	4.05	0	S	0274	3.8759	202.13		

HCPCS	DESCRIPTION	Facility PE RVU	Non-Facility PE RVU	Incremental Facility Payment ($)	Outpatient PPS Status Codes, Classification Groups, Relative Weights, and Payment Rates: Status Code[a]	APC	Relative Weight	Payment Rate ($)	ASC Payment Groups and Payment Rates: Group	Payment Rate ($)
72265	Contrast x-ray, lower spine	0.26	0.26	0	S	0274	3.8759	202.13		
73030	X-ray exam of shoulder	0.63	0.63	0	X	0260	0.7655	39.92		
73030	X-ray exam of shoulder	0.57	0.57	0	X	0260	0.7655	39.92		
73030	X-ray exam of shoulder	0.06	0.06	0	X	0260	0.7655	39.92		
73110	X-ray exam of wrist	0.59	0.59	0	X	0260	0.7655	39.92		
73110	X-ray exam of wrist	0.53	0.53	0	X	0260	0.7655	39.92		
73110	X-ray exam of wrist	0.06	0.06	0	X	0260	0.7655	39.92		
73130	X-ray exam of hand	0.59	0.59	0	X	0260	0.7655	39.92		
73130	X-ray exam of hand	0.53	0.53	0	X	0260	0.7655	39.92		
73130	X-ray exam of hand	0.06	0.06	0	X	0260	0.7655	39.92		
73140	X-ray exam of finger(s)	0.46	0.46	0	X	0260	0.7655	39.92		
73140	X-ray exam of finger(s)	0.42	0.42	0	X	0260	0.7655	39.92		
73140	X-ray exam of finger(s)	0.04	0.04	0	X	0260	0.7655	39.92		
73220	MRI upper extremity w/o & w/dye	25.52	25.52	0	S	0337	9.244	482.08		
73220	MRI upper extremity w/o & w/dye	24.78	24.78	0	S	0337	9.244	482.08		
73220	MRI upper extremity w/o & w/dye	0.74	0.74	0	S	0337	9.244	482.08		
73221	MRI joint upper extremity w/o dye	11.62	11.62	0	S	0336	6.5987	344.13		
73221	MRI joint upr extremity w/o dye	11.16	11.16	0	S	0336	6.5987	344.13		
73221	MRI joint upr extremity w/o dye	0.46	0.46	0	S	0336	6.5987	344.13		
73560	X-ray exam of knee, 1 or 2	0.58	0.58	0	X	0260	0.7655	39.92		
73560	X-ray exam of knee, 1 or 2	0.52	0.52	0	X	0260	0.7655	39.92		
73560	X-ray exam of knee, 1 or 2	0.06	0.06	0	X	0260	0.7655	39.92		
73562	X-ray exam of knee, 3	0.63	0.63	0	X	0260	0.7655	39.92		
73562	X-ray exam of knee, 3	0.57	0.57	0	X	0260	0.7655	39.92		
73562	X-ray exam of knee, 3	0.06	0.06	0	X	0260	0.7655	39.92		
73564	X-ray exam, knee, 4 or more	0.7	0.7	0	X	0260	0.7655	39.92		
73564	X-ray exam, knee, 4 or more	0.62	0.62	0	X	0260	0.7655	39.92		
73564	X-ray exam, knee, 4 or more	0.08	0.08	0	X	0260	0.7655	39.92		
73610	X-ray exam of ankle	0.59	0.59	0	X	0260	0.7655	39.92		
73610	X-ray exam of ankle	0.53	0.53	0	X	0260	0.7655	39.92		
73610	X-ray exam of ankle	0.06	0.06	0	X	0260	0.7655	39.92		
73630	X-ray exam of foot	0.59	0.59	0	X	0260	0.7655	39.92		
73630	X-ray exam of foot	0.53	0.53	0	X	0260	0.7655	39.92		
73630	X-ray exam of foot	0.06	0.06	0	X	0260	0.7655	39.92		
73720	MRI lower extremity w/o & w/dye	25.51	25.51	0	S	0337	9.244	482.08		
73720	MRI lower extremity w/o & w/dye	24.78	24.78	0	S	0337	9.244	482.08		
73720	MRI lower extremity w/o&w/dye	0.73	0.73	0	S	0337	9.244	482.08		
73721	MRI jnt of lower extremity w/o dye	11.62	11.62	0	S	0336	6.5987	344.13		
73721	MRI jnt of lower extremity w/o dye	11.16	11.16	0	S	0336	6.5987	344.13		
73721	MRI jnt of lower extremity w/o dye	0.46	0.46	0	S	0336	6.5987	344.13		
90780	IV infusion therapy, 1 hour	1.1	1.1	0	E	0	0	0		
90782	Injection, sc/im	0.11	0.11	0	X	0353	0.3973	20.72		
90801	Psy dx interview	0.96	1.19	9	S	0323	1.841	96.01		
90806	Psytx, off, 45-50 min	0.62	0.72	4	S	0323	1.841	96.01		
90807	Psytx, off, 45-50 min w/ e & m	0.65	0.72	3	S	0323	1.841	96.01		
90808	Psytx, office, 75-80 min	0.93	1.05	5	S	0323	1.841	96.01		

					Outpatient PPS Status Codes, Classification Groups, Relative Weights, and Payment Rates				ASC Payment Groups and Payment Rates	
HCPCS	DESCRIPTION	Facility PE RVU	Non-Facility PE RVU	Incre-mental Facility Payment ($)	Status Code[a]	APC	Relative Weight	Payment Rate ($)	Group	Payment Rate ($)
90853	Group psychotherapy	0.24	0.26	1	S	0325	1.4244	74.28		
90862	Medication management	0.33	0.41	3	X	0374	1.1434	59.63		
90901	Biofeedback train, any method	0.19	0.86	26	S	0321	1.2112	63.17		
92002	Eye exam, new patient	0.35	0.94	23	V	0601	0.969	50.53		
92004	Eye exam, new patient	0.7	1.66	37	V	0602	1.4631	76.3		
92012	Eye exam established patient	0.3	0.99	27	V	0600	0.843	43.96		
93000	Electrocardiogram, complete	0.51	0.51	0	E	0	0	0		
93005	Electrocardiogram, tracing	0.45	0.45	0	S	0099	0.3682	19.2		
93010	Electrocardiogram report	0.06	0.06	0	A	0	0	0		
95831	Limb muscle testing, manual	0.13	0.53	16	N	0	0	0		
95851	Range of motion measurements	0.08	0.57	19	N	0	0	0		
95860	Muscle test, 1 limb	1.62	1.62	0	S	0218	1.0077	52.55		
95860	Muscle test, 1 limb	1.19	1.19	0	S	0218	1.0077	52.55		
95860	Muscle test, 1 limb	0.43	0.43	0	S	0218	1.0077	52.55		
95861	Muscle test, 2 limbs	1.44	1.44	0	S	0218	1.0077	52.55		
95861	Muscle test, 2 limbs	0.74	0.74	0	S	0218	1.0077	52.55		
95861	Muscle test, 2 limbs	0.7	0.7	0	S	0218	1.0077	52.55		
95900	Motor nerve conduction test	1.12	1.12	0	S	0218	1.0077	52.55		
95900	Motor nerve conduction test	0.93	0.93	0	S	0218	1.0077	52.55		
95900	Motor nerve conduction test	0.19	0.19	0	S	0218	1.0077	52.55		
95903	Motor nerve conduction test	1.07	1.07	0	S	0218	1.0077	52.55		
95903	Motor nerve conduction test	0.8	0.8	0	S	0218	1.0077	52.55		
95903	Motor nerve conduction test	0.27	0.27	0	S	0218	1.0077	52.55		
95904	Sense nerve conduction test	0.95	0.95	0	S	0215	0.5814	30.32		
95904	Sense nerve conduction test	0.8	0.8	0	S	0215	0.5814	30.32		
95904	Sense nerve conduction test	0.15	0.15	0	S	0215	0.5814	30.32		
95920	Intraop nerve test add-on	2.26	2.26	0	S	0216	2.8972	151.09		
95920	Intraop nerve test add-on	1.3	1.3	0	S	0216	2.8972	151.09		
95920	Intraop nerve test add-on	0.96	0.96	0	S	0216	2.8972	151.09		
95925	Somatosensory testing	1.14	1.14	0	S	0216	2.8972	151.09		
95925	Somatosensory testing	0.91	0.91	0	S	0216	2.8972	151.09		
95925	Somatosensory testing	0.23	0.23	0	S	0216	2.8972	151.09		
95934	H-reflex test	0.44	0.44	0	S	0215	0.5814	30.32		
95934	H-reflex test	0.21	0.21	0	S	0215	0.5814	30.32		
95934	H-reflex test	0.23	0.23	0	S	0215	0.5814	30.32		
96100	Psychological testing	1.75	1.75	0	X	0373	2.2577	117.74		
96117	Neuropsychological test battery	1.75	1.75	0	X	0373	2.2577	117.74		
97010	Hot or cold packs therapy	0.05	0.05	0	A	0	0	0		
97014	Electric stimulation therapy	0.19	0.19	0	A	0	0	0		
97035	Ultrasound therapy	0.11	0.11	0	A	0	0	0		
97110	Therapeutic exercises	0.28	0.28	0	A	0	0	0		
97124	Massage therapy	0.24	0.24	0	A	0	0	0		
97140	Manual therapy	0.27	0.27	0	A	0	0	0		
97530	Therapeutic activities	0.31	0.31	0	A	0	0	0		
97750	Physical performance test	0.31	0.31	0	A	0	0	0		
98940	Chiropractic manipulation	0.13	0.24	4	S	0060	0.3294	17.18		
99183	Hyperbaric oxygen therapy	0.75	0.75	0	E	0	0	0		
99203	Office/outpatient visit, new	0.49	1.1	24	V	0601	0.969	50.53		
99204	Office/outpatient visit, new	0.72	1.49	30	V	0602	1.4631	76.3		
99205	Office/outpatient visit, new	0.95	1.79	33	V	0602	1.4631	76.3		
99212	Office/outpatient visit, est	0.16	0.52	14	V	0600	0.843	43.96		
99213	Office/outpatient visit, est	0.24	0.69	18	V	0601	0.969	50.53		
99214	Office/outpatient visit, est	0.4	1.03	25	V	0602	1.4631	76.3		
99215	Office/outpatient visit, est	0.64	1.34	27	V	0602	1.4631	76.3		
99244	Office consultation	0.94	1.8	34	V	0602	1.4631	76.3		

					Outpatient PPS Status Codes, Classification Groups, Relative Weights, and Payment Rates				ASC Payment Groups and Payment Rates	
HCPCS	DESCRIPTION	Facility PE RVU	Non-Facility PE RVU	Incre-mental Facility Payment ($)	Status Code[a]	APC	Relative Weight	Payment Rate ($)	Group	Payment Rate ($)
99245	Office consultation	1.24	2.26	40	N	0	0	0		
99283	Emergency department visit	0.32	0.32	0	N	0	0	0		

SOURCE: DHHS (2002c, 2003a, 2003c).

NOTES: Blank cells in this table are not applicable to the category.

Procedure descriptions are listed here as they appear in the DHHS physician schedule.

[a]Status code definitions:

A = Paid under a different fee schedule.
C = Inpatient services not payable under OPPS.
E = Payment not allowed under OPPS or not covered by Medicare.
N = Payment packaged into another service or APC group.
S = Significant procedure but multiple procedure payment reduction does not apply.
T = Significant procedure to which multiple procedure payment reduction applies.
V = Medical visit paid under OPPS.
X = Ancillary services paid under OPPS.

REFERENCES

BLS. *See* U.S. Department of Labor, Bureau of Labor Statistics.

CMS. *See* Centers for Medicare and Medicaid Services.

CHSWC. *See* The California Commission on Health and Safety and Workers' Compensation.

CWCI. *See* California Workers' Compensation Institute.

DHHS. *See* U.S. Department of Health and Human Services.

MedPAC. *See* Medicare Payment Advisory Commission.

American Medical Association, *Physicians' Current Procedural Terminology,* 4th ed., (CPT-4), Chicago: AMA, 2002.

The Boards of Trustees, Federal Hospital Insurance and Federal Supplementary Medical Insurance Trust Funds, *2003 Annual Report of the Boards of Trustees of the Federal Hospital Insurance and Federal Supplementary Medical Insurance Trust Funds,* Washington, D.C.: The Boards of Trustees, 2003 (available at www.cms.gov/publications/trusteesreport/ as of August 2003).

The California Commission on Health and Safety and Workers' Compensation, State of California, Department of Industrial Relations, *2001–2002 Annual Report,* August 2002 (available at http://www.dir.ca.gov/chswc/CHSWC_AnnualReport2002/CHSWCAnnualReport_2002.HTML as of September 2003).

The California Commission on Health and Safety and Workers' Compensation, State of California, Department of Industrial Relations, *Workers' Compensation Medical Payment Systems: A Proposal for Simplification and Administrative Efficiency,* April 2003 (available at http://www.dir.ca.gov/CHSWC/CHSWC_WCMedicalPaymentSystem/CHSWC_WCMedicalPaymentSystem.pdf as of August 2003).

California Workers' Compensation Institute, Industry Claims Information System, *Clinical Severity in Workers' Compensation Inpatient Care,* Oakland, Calif.: California Workers' Compensation Institute, July 2001a.

California Workers' Compensation Institute, Industry Claims Information System, "Financial Impact of Proposed Inpatient Fee Schedule Revisions," *ICIS Says,* 2001b (available at http://www.cwci.org/icis as of March 2003).

California Workers' Compensation Institute, Industry Claims Information System, "Shifting Age and Gender Demographics Among California Workers' Compensation Injured Workers," *ICIS Says,* 2003 (available at http://www.cwci.org/icis as of March 2003).

Centers for Medicare and Medicaid Services, *Acute Inpatient Prospective Payment System,* "DRG Relative Weights," tables from 1998–2000, public use files for download from the Prospective Payment System, Baltimore, Md.: CMS (current tables available at http://cms.hhs.gov/providers/hipps/ippspufs.asp as of September 2003).

Code of Federal Regulations, Title 42, Vol. 2, Public Health, Human Services, Part 414 (42CFR414), "Payment for Part B Medical and Other Health Services," revised as of October 1, 2002.

Department of Defense, Office of the Assistant Secretary of Defense for Health Affairs, Tricare Management Activity, *Tricare Reimbursement Manual*, Chapter 7, Section 1, "TRICARE/CHAMPUS Inpatient Mental Health Per Diem Payment System," March 15, 2003 (available at http: tricare.osd.mil/trm/C7S1.pdf as of August 2003).

Division of Workers' Compensation, State of California, Department of Industrial Relations, *California Workers' Compensation Official Medical Fee Schedule,* Chapter 4.5, Subchapter 1, "Administrative Director—Administrative Rules," Article 5.5, "Application of the Official Medical Fee Schedule (Treatment)," San Francisco: Division of Workers' Compensation, April 1, 1999.

Dobson, A., J. DaVanzo, J. Gilani, M. Consunji, L. Koenig, and J. T. Black, *The Relative Work Content of Evaluation and Management Codes: The Physician Work Study,* report prepared for the California Department of Industrial Relations, Industrial Medical Council, Falls Church, Va.: The Lewin Group, July 18, 2002a.

Dobson, A., L. Koenig, J. Siegel, J. Gilani, S. Ho, and J. DaVanzo, *Practice Expense Study of Evaluation and Management Services,* report prepared for the California Department of Industrial Relations, Industrial Medical Council, Falls Church, Va.: The Lewin Group, September 19, 2002b.

Eccleston, S. M., A. Laszlo, Xiaoping Zhao, and M. Watson, *Benchmarks for Designing Workers' Compensation Medical Fee Schedules,* Cambridge, Mass.: Workers' Compensation Research Institute (WC-02-2), 2002.

Hunt, S., S. Maerki, D. Porter, and J. Fang, *Applying RBRVS to Medi-Cal: Case Studies in Seven States,* report prepared for the Medi-Cal Policy Institute, Oakland, Calif.: Price Waterhouse Coopers, 2001.

Kominski, G. F., and L. B. Gardner, *Inpatient Hospital Fee Schedule and Outpatient Surgery Study: Final Report to the Commission on Health and Safety and Workers' Compensation,* UCLA Center for Health Policy Studies, Los Angeles, Calif.: UCLA Center for Health Policy Studies, 2001 (available at http://www.healthpolicy.ucla.edu/pubs/pubLIST.asp as of September 2003).

Kominski, G. F., N. Pourat, and J. T. Black, *The Use of Relative Value Scales for Provider Reimbursement in State Workers' Compensation Programs,* Los Angeles, Calif.: UCLA Center for Health Policy Research, 1999 (available at http://www.healthpolicy.ucla.edu/pubs/pubLIST.asp as of September 2003).

The Lewin Group, *California Workers' Compensation RBRVS Study,* draft report prepared for the Industrial Medical Council, Department of Industrial Relations, Falls Church, Va.: The Lewin Group, October 8, 2002.

Medicare Payment Advisory Commission, *Report to the Congress, Medicare Payment Policy 2001,* Washington, D.C.: Medicare Payment Advisory Commission, 2001a.

Medicare Payment Advisory Commission, *Report to the Congress, Paying for Interventional Pain Services in Ambulatory Settings,* Washington, D.C.: Medicare Payment Advisory Commission, 2001b.

Medicare Payment Advisory Commission, *Report to the Congress, Medicare Coverage of Nonphysician Practitioners,* Washington, D.C.: Medicare Payment Advisory Commission, 2002a.

Medicare Payment Advisory Commission, *Report to the Congress, Medicare Payment to Advanced Practice Nurses and Physician Assistants,* Washington, D.C.: Medicare Payment Advisory Commission, 2002b.

Medicare Payment Advisory Commission, *Report to the Congress, Medicare Payment Policy 2002,* Washington, D.C.: Medicare Payment Advisory Commission, 2002c.

Medicare Payment Advisory Commission, *Report to the Congress, Medicare Payment Policy 2003,* Washington, D.C.: Medicare Payment Advisory Commission, 2003.

Neuhauser, F., A., Sedlow, L. Gardner, and E. Edelstein, *Cost of Pharmaceuticals in Workers' Compensation,* report prepared for the Commission on Health and Safety and Workers' Compensation, 2000 (available at http://www.dir.ca.gov/CHSWC as of January 2003).

Schoenman, J. A., and J. J. Feldman, *Results of the Medicare Payment Advisory Commission's 2002 Survey of Physicians,* report prepared by The Project HOPE Center for Health Affairs for MedPAC, Bethesda, Md.: The Project HOPE Center for Health Affairs, December 2002, Chapter 3.

The State of California, *Code of Regulations,* Title 8, Chapter 4.5, Division of Workers' Compensation, Subchapter 1, "Administrative Director—Administrative Rules," Article 5.5, Application of the Official Medical Fee Schedule (Treatment), Para. 9792.1, Payment of Inpatient Services of Health Facilities, December 1, 2000.

The State of California, Assembly Bill 749, *Workers' Compensation: Administration and Benefits,* February 19, 2002.

U.S. Department of Health and Human Services, Health Care Financing Administration, "Medicare Program; Revisions to Payment Policies Under the Physician Fee Schedule for Calendar Year 1999; Proposed Rule," *Federal Register,* Vol. 63, No. 108, June 5, 1998a, p. 30818.

U. S. Department of Health and Human Services, Health Care Financing Administration, "Medicare Program; Update of Rate Setting Methodology, Payment Rates, Payment Policies, and the List of Covered Procedures for Ambulatory Surgical Centers Effective October 1, 1998b; Proposed Rule," *Federal Register,* Vol. 63, No. 113, June 12, 1998b, p. 32290.

U. S. Department of Health and Human Services, Health Care Financing Administration, "Medicare Program; Update of Rate Setting Methodology, Payment Rates, Payment Policies, and the List of Covered Procedures for Ambulatory Surgical Centers Effective October 1, 1998, Reopening of Comment Period and Delay in Adoption of the Proposed Rule as Final," *Federal Register,* Vol. 63, No. 190, October 1, 1998c, p. 52663-5.

U.S. Department of Health and Human Services, Health Care Financing Administration, "Medicare Program; Changes to the Hospital Inpatient Prospective Payment Systems and Fiscal Year 2000 Rates; Final Rule," *Federal Register,* Vol. 64, No. 146, June 3, 1999, p. 41490.

U.S. Department of Health and Human Services, Health Care Financing Administration, "Medicare Program; Changes to the Hospital Inpatient Prospective Payment Systems and

Fiscal Year 2001 Rates; Proposed Rule," *Federal Register,* Vol. 65, No. 88, May 5, 2000a, p. 26282.

U.S. Department of Health and Human Services, Health Care Financing Administration, "Medicare Program; Changes to the Hospital Inpatient Prospective Payment Systems and Fiscal Year 2001 Rates; Final Rule," *Federal Register,* Vol. 65, No. 148, August 1, 2000b, p. 47054.

U.S. Department of Health and Human Services, Health Care Financing Administration, "Medicare Program; Revisions to Payment Policies Under the Physician Fee Schedule for Calendar Year 2001," *Federal Register,* Vol. 65, No. 212, November 1, 2000c, p. 65375.

U. S. Department of Health and Human Services, Centers for Medicare and Medicaid Services, "Medicare Program; Changes to the Hospital Inpatient Prospective Payment Systems and Rate and Costs of Graduate Medical Education; Fiscal Year 2002 Rates; Provisions of the Balanced Budget Refinement Act of 1999; and Provisions of the Medicare, Medicaid, and SCHIP Benefits and Improvement Act of 2000," *Federal Register,* Vol. 66, No. 148, August 1, 2001, p. 39828.

U.S. Department of Health and Human Services, Centers for Medicare and Medicaid Services, Program Memorandum: Intermediaries/Carriers, "Update of Rates and Wage Index for Ambulatory Surgical Center (ASC) Payments Effective October 1, 2002 [Transmittal AB-02-124]," Washington, D.C.: Centers for Medicare and Medicaid Services, August 28, 2002a.

U.S. Department of Health and Human Services, Health Care Financing Administration, "Medicare Program; Changes to the Hospital Outpatient Prospective Payment System and Calendar Year 2003 Payment Rates, and Changes to Payment Suspension for Unfiled Cost Reports; Final Rule," *Federal Register,* Vol. 67, No. 212, November 1, 2002b, p. 66718.

U.S. Department of Health and Human Services, Centers for Medicare and Medicaid Services, *Program Memorandum: Intermediaries/Carriers,* "2003 Clinical Laboratory Fee Schedule and Laboratory Services Subject to Reasonable Charge Payment Method," Washington, D.C.: Centers for Medicare and Medicaid Services, Transmittal AB-02-163, November 8, 2002c.

U. S. Department of Health and Human Services, Centers for Medicare and Medicaid Services, "Medicare Program; Revisions to Payment Policies Under the Physician Fee Schedule for Calendar Year 2003 and Inclusion of Registered Nurses in the Personnel Provision of the Critical Access Hospital Emergency Services Requirement for Frontier Areas and Remote Locations; Final Rule," *Federal Register,* Vol. 67, No. 251, December 31, 2002d, p. 79968.

U.S. Department of Health and Human Services, Health Care Financing Administration, "Medicare Program; Changes to the Hospital Outpatient Prospective Payment System and Calendar Year 2003 Payment Rates, and Changes to Payment Suspension for Unfiled Cost Reports; Correction," *Federal Register,* Vol. 68, No. 27, February 10, 2003a, p. 6636.

U.S. Department of Health and Human Services, Centers for Medicare and Medicaid Services, "Medicare Program; Prospective Payment System for Long-Term Care Hospitals; Proposed Annual Payment Rate Updates and Policy Changes; Proposed Rule," *Federal Register,* Vol. 68, No. 45, March 7, 2003b, p. 11234.

U. S. Department of Health and Human Services, Health Care Financing Administration, "Medicare Program; Update of Ambulatory Surgical Center List of Covered Procedures

Effective July 1, 2003, Final Rule," *Federal Register,* Vol. 68, No. 60, March 28, 2003c, p. 15268.

U.S. Department of Labor, Bureau of Labor Statistics, *State and County Employment and Wages from Covered Employment and Wages Overview,* Washington, D.C.: Bureau of Labor Statistics, 2003a.

U.S. Department of Labor, Bureau of Labor Statistics, "How Does the Producer Price Index Differ from the Consumer Price Index?" *PPI Program Spotlight,* No. 98-3, 2003b (available at http://stats.bls.gov/ppi/ppivcpi.pdf as of August 2003).

Workers' Compensation Insurance Rating Bureau of California, *WCIRB California Annual Report 2001,* San Francisco: WCIRB, July 2002 (available as of September 2003 at www.wcirbonline.org).